Journal
of
Romanian Studies

Vol. 2, No. 1 (2020)

JRS editors
Peter Gross and Diane Vancea

JRS review editor
Iuliu Ratiu

JRS Editorial Assistant
Claudia Lonkin

About the Society for Romanian Studies

THE SOCIETY FOR ROMANIAN STUDIES (SRS) *is an international interdisciplinary academic organization founded in 1973 and dedicated to promoting research and critical studies on all aspects of Romanian and Moldovan culture and society. The SRS is recognized as the major North American professional organization for scholars concerned with Romania, Moldova, and their diasporas.*

SRS is affiliated with the South East European Studies Association (SEESA); the Association for Slavic, East European and Eurasian Studies (ASEEES—formerly known as the American Association for the Advancement of Slavic Studies or AAASS); the American Political Science Association (APSA); the American Historical Association (AHA); and the Romanian Studies Association of America (RSAA).

SRS offers a number of programs and activities to its members, including the peer-reviewed *Journal of Romanian Studies*, a biannual newsletter, the Romanian Studies book series published in collaboration with the publishing house Polirom in Iași, a mentoring program, prizes for exceptional scholarship in two different categories, as well as an international conference organized every three years in Romania.

More information about the SRS, including current officers, the national board, and membership information, can be found on the SRS website at *https://society4romanianstudies.org*.

www.society4romanianstudies.org
The Society for Romanian Studies

Editorial Board:

PETER GROSS (pgross@utk.edu) and
DIANE VANCEA (economics@ovidius-university.net)
JRS editors

IULIU RATIU (ratiu.pfa@gmail.com)
JRS review editor

CLAUDIA LONKIN (claudia.lonkin@gmail.com)
JRS Editorial Assistant

Advisory Board:

DENNIS DELETANT (Georgetown University, USA)
JON FOX (University of Bristol, UK)
VALENTINA GLAJAR (Texas State University, USA)
PETER GROSS (University of Tennessee, USA)
BRIGID HAINES (Swansea University, UK)
IRINA LIVEZEANU (University of Pittsburgh, USA)
MIHAELA MIROIU (National School of Political Science and Public Administration, Romania)
STEVE D. ROPER (Florida Atlantic University, USA)
DOMNICA RADULESCU (Washington and Lee University, USA)
PAUL E. SUM (University of North Dakota, USA)
CRISTIAN TILEAGA (Loughborough University, UK)
VLADIMIR TISMANEANU (University of Maryland, College Park, USA)
LUCIAN TURCESCU (Concordia University, Montreal, Canada)

Bibliographic information published by the Deutsche Nationalbibliothek
The Deutsche Nationalbibliothek lists this publication in the Deutsche Nationalbibliografie; detailed bibliographic data are available on the Internet at
http://dnb.dnb.de.

Bibliografische Information der Deutschen Nationalbibliothek
Die Deutsche Nationalbibliothek verzeichnet diese Publikation in der Deutschen Nationalbibliografie; detaillierte bibliografische Daten sind im Internet über http://dnb.d-nb.de abrufbar.

Journal of Romanian Studies
Vol. 2, No. 1 (2020)

Stuttgart: *ibidem*-Verlag / *ibidem* Press

Erscheinungsweise: halbjährlich / Frequency: biannual

ISBN 978-3-8382-1419-1

ISSN 2627-5325

Ordering Information:
PRINT: Subscription (two copies per year): € 58.00 / year (+ S&H: € 6.00 / year within Germany, € 10.00 / year international). The subscription can be canceled at any time.
Single copy or back issue: € 34.00 / copy (+ S&H: € 3.00 within Germany, € 4.50 international).

E-BOOK: Subscription (two copies per year): € 35.99 / year, individual copy or back issue: € 24.99 / copy. Available via ibidem.eu.

For further information please visit www.ibidem.eu/jrs.htm

© *ibidem*-Verlag / *ibidem* Press
Stuttgart, Germany 2020

Alle Rechte vorbehalten
Das Werk einschließlich aller seiner Teile ist urheberrechtlich geschützt. Jede Verwertung außerhalb der engen Grenzen des Urheberrechtsgesetzes ist ohne Zustimmung des Verlages unzulässig und strafbar. Dies gilt insbesondere für Vervielfältigungen, Übersetzungen, Mikroverfilmungen und elektronische Speicherformen sowie die Einspeicherung und Verarbeitung in elektronischen Systemen.

All rights reserved

No part of this publication may be reproduced, stored in or introduced into a retrieval system, or transmitted, in any form, or by any means (electronical, mechanical, photocopying, recording or otherwise) without the prior written permission of the publisher.
Any person who performs any unauthorized act in relation to this publication may be liable to criminal prosecution and civil claims for damages.

Printed in the EU

Contents

Note from the Editors
PETER GROSS, DIANE VANCEA, IULIU RATIU, CLAUDIA LONKIN 7

Ephemeral Modernisms, Transnational Lives: Reconstructing Avant-Garde Performance in Bucharest
ALEXANDRA CHIRIAC 9

Compulsory Primary Education and State Building in Rural Bessarabia (1918–1940)
PETRU NEGURĂ 35

Record Weak: Romanian Judiciary in Occupied Transnistria
VLADIMIR SOLONARI 59

A Political Palimpsest: Nationalism and Faith in Petre Țuțea's Thinking
DELIA POPESCU 83

What Is too Long and When Is too Late for Transitional Justice? Observations from the Case of Romania
CYNTHIA M. HORNE 109

Searching for a Future: Mass Media and the Uncertain Construction of Democracy in Romania
BRINDUSA ARMANCA AND PETER GROSS 139

Ionuț Butoi, Mircea Vulcănescu. O microistorie a interbelicului românesc.
Review by EMANUEL COPILAȘ 163

Henry P. Rammelt. Activistes protestataires en Hongrie et en Roumanie.
Review by DANA S. TRIF 167

Note from the Editors

After successfully guiding the first three inaugural issues, the founding editors of the *Journal of Romanian Studies*—Lavinia Stan, Jules Leger Research Chair and professor of comparative politics at St. Francis Xavier University, Canada; Margaret Hiebert Beissinger, Professor in the Department of Slavic Languages and Literatures at Princeton University, and Radu Cinpoeș, head of the Department of Politics and senior lecturer at Kingston University, London, England—have handed over the reins of the publication to us.

Together with the Society for Romanian Studies and its members, we owe a tremendous debt of gratitude to Professors Stan, Beissinger and Cinpoeș for their vision, persistence, expertise and hard work in creating the *JRS*. By doing so, they forged a vehicle that enlarges the global scope and extent for scholarship on Romanian and Moldovan topics.

A sincere thank you and "well done" to our three predecessors.

We take seriously our fiduciary responsibility to complete the vision of the founding editors and make the JRS the premier publication that disseminates notable, multi-disciplinary scholarship on Romanian and Moldovan topics.

In the next three years, we aim to unrelentingly enhance the quality of *JRS*'s content, increase the number and disciplinary variety of submissions, persistently pursue top established and up-and-coming intellectuals/academics to contribute to the journal, and magnify the journal's visibility and standing in and outside the academic community.

The editorial team cannot do its work without the aid of the members of the Society of Romanian Studies and its Board, as well other subscribers. We fervently hope that you, our readers, will help us achieve the above-stated goals by submitting articles, identifying potential contributors, serving as reviewers and, when necessary, as translators. And of course, we urge you to spread the word that our journal is an exceptional reference for scholars, students, policy makers, the media, and all who have an interest in the myriad of topics related to Romania and Moldova.

Thank you for your support.

Peter Gross, Co-Editor

Professor Emeritus & former Director
School of Journalism & Electronic Media
The University of Tennessee
Knoxville, TN, U.S.A.

Diane Vancea, Co-Editor

Professor & Vice-rector
Ovidius University
Constanta, Romania

Iuliu Ratiu, Book Editor

Associate lecturer
Department of Modern Languages & Business Communication
The Faculty of Economics & Business Administration
Babeş-Bolyai University
Cluj-Napoca, Romania

Claudia Lonkin, Editorial Assistant

Graduate Student
Department of History & Classics
University of Alberta
Edmonton, AB, Canada

Ephemeral Modernisms, Transnational Lives: Reconstructing Avant-Garde Performance in Bucharest

Alexandra Chiriac

> "Was there or wasn't there a revolution in our town?"
> *12:08 East of Bucharest* (2006, dir. Corneliu Porumboiu)

Abstract: *During the mid-1920s Bucharest became home to the Vilna Troupe, an ensemble formed in Vilnius in 1915 and famed for its groundbreaking Yiddish-language productions that toured all over the world. Its collaborations with the Romanian artist M. H. Maxy are the subject of this essay, which demonstrates the experimental nature of several productions that took place in Bucharest during this period. New research material from sources on both sides of the Atlantic makes it possible to reconstruct the outputs of this richly innovative partnership to a much greater extent than before, demonstrating that the vitality of avant-garde theatre in Bucharest has been heretofore underestimated by scholars, its existence obscured by the ephemerality of the performative and by its unwieldy transnational trajectory. An earlier version of this essay won the Graduate Student Essay Prize offered in 2018 by the Society for Romanian Studies.*

Introduction

In 2006, the Romanian film *A fost sau n-a fost?* won the Caméra d'Or Prize at the Cannes Film Festival. During its subsequent international release the film was renamed *12:08 East of Bucharest*, playing on that paradigm of liminality, something that is East of the East. The original Romanian title is different, but interrogates this same premise. Literally meaning "Was there or wasn't there?" it refers to the characters' quest to establish whether the 1989 Romanian revolution also took place in their provincial town, an impossible pursuit made into satire by the film's director Corneliu Porumboiu. This central question—was there or was there not a revolution?—applies equally well to the status of avant-garde theatre in Romania during the interwar period. Among Romanian scholars, there seems to be a consensus that truly experimental theatre had no significant presence in Bucharest, or that, as Paul Cernat writes, "the attempts of the

Romanian avant-gardes to revolutionise theatre in the 1920s remained only a good intention."¹

Could it be that a revolution really did take place, yet its traces have become obscured? In the context of Eastern European history, there are good reasons for this omission beyond the essentially ephemeral nature of the performative arts. Firstly, Romania's turbulent trajectory in the twentieth century has left its mark on local archives, libraries, and museums. Recovering visual evidence of performances has been a challenging process of trial and error for the author of this essay, with items erroneously catalogued or stored in unexpected locations as far afield as Boston or New York. Secondly, recent attempts to create a more inclusive account of modernism have understandably focused, as Polish scholar Piotr Piotrowski noted, on the "reconstruction of the national sources of avant-garde art."² However, as the extent of the avant-gardes' mobility becomes increasingly evident, the construction of national and even regional histories may prove too timid a solution, stymied by the geopolitical changes of the twentieth century.

This is especially true in the case of the Vilna Troupe, an itinerant ensemble that brought a new vision of theatre through its radical productions during its time in Romania from 1923 to 1927. Formed in Vilnius in 1915, the group had rapidly forged an international reputation due to its innovative Yiddish-language productions. According to Debra Caplan:

> within a year, they [were] the most famous Jewish theatre company in Eastern Europe [...]. [Within] five years, they [became] a global sensation, drawing the attention of prominent Jewish and non-Jewish theatre artists, politicians, and intellectuals from across Eastern and Western Europe, North and South America, and beyond. They [were] widely regarded as one of the foremost avant-garde theatre companies in the world.³

---

1   Paul Cernat, *Avangarda românească și complexul periferiei* (Bucharest: Cartea Românească, 2007), 269, and Ion Cazaban, "Futurismul ca model teatral," *Studii și cercetări de istoria artei. Arta plastică*, special issue (2010): 33–45. Cazaban concluded that the Romanian avant-garde's rhetoric with regards to new theatrical practices, as seen in their periodicals, remained a theoretical debate. On what constitutes avant-garde and/or modernist theatre, see Günter Berghaus, *Theatre, Performance, and the Historical Avant-Garde* (New York: Palgrave Macmillan, 2005); Olga Taxidou, *Modernism and Performance. Jarry to Brecht* (New York: Palgrave Macmillan, 2007); and Claire Warden, *Modernist and Avant-Garde Performance. An Introduction* (Edinburgh: Edinburgh University Press, 2015).
2   Piotr Piotrowski, *Art and Democracy in Post-Communist Europe* (London: Reaktion Books, 2012), 39.
3   Debra Caplan, "Nomadic Chutzpah: The Vilna Troupe's Transnational Yiddish Theatre Paradigm, 1915–1935," *Theatre Survey*, 55, no. 3 (September 2014): 296–317. For a comprehensive account of the Vilna Troupe's international history, see Debra

Amongst their audience they could count Sarah Bernhardt, Max Reinhardt, Augustus John, Walter Sickert, and Eugen Ionesco.[4] The Vilna Troupe's success benefited from its frequent collaborations with local artists and directors, helping to develop their wide-ranging repertoire and to foster visual experimentation. During 1925 and 1926, M. H. Maxy, a prominent member of the Romanian avant-garde, became one of their foremost collaborators, producing stage designs and promotional materials for the troupe. His work in the theatrical realm is closely interconnected with his other activities during this period, including his collaboration with an educational and commercial venture for modern applied arts and design, and the launch of his own avant-garde periodical, *Integral*. This essay examines Maxy's collaborations with the Vilna Troupe in an attempt to reconstitute these theatrical productions. It is based on detailed searches through the period press and extensive archival research, bringing to light material located in the National Museum of Art of Romania, the Romanian Academy, Widener Library at Harvard University, and the YIVO Institute for Jewish Research in New York.

The Vilna Troupe in Romania

Few scholarly accounts exist of the Vilna Troupe's time in Bucharest. One of the more comprehensive is the section dedicated to the troupe by Israel Bercovici in his history of Jewish theatre in Romania.[5] According to Bercovici, the ensemble's first two seasons in Bucharest drew large crowds, including actors from the local theatres and even members of the Romanian royal family, and received glowing reviews. The newspaper *Adevărul* considered its productions "worthy of being seen even by those who do not understand the language."[6] Its greatest Romanian success came in 1925 with a production of Osip Dymov's *The Singer of His Sorrow* which was so popular that it ran for over 150 performances.[7]

Caplan, *Yiddish Empire: The Vilna Troupe, Jewish Theater, and the Art of Itinerancy* (Ann Arbor: University of Michigan Press, 2018).

4   Caplan, "Nomadic Chutzpah," and Caplan, *Yiddish Empire*.
5   Israil Bercovici, *O sută de ani de teatru evreiesc în România*, 2nd edition, revised and augmented by Constantin Măciucă (Bucharest: Integral, 1998), 125–46.
6   Bercovici, *O sută de ani*, 127. All translations from Romanian are my own unless otherwise specified.
7   Camelia Crăciun, "Bucureștiul interbelic, centru emergent de cultura idiș," *Revista de istorie a evreilor din România*, 16–17, no. 1 (2016): 65–81. Osip Dymov (1878–1950) was a writer and playwright born in Białystok and active in Russia, Germany and the United States. One of his most popular works was *Yoshke muzikant* (Yoshke the Musician), also known as *Der zinger fun zayn troyer* (The Singer of His Sorrow), which Dymov wrote in 1914. See Vassili Schedrin, "Dymov, Osip," *YIVO*

Despite this great commercial and critical success, the Vilna Troupe has made few appearances in scholarly accounts on theatrical life in Romania. The existence of a certain narrative regarding the "acceptable" influence being that of West European culture, in particular that of France, means that certain theatrical visits have acquired a larger body of scholarship than others. The influence of French troupes, such as that of Georges Pitoëff, is the subject of a detailed article by Vera Molea, while the lasting impact of German director Karl Heinz Martin has been frequently discussed by Ion Cazaban, one of the foremost theatrical scholars in Romania.⁸ The legacy of such visiting theatrical luminaries is frequently acknowledged, whereas that of the Vilna Troupe's productions rarely is, despite accounts that describe local cultural figures attending their performances with enthusiasm. Nonetheless, contemporary commentators recognised their value, acknowledging that the Vilna Troupe's performances were "a revelation for our theatre" and "a school for the new generation of actors."⁹ According to Joseph Buloff, one of the Troupe's rising stars, these performances even inspired prominent modernist playwright Eugen Ionesco, who attended them as a young man. Years later, when Ionesco had made his name as a pioneer of the Theatre of the Absurd, Buloff recalled having received an enthusiastic phone call from the unknown young playwright some years before.[10]

Saul: The Constructivist Experiment That Never Was

If theatrical initiatives of an experimental nature did take place in Bucharest, scholarly accounts of the subject have been few and far between.[11] The ephemerality of the theatrical arts does explain such an absence. Productions were poorly documented, and the intervening years of

---

    Encyclopedia of Jews in Eastern Europe (2011), available at: http://www.yivoencyclopedia.org/article.aspx/Dymov_Osip, accessed on 28 March 2018.

8   Vera Molea, "Actori și trupe de teatru franceze la București (1830–1940)," *Lettre Internationale*, 88 (Winter 2013–2014): 9–15; Ion Cazaban, *Scena românească și expresionismul* (Bucharest: Cheiron, 2012); Ion Cazaban, "La scene roumaine et l'expressionisme (II)," *Studii și cercetări de istoria artei. Teatru, muzică, cinematografie* 45, no. 1 (2007): 103–16. The Vilna Troupe had not fared much better in international scholarship until the publication of Caplan's recent monograph *Yiddish Empire*, the first scholarly work to discuss this pioneering ensemble at length.

9   Bercovici, *O sută de ani*, 144–5, quoting an article from *Clipa*, 18 September 1927.

10   Luba Kadison and Joseph Buloff, *On Stage, Off Stage: Memories of a Lifetime in the Yiddish Theatre* (Cambridge, Mass.: Harvard University Library, 1992), 54.

11   The most comprehensive work on this subject was done during the communist period by theatre historian Simion Alterescu, who published his findings in the journals of the Romanian Institute of Art History. See Simion Alterescu, "Teatrului românesc din primele decenii ale secolului al XX-lea și inovarea artei scenice

communist dictatorship have further impeded the recuperation of memories, images, or documents relating to avant-garde artistic practices. Furthermore, Romanian scholarship on the avant-garde has been preoccupied with its literary output to the detriment of other disciplines and has fetishized in particular the avant-garde's printed publications, such as *Integral* and *Contimporanul*.[12] Whilst these are important sources of information, their frequency could be inconsistent and their rhetoric unreliable, and thus they cannot be relied upon to provide an accurate and coherent picture of the productions that made it to the stage. As a result of this approach, Maxy's work in the theatre hardly makes an appearance in existing scholarship on the artist and when it does it is strewn with errors that have become self-perpetuating, as is the case with Maxy's first foray into scenography. In March 1925, the first issue of *Integral* announced:

> The group INTEGRAL, which does not have the means at present to manifest itself independently and on its own terrain, is undertaking its first [theatrical] experiment at the Central Theatre of the Vilna Troupe with a production of *Saul* by André Gide directed by I. M. Daniel, with decor and costumes by M. H. Maxy. The event must be emphasised: these are the first scenic constructions in our country.[13]

The following month, the second issue of the magazine printed three images relating to the play. These were Maxy's designs for six costumes and for the set itself. Of the production itself there was no written account, however, and the images accompanied an article by Maxy on modernism in theatre in France, Germany, and Russia.[14] French theatre was judged to be lacking in innovation in comparison to the experimental practices flourishing in Germany and Russia. According to the author, Germany had

---

interbelice (Avangarda. Semnificația conceptului și a mișcării artistice)," *Studii și cercetări de istoria artei. Teatru, muzică, cinematografie*, 30 (1983): 46–55, and Simion Alterescu, "Le Théâtre d'Avant-Garde. Conceptions théoriques et activité créative en Roumanie au début du XXeme siècle," *Revue roumaine d'histoire de l'art. Série Théâtre, musique, cinema*, 20 (1983): 21–33. After his death, Ion Cazaban and Paul Cernat became the authorities on the Romanian avant-garde's involvement with theatre, yet they do not believe this involvement was significant. See Cazaban, *Scena românească*, and Cernat, *Avangarda românească*.

12 The majority of scholarship published in Romania on the avant-garde journals has been by literary scholars such as Paul Cernat, Ovidiu Crohmălniceanu or Ion Pop. Cernat, *Avangarda românească*; Ion Pop, *Introducere în avangarda literară românească* (Bucharest: ICR, 2007); Ovidiu Crohmălniceanu, *Evreii în mișcarea de avangardă românească* (Bucharest: Hasefer, 2001).

13 *Integral*, 1 (1 March 1925): 16. *Saül* was one of Gide's first plays, written in 1897–1898 and published in 1903 but staged for the first time in 1922 by Jacques Copeau. See D. M. Church, "Structure and Dramatic Technique in Gide's *Saül* and *Le Roi Candaule*", *PMLA* 84, no. 6 (1969): 1640.

14 M. H. Maxy, "Regia scenică—decor—costum," *Integral*, no. 2 (1 April 1925), 4–5.

taken the lead in scenic inventions, bringing new technologies to the stage, as well as the concept of the "scenic cube," which incorporated the actors and the décor into one "plastic image" that could be manipulated according to dramatic requirements. In Russia, by contrast, it was the actor who took primacy through Vsevolod Meyerhold's biomechanics, and the stage environment was changing to accommodate the three-dimensionality of the new dynamic body.

Despite the lack of a textual link between these affirmations and the accompanying reproductions by Maxy, the idea of the "scenic cube" is translated literally into the stage design which is shaped like a cube, rather than the more usual oblong format. The set is fashioned from interconnected geometric elements grouped around a multi-level podium that may well form a mechanised assemblage. The geometric rigidity of the set is mirrored by the costume compositions for the characters of Saul, David, Jonathan and the three Devils, which reconfigure the same shapes into human form (see Figure 1). These do not appear to be practical designs—the figures lack sections of various limbs—but rather the pictorial representation of a mechanical union between actor and stage as well as a rejection of theatrical naturalism. The lack of concern for feasibility in these sketches and the lack of information about the production in the press of the period corroborate a later account that *Saul* never actually made it to the stage.[15] This information is unclear in scholarly accounts of Maxy's career and studies of avant-garde theatre in Romania, which frequently use *Integral* as their only printed source from the period.[16] Furthermore, due to *Integral*'s prominence for scholars of the avant-garde, Maxy's theatrical portfolio is often thought to consist only of the productions described within.

---

15 Israel Marcus, *Șapte momente din istoria evreilor în România* (Haifa: Glob, 1977), 54. The author spent several months interviewing Maxy in later life and claimed that the artist checked the resulting biographical account for accuracy shortly before he died.

16 Michael Ilk, *Maxy: der integrale Künstler* (Ludwigshafen: Michael Ilk, 2003), 44 and 176. Ilk's monograph includes Saul in the lists of theatrical productions the artist was involved in and the chronology of Maxy's life which suggests he created sets for this play on the stage of the Central Theatre in March 1925. This misrepresentation may also stem from Maxy's own accounts of his career, as is the case with the chronology of his 1965 retrospective where the designs for *Saul* appear under his activities for 1926. See *Expoziția retrospectivă M. H. Maxy*, Sala Dalles, October–November 1965 (Bucharest: Arta Grafică, 1965), and Petre Oprea, *M. H. Maxy* (Bucharest: Arta Grafică, 1974). For studies of the avant-garde theatre in Romania, see Ion Cazaban, "Scenografi ai teatrului românesc interbelic (I)," *Studii și cercetări de istoria artei. Teatru, muzică, cinematografie*, 40 (1993): 55–62, and Andrei Pintilie, "Considerații asupra mișcării de avangardă în plastica românească," in *Bucharest in the 1920s and 1930s: Between Avant-Garde and Modernism*, ed. Magda Cârneci (Bucharest: Simetria, 1994), 27–37.

Figure 1: M. H. Maxy. Costume designs for the Devils in *Saul*. Printed in *Integral* no. 2, April 1925.

Other than *Integral*, visual evidence of Maxy's stage and costume designs for the Vilna Troupe are located in the graphic arts collections of the National Art Museum of Romania and the Romanian Academy.[17] Prepared on the same type of paper and in the same style, these works are all signed and dated and contain information about the productions they represent. They are highly finished and do not appear to be working sketches. It is thus likely that they are later recreations of working designs, perhaps for an exhibition, despite being dated with the actual year of the individual productions. Such a possibility is all the more plausible since Irina Cărăbaș has found further instances of Maxy recreating earlier works, probably for his 1965 retrospective. Organised during a period of ideological thaw, the exhibition was an important moment of validation from the communist regime for Maxy's entire artistic career, and thus the inclusion of avant-garde works was important. According to Cărăbaș, at least two paintings from the 1920s were recreated: a portrait of Tristan Tzara from 1923–1924 and another of actress Florentina Ciricleanu from

---

17 National Art Museum of Romania, Graphic Arts Collection, Fond Maxy; Romanian Academy, Graphic Arts Collection, Fond Maxy.

1926, and in both cases Maxy signed and dated the new works retrospectively.[18] It seems likely that the stage designs were also recreated for this purpose, especially as they do not appear in other previous exhibition catalogues.[19]

Within this group of works on paper two are related to *Saul* and to the prints that appeared in *Integral* in 1925. The set design, which closely resembles the version printed in *Integral*, is dated 1924, although as shown above it may have been created at a later date (see Figure 2). Unlike the other drawings in the group, it is not annotated with the name of the director or the theatrical ensemble, thus confirming the fact that this production never took place. It reveals a constructivist stage with three distinguishable elements: a backdrop with a geometric composition dominated by a half-moon shape, the stage-side tormentors with jagged zig-zag designs, and a multi-level centrepiece topped by a rectangular contraption from which two beams reach out to the two sides of the stage. Perhaps Maxy envisioned the elements to be mechanised or to serve as acrobatic supports for a new breed of biomechanical actors. The actors themselves are imagined by Maxy in the second highly finished work on paper. This is another version of the print representing the three Devils in *Integral*, and the disjointed bodies, made up of primary-coloured geometric shapes and robotic elements, are even more evident in this drawing. One character is missing its arms, while another seems to have had them replaced by chevron-shaped springs. Like the set designs, the costumes are a futuristic flight of fancy that could not be realised and which may well have proven a step too far even for the ground-breaking Vilna Troupe. As shown later in this essay, these were by far Maxy's most severely avant-garde designs, eschewing all naturalistic elements and fully embracing constructivist aesthetics on stage. Yet this particular vision remained only an imagined one.

---

18   Irina Cărăbaș, "Avangarda românească în viața de dincolo. M. H. Maxy—pictor comunist," in *Arta în România între anii 1945–2000. O analiză din perspectiva prezentului*, eds. Dan Călin, Iosif Kiràly, Anca Oroveanu and Magda Radu (Bucharest: UNArte, 2016), 36–51. According to Cărăbaș, Ilk was the first Maxy scholar to draw attention to the differences between the paintings of Tzara and Ciricleanu currently in the collection of the National Art Museum of Romania and the period reproductions from *Integral* and *Contimporanul*. In 2019, following technical analysis, the Museum concluded that Maxy repainted sections of Tzara's portrait on several occasions.

19   This is based on the extensive solo and group exhibition catalogue archive in the Fond Maxy at the National Art Museum of Romania, as well as period press searches.

Figure 2:   M. H. Maxy. Set design for *Saul.* Pencil, ink, watercolour, and gouache. 1960s (National Art Museum of Romania).

The fact that the "first scenic constructions" Maxy imagined for *Saul* failed to become reality was perhaps to be expected. In Romania, set design had been primarily developed by a number of Italian artists who worked in Bucharest during the second half of the nineteenth century. Elaborate, yet generic and interchangeable, painted décor was the norm. The 1889 obituary of Gaetano Labo, the most prominent of these artists, specifically referred to the complex skill required to obtain the correct perspective in painted backdrops.[20] According to Ion Cazaban, the first truly modern stage design was seen in Bucharest only in 1922 when Karl Heinz Martin, a disciple of Max Reinhardt, came from Berlin to direct four plays at the Bulandra Theatre.[21] His theatrical aesthetic was pared back, with monochrome backdrops and a limited number of essential props, relying on lighting to create the desired atmosphere.[22] Although innovative in their

---

20 Ana Traci, "Pictori scenografi in secolul al XIX-lea la Teatrul cel Mare din București," *Studii și cercetări de istoria artei. Teatru, muzică, cinematografie,* 51–53, nos. 7–9 (2013–2015): 3–23.
21 Cazaban, Scena românească și expresionismul, 56.
22 Ibid, 19, quoting *Rampa,* 8 March 1922.

sparseness, the sets still had some semblance to reality, with domestic objects used to suggest an interior. What had previously been a two-dimensional fantasy brought to life through the illusion of perspective could now be seen on stage, albeit in a more streamlined version. Maxy's scenic constructions made the leap much further, to a stage that resembled nothing familiar, except perhaps an abstract painting. In his writings, Maxy mused on the need for removing painterly illusion in favour of the three-dimensionality of the "scenic cube" and increasingly strove to replace the pictorial with the spatial in his theatre designs, as this essay reveals.[23] Another endeavour of avant-garde theatre practitioners was mechanisation. Their efforts surpassed Martin's use of lighting technology, for example, by experimenting with multi-level platforms and moving elements on stage, as Meyerhold often did.[24] Perhaps Maxy intended for his stage design to include such elements, especially when considering his robot-inspired vision for the actors' costumes. However, this might have been challenging to achieve in reality, particularly given the Vilna Troupe's demanding touring schedule and the attachment to traditional décor in contemporary Romanian theatre.

Shabbsai Tsvi: A Transnational Performance Retrieved

The very first production with designs by Maxy to reach the stage was *Shabbsai Tsvi*, which premiered almost a year later, in February 1926.[25] The production was an amalgamation of dramas by Jewish writer Sholem Asch and Polish intellectual Jerzy Żuławski, and it recounted the downfall of the eponymous seventeenth century hero who abjured his faith in front of the Ottoman sultan Mehmet IV, thus proving to be a false messiah.[26]

---

23 M. H. Maxy, "Regia scenică—decor—costum," 4.
24 For a detailed study of Meyerhold's innovations see Konstantin Rudnitsky, *Meyerhold the Director* (Ann Arbor: Ardis, 1981).
25 A. Sch., "Premiera de astă seară. Teatrul Central," *Rampa*, 24 February 1926. The spelling of the title varies even within the same article in the period press, so I have chosen the version used by Yiddish theatre scholar Debra Caplan.
26 Sholem Asch's three act poetic drama was first published in 1908 in a Vilnius periodical. Polish writer Jerzy Żuławski may have been inspired by it when he wrote *The End of the Messiah*, a four-act play about the same subject first published in 1911. The Bucharest performance was adapted by Joseph Buloff from both of these works. For more information about these plays see Joseph Sherman, "Asch, Sholem," YIVO Encyclopedia of Jews in Eastern Europe (2010), available at: http://www.yivoencyclopedia.org/article.aspx/Asch_Sholem, accessed on 9 January 2017; Krzysztof Niweliński, "Shabbetai Sevi on Stage: Literary, Theatrical and Operatic Creations of the Messiah," *El Prezente. Journal for Sephardic Studies*, no. 10 (December 2016), 55–69; Sonia Gollance, "Plotting Yiddish Drama. Shabse

The production enjoyed great success: the cultural daily *Rampa* quoted positive reviews from eight other publications. The reviewers were unanimous in their praise of the four scenes that made up the production which were "grandiose," "breath-taking" and "a delight for the eye." The design of the sets and costumes, "superbly coloured and harmonious, was proof they were arranged and executed by an artist," forming "a true poem of light and colour."[27]

Until recently, it might have been difficult to imagine what this performance actually looked like. The surviving designs by Maxy, located in the collections of the Romanian Academy, have not been very widely discussed or reproduced, compared to *Saul*, for example.[28] *Shabbsai Tsvi* was not mentioned in *Integral* (which only had one issue printed in 1926) and has thus escaped the attention of scholars of the Romanian avant-garde. The three designs are part of the same group of highly-finished works on paper discussed earlier and are thus more likely to date from the 1960s than 1926 when the productions took place. Nonetheless, they provide an important visual clue to what *Shabbsai Tsvi* looked like on stage, especially when examined alongside a group of period photographs that have emerged during my research for this project. Unconnected to Maxy's name, the images have been part of the Joseph Buloff Jewish Theater Archive housed by the Judaica Division at Harvard's Widener Library since 1987, when they were bequeathed by his wife Luba Kadison and their daughter Barbara.[29] The collection documents the international career of actors Buloff and Kadison, who were part of the original nucleus of the Vilna Troupe and who settled in the United States in the late 1920s. The images of *Shabbsai Tsvi* in the collection were dated 1924 and were catalogued without reference to the play's designer, which explains their absence from any studies of Maxy's work, despite the fact that he appears in one of the photographs together with Buloff.[30] According to Luba Kadison, "the sets were designed by Maxim [sic], a renowned Rumanian painter,

---

Tsvi," Digital Yiddish Theatre Project, no date, available at: https://web.uwm.edu/yiddish-stage/plotting-yiddish-drama/shabse-tsvi, accessed on 28 August 2019.
27 "Cronica dramatică despre *Sapsay Zwi* cu Trupa din Vilna," *Rampa*, 6 March 1926.
28 Romanian Academy, Graphic Arts Collection, Fond Maxy. They are briefly discussed in Ion Cazaban, "Scenografi ai teatrului românesc interbelic (I)," 61, and illustrated in Magda Cârneci, ed., *Rădăcini și ecouri ale avangardei în colecțiile de grafică ale Bibliotecii Academiei Române* (Bucharest: Academia Română, 2011).
29 Gladys Damon, "Harvard Library Receives," clipping from unidentified newspaper. YIVO Institute for Jewish Research, Joseph Buloff and Luba Kadison Collection.
30 Harvard Library, Joseph Buloff Jewish Theater Archive, Photographs Collection. Following my research visit in October 2017, the catalogue records of the relevant photographs in the collection were updated with the correct information, including the date of the production and Maxy's name.

who brought the leading personalities of Bucharest to see this highly stylized, surreal production that took the Vilna Troupe still further away from its earlier realistic style. The response was overwhelming."[31]

The photographs and the designs can now present a much more accurate account of the production than what had been previously thought possible. The surviving visual material reveals three very different scenes that hover between the abstract and the figurative. A photograph from Act I with Buloff in the title role was printed in *Rampa* shortly after the premiere.[32] It shows the hero standing on a pedestal outside the gates of a city, as his followers prostrate themselves.[33] The cubo-futurist outlines of the metropolis rise up behind him, juxtaposing historicist and contemporary architectural forms. The stylised turrets of a tower can be distinguished in the centre of the composition, alongside a shape resembling a multi-storey modernist apartment block with a flat roof and fashionable ocean-liner styling, including a wave motif. Its porthole-shaped windows contrast with the latticed shapes above and below that evoke medieval portcullises. Although the staging still follows the theatrical convention of the painted backdrop, it has renounced all attempts at an illusionistic effect. Maxy's sketch for Act I emphasises the three-dimensional quality of the theatrical stage itself: the space in front of the backdrop is clearly delineated by a striped border, and the prompt box is visible at the front edge of the stage, whilst the upper edges of the city seep out from the pictorial space culminating in a puff of chimney smoke that escapes the confines of the drawing's edge. The set's flatly sparse yet monumental quality serves to re-enforce the action taking place on the stage in front of it. Reflecting the tenets of modern theatrical innovation, in particular those of Meyerhold, it is the actors that provide the set with contrast, structure, and volume through collective movements and configurations, emphasised by their costumes.

---

31 Kadison and Buloff, *On Stage, Off Stage*, 53.
32 Scarlat Fronda, "Cronica dramatică. Teatrul Central. Sapsay Zwi (Falsul Messia)," *Rampa*, 26 February 1926. A better quality version of this image is included in the Fond Maxy, Documentation Department, National Art Museum of Romania.
33 Żuławski's play is "set in Ottoman Adrianople, today's Turkish city of Edirne, about mid-September 1666," according to Niweliński, "Shabbetai Șevi on Stage," 58.

Figure 3: M. H. Maxy. Set design for *Shabbsai Tsvi*, Act II. Pencil, ink, and gouache, 1960s (Romanian Academy Library).

In Act II, Maxy's sketch displays a riot of primary colours that suggest the sumptuous setting of the Sultan's court, yet they are tempered by geometrical shapes and patterns, rejecting the fashion for unbridled theatrical orientalism exemplified by ensembles such as the Ballet Russes (Figure 3). Even the Sultan and his two attendants form a symmetrical group wearing lavish, yet crisply abstract, garments. The potentiality of the stage space is once again carefully considered: there are curtains, steps, and multi-level platforms in Maxy's sketch drawn according to perspective conventions, in contrast to the flat background. Several photographs show how the design was used in practice during different scenes in the play's narrative. In one image Shabbsai Tsvi can be seen in combat with the Sultan's Janissaries, wearing his messianic crown (Figure 4), while two other photographs show him being captured and paying obeisance to the Ottoman ruler. All of these scenes make full use of the set's structure: Shabbsai Tsvi's downfall is mirrored by this descent from the pyramidal podium to its base, and the Sultan's underlings gather in compact formations, using the stepped platforms to create diagonal lines that frame the action. Maxy's costume designs are equally stylised. The striped garments of the guards alternate with patches of plain colour, whilst Shabbsai Tsvi is set apart by his white robes. The Sultan's costume is the most elaborate, consisting of a robe with an abstract asymmetrical composition and a turban topped with geometric patterns. The Sultan's oversized headgear and his bulging belly turn him into an antagonist that is perhaps too comical to be effective—a critique brought also by the Romanian press, yet Żuławski did mean to portray him as a weak and ineffectual ruler.[34]

Figure 4: The Vilna Troupe in *Shabbsai Tsvi*, Act II, 1926 (Harvard Library, Joseph Buloff Jewish Theater Archive).

Ultimately, Shabbsai Tsvi's battle is with his own self, as the production's concluding act suggests. The design for this scene makes its visual impact though arresting simplicity, with an elongated pentagon shape emerging out of the darkness of the stage to enclose a step pyramid on which the protagonist stands, a barely human figure composed of interlocking geometric

---

34 J. Blumberg, "Sabetai Zwi. Câteva observațiuni cu ocazia Jubileului de 25 reprezentații a piesei *Sapsay-Zwi*," *Renașterea*, 27 March 1926; Niweliński, "Shabbetai Șevi on Stage," 60.

shapes. Shabbsai Tsvi, having lost his white messianic robes, is juxtaposed on stage with his temptress Sarah, his position uncertain, hovering somewhere between heaven and earth. As Luba Kadison later revealed, Sarah's white dress was Buloff's means of signalling that she "symbolized the false messiah's alter-ego" and thus his struggle with his own nature rather than a physical being. For one reviewer, this last scene was truly memorable and offered "a majestic simplicity in its decorative concept."[35]

Shabbsai Tsvi was one of the Vilna Troupe's most notable successes in Bucharest. The mise-en-scène was reputedly the most sumptuous the Central Theatre had ever seen,[36] weaving together "decor, lights, apparitions, tempo, [and] acting" into one inspired performance, akin to the experiments of Max Reinhardt whom the Vilna Troupe had met in Berlin.[37] Maxy's work had "great artistic value," and "Romanian theatre [could] count on him as a craftsman of admirable talent."[38] One month after the premiere, an article celebrated the play's 25th performance and several newspapers ran serialised accounts of Shabbsai Tsvi's life.[39]

The play had also propelled Buloff to critical and popular acclaim in Romania, and perhaps contributed to his decision to advance his career in the United States. This, however, was not the end of *Shabbsai Tsvi*, which enjoyed its own transnational afterlife. Buloff's revival on the stage of the Jewish People's Institute in Chicago in the autumn on 1927 preserved Maxy's scenography, crediting its maker in the play's programme.[40] This programme, located in two similar versions in both the YIVO Institute and the Harvard University archives, has not been previously identified by scholars of Maxy's work, and thus the transatlantic reach of this scenography has never been explored.[41] The archives also contain detailed scrapbooks with press reviews, assembled by Buloff. Chicago critics lauded the production as "an artistic triumph of the first order

---

35 L.B. Wechsler, "Cronica dramatică. Trupa din Vilna. *Sabsay Zwi*. Mister în 3 acte de Schalom Asch prelucrat de J. Jurlowsky," *Renașterea*, 27 February 1926.
36 Sch., "Premiere de astă seară. Teatrul Central."
37 I. Sing, "Cronica dramatică. Sapsay *Zwi* la Trupa din Wilna," *Hasmonaea*, February 1926.
38 Wechsler, "Cronica dramatică."
39 Blumberg, "Sabetai Zwi. Câteva observațiuni," and the serialisation of "Sabetay Zewi" by Israel Zangwil in *Renașterea*, starting on 13 March 1926.
40 According to Kadison and Buloff, *On Stage, Off Stage*, 70, this happened in 1928, but the production took place the previous year. See "The Chicago Dramatic Society to Present Sabati Zwi," *The Sentinel*, 4 November 1927.
41 Harvard Library, Judaica Division, Joseph Buloff Jewish Theater Archive, Programmes Collection; YIVO Institute for Jewish Research, Esther-Rachel Kaminska Theater Museum Collection.

[...] upon a stage lit up with scenic wonder" and "a revelation" with "enchanting music and [...] fantastic, almost bizarre, scenery."[42] According to reporter Meyer Levin, "the play was staged in the "modern way." The scenery was in sections and parcels of color that suggested the forms of actual things. There were platforms and steps for the actors to group upon; there were costumes that moved as part of the scenery."[43]

Levin reported in detail about the drama unfolding on stage, providing some additional clues which render the performance even more innovative. The Sultan's dais for example was multi-functional, turning to reveal the staircase that prefaces Shabbsai Tsvi's downfall. Furthermore, Levin makes explicit the symbolic implications of the sets and costumes which signal the characters' paths, such as the use of black and white ensembles for Shabbsai Tsvi or the multi-level platforms that allow the hero and his antagonists, the Sultan and Sarah, to switch places both physically and metaphorically.

Comparing the physical manifestations of *Shabbsai Tsvi* with the prototypes for *Saul,* it becomes clear that although the strict, strongly utopian constructivism of the latter was unrealisable, aspects of it did inform the former. The mask-like make-up, the multi-functional set with its ramps and stairs, the flatness of the backdrops infused with cubist shapes, and echoes of modernist architecture all echoed contemporary developments in stage design and performance. If some conventions were preserved, such as the backcloth, illusionistic effects were discarded as were any aspirations of mimicking reality. The play's success may have stemmed from its conciliation of the traditional and the avant-garde, which is also visible in an intriguing photograph of the play's lead actor and designer standing in front of the Act I backdrop. Buloff, in full costume and makeup, strikes a pose next to Maxy, tall and elegantly dressed. Although their trajectories converged for only a short period on the stage of Bucharest's Central Theatre, what emerged from this encounter was a transportable and transmutable vision of modern performance that found success in a transnational context.

---

42   Clippings from unidentified publications found in Scrapbook 2 in the Harvard Library, Judaica Division, Joseph Buloff Jewish Theater Archive, Scrapbooks Collection.
43   This is a clipping from Scrapbook 2, Harvard Library, Judaica Division, Joseph Buloff Jewish Theater Archive, Scrapbooks Collection. It was most likely taken from *The Chicago Daily News,* where Levin, later a prominent novelist, worked as a reporter until 1928. See Herbert Mitgang, "Meyer Levin, Writer, 75, Dies; Books Included *Compulsion*" (1981), available at: https://www.nytimes.com/1981/07/11/obituaries/meyer-levin-writer-75-dies-books-included-compulsion.html, accessed on 12 April 2018.

The Sentimental Mannequin: Modern Life on the Theatrical Stage

Cultural collaboration was also apparent in another Vilna Troupe production in Bucharest which took place after Buloff's departure and which represented a new step for the ensemble: exploring contemporary Romanian dramaturgy. *The Sentimental Mannequin* by Romanian poet and playwright Ion Minulescu had made its debut in early 1926 at the National Theatre in Bucharest, so it was a brave choice for the Yiddish troupe to present their own version in translation in November of that same year. A Pirandellian play-within-a-play, it charted the attempts of a playwright to find inspiration for his forthcoming oeuvre. Minulescu's wish was for the play to resemble a puppet show, and he included detailed stage directions in his script.[44] The characters were described as "mannequins" exposed in displays that reflected Romania's social classes and included a young and ambitious playwright, a high-society dame, and her ageing millionaire husband. The play was to be performed through a shop window, obscured by blind in-between scenes as though closed for business, and framed by a sign inscribed "La Dernière Mode pour Dames et Messieurs. Confections, Opinions, Sentiments." Furthermore, the play's scenes were to be called vitrines instead of acts.[45] *The Sentimental Mannequin* was thus a clear product of its age, reflecting both contemporary social mores and current theories of experimental theatre, including an interest in marionettes and an emphasis on the illusory quality of the stage. It also provided a commentary on the impact of modern life on domestic spaces, which in *The Sentimental Mannequin* are more than a backdrop, becoming a reflection of the characters that inhabit them. The first vitrine for example, is the garret room of playwright Radu Cartian, decorated with good taste yet exhibiting a bohemian disarray, while the next two acts take place in the luxuriously modern dwelling of socialite Jeana Ionescu-Potopeni.

Maxy's set designs have been preserved in the collection of the National Art Museum of Romania.[46] In Maxy's vision, Radu's dwelling is full of jagged edges, geometric furniture, and curious angles. The walls slope in different directions, and a latticed triangular shape hovers over the room. If in *Shabbsai Tsvi* the traditional theatrical backdrop was still employed, albeit with a near-abstract design, in *The Sentimental Mannequin* Maxy seems to have done away with it altogether instead utilising the

---

44   Ion Minulescu, *Manechinul sentimental* (Bucharest: Cultura națională, 1926).
45   Ibid, 9–10.
46   National Art Museum of Romania, Graphic Art Collection, Fond Maxy.

three-dimensional potential of the stage space. The interplay of surfaces that are both solid and transparent render Cartian's home spatially plausible yet also evidently illusory. This apparent contradiction is particularly manifest in Maxy's sketch. The lines that dissect the floor and the walls recall a perspective grid, yet they lead the eye in strange and disorienting directions. Disregarding Minulescu's instructions, Maxy did away with the shop sign framing. The plain colour palette, together with the geometric furniture, a functional wall niche, and uncluttered space, suggests that perhaps the artist was using the opportunity to educate the public about the clean lines of modern interior design, having recently become involved with the Academy of Decorative Arts, a private venture for design education opened in Bucharest in 1924 which counted Minulescu amongst its patrons.[47]

If Maxy dispensed with the shop window framing in the first act, in the second vitrine he boldly turned the entire stage into a stylish boutique with flowing curtains and constructivist home accessories seen from "outside" its window (Figure 5). Minulescu's shop sign slogans surround this tableau, allowing the audience to voyeuristically peer through the make-believe glass. The objects dotted around the display would not be easily identifiable—they could be construed as sculptures perhaps—if they did not resemble objects displayed in the showroom of the Academy of Decorative Arts which had only just opened in October 1926. The distinctive shapes recall the sharply geometric lamps and vases produced by designer Andrei Vespremie, the Academy's artistic director, and subsequently by Maxy, which are immediately recognisable as the inspiration behind the objects that crowd the imaginary shop window (Figure 6). It is not yet known whether the items in *The Sentimental Mannequin* were simply props made in the image of modernist design objects or whether they were the Academy's actual output. Either way, the stage thus set became both a real and a fictitious shop window, mirroring the Academy's newly opened commercial space.

---

47 For recent studies of the Academy's activities, see Irina Cărăbaș, "The Shadow of the Object. Modernity and Decoration in Romanian Art," in *Dis(continuities). Fragments of Romanian Modernity in the First Half of the Twentieth Century*, ed. Carmen Popescu (Bucharest: Simetria, 2010), 101–42, and Alexandra Chiriac, "Myth, Making, and Modernity: The Academy of Decorative Arts and Design Education in Bucharest," *Caietele Avangardei*, 6, no. 12 (2018), 96–107.

Figure 5: M. H. Maxy. Set design for *The Sentimental Mannequin*, Act II. Pencil, ink, and gouache, 1960s (National Art Museum of Romania).

The living room of Jeana, the woman whom Cartian wishes to use as inspiration for the leading lady in his new play, should be "a luxurious room with few pieces of furniture in a pure style," perhaps an antithesis to the cluttered orientalised interiors of Bucharest's middle classes which had made their way onto the theatrical stage.[48] In one such example, a play titled *Anuța* staged at the National Theatre in Bucharest in November 1925, the stage space was virtually undistinguishable from an upper-class Bucharest dwelling, with heavy wooden furniture, oriental-style carpets, an oversized chandelier, and even a glimpse into a dining room ready to welcome guests.[49] By contrast, Maxy filled his stage design with the sleek contours of modernist objects and little more than that, presenting a literal depiction of the commercial space alluded to by Minulescu. One of his sketches even includes the entrance to the shop, its design replete with modernist architectural detail, suggesting a metal frame with rectangular

---

48   Minulescu, *Manechinul sentimental*, 53.
49   From an album of stage designs, National Theatre, 1925–26 theatrical season (Archives of the National Theatre Museum, Bucharest). *Anuța* (1925) is a morality play by Lucreția Petrescu in which the innocent daughter of a kept woman is introduced to her mother's entourage, but succeeds in escaping the same fate.

patterns and a cubist-inspired door handle. The composition evokes the cover of *Integral*'s December 1926 issue, in which a vase by Vespremie can be glimpsed amongst the elegant assemblage of objects in the Academy's showroom, above the caption "Modern Interior by M. H. Maxy: Furniture, Cushions, Carpets, Paintings"[50] (see Figure 6). Although this particular sign may not say "La Dernière Mode," it certainly implies it. Thus, the stage designs for *The Sentimental Mannequin* observed the same modernist parameters that construed the new urban interiors, blurring modern art and modern life in the most avant-garde of fashions.

Figure 6:   Image from the cover of Integral no. 9, December 1926.

---

50   *Integral*, no. 9 (December 1926).

Man, Beast and Virtue: **The Permeability of the Fourth Wall**

Only one month after *The Sentimental Mannequin*, in December 1926, the Vilna Troupe premiered Luigi Pirandello's *Man, Beast and Virtue* with designs by Maxy. The Italian playwright, an important figure for the Romanian avant-garde, was interviewed in *Integral* in November 1925 by Maxy's colleague, Mihail Cosma.[51] According to Pirandello, his ultimate goal was to uncover the scenic potential in any situation, transforming "any street corner" into a theatrical stage and any passers-by into "characters in search of an author." Despite Pirandello's reputation, his plays had not been widely performed in Romania, and the Vilna Troupe's production was only the third work by the playwright to see the light of the stage in Bucharest.[52] *Man, Beast and Virtue,* Pirandello's so called "tragifarce" first published in 1919, has a simple plot: Signora Perella, the wife of a sea-captain, falls for Paolino, her son's tutor. She becomes pregnant and conspires with her lover to make the husband believe the child is his. There is only one problem: the sea-captain prefers to avoid his wife even on the rare occasions when he is ashore. Thus, the scheming couple have only a small window of opportunity to induce the captain to accept his wife's amorous advances.

Perhaps due to its on-stage success, *Man, Beast and Virtue* is one of Maxy's better documented plays. As well as a front cover and feature in *Integral*'s January 1927 issue, further visual material is located in the collections of the National Art Museum of Romania: two photographs and two set designs from the same group of highly finished works on paper by Maxy that probably date from the 1960s.[53] The sketch for Act I reveals a domestic interior similar to the opening scene of *The Sentimental Mannequin*. Maxy takes one step further in this case, dispensing with walls altogether and opting instead for a structure so permeable that the latticed panels edging one side seem almost compact by comparison. The interior is sparsely decorated with bookshelves, a table, chair, and carpet, elements common to both productions, as are the jagged edges and the underwhelming colour palette. The juxtaposition of flat and three-dimensional elements positions this space, like that of Act I in *The Sentimental Mannequin,* somewhere between the real and the illusory. Furthermore, the uncanny proportions of the objects in this sketch—the chair towering over the table and the oversized plant pot—propel this further into the realm of

---

51 Mihail Cosma, "De vorbă cu Luigi Pirandello," *Integral*, no. 8 (November 1925), 2–3.
52 "O piesă de Pirandello la Teatrul Central," *Rampa*, 2 December 1926.
53 National Art Museum of Romania, Documentation Department, Fond Maxy and Graphic Arts Collection, Fond Maxy.

the surreal. The existence of photographs in the case of *Man, Beast and Virtue* reveals how such a design was translated into reality. Maxy placed the characters in a simulacrum of a home with walls that were present yet invisible, so that their trials and tribulations, though contained within, were visible for all to see. The structures that sketched out the walls, although geometric, were uneven, creating a disorienting, distorted perspective that mirrored both the naval theme of the play and its moral morass. The front "wall" sloped upwards while the back "wall" sloped downwards, as did the latticed door attached to it, a device Maxy previously experimented with in *The Sentimental Mannequin* but which evidently came to fruition in the structurally lighter design for *Man, Beast and Virtue*.

Figure 7: M. H. Maxy. Set design for *Man, Beast and Virtue*, Act II. Pencil, watercolour, ink, and gouache, 1960s (National Art Museum of Romania).

In the design for Act II a second interior was sketched out with beams forming an octagonal shape that enclosed a table with four chairs, a shelving unit for dishes, and several potted plants (Figure 7). According to *Integral*'s reviewer, "the sea captain's room is constructed from naval elements: the table slopes like the crest of a wave, the chairs are capped by anchors, the lamp is an anchor, the shelves are made from the sterns and prows of ships."[54] The same spatial instability is present in this second mise-en-scène, with surfaces that slope when they should be balanced and walls that are permeable when they should be solid. Although Maxy's sketch suggests that the view from the sitting room towards the zig-zagging surface of the sea could be a painted backdrop, photographs reveal this was not the case (Figure 8). The latticed balcony doors and the anchor-shaped chandelier were free-standing elements of the decor, while a small rectangular panel with abstract shapes—barely visible behind the actors on stage—was perhaps suggestive of the water's turbulent surface. As we have seen with *The Sentimental Mannequin*, Maxy's sets were fully transitioning into the realm of the three-dimensional, yet producing disorienting illusions of reality that slipped away from spectators just like the mirage of a painted backcloth. A review of the play published in *Rampa* praised the "bizarre cubist-expressionist" mise-en-scène and explained the presence of the flower pots with their stylised blooms attached to grid-like structures.[55] Signora Perella was to move the five plants from one window to another as a signal to her lover that their stratagem has succeeded. In the archival photograph, she stands on a stool in the pose of a mock Madonna between her husband and the tutor Paolino, who is offering her one of the plants as a tribute (Figure 8). The potted plants, or rather the pots, hold further significance. Like the mystery objects in *The Sentimental Mannequin*, they are the product of the Academy of Decorative Arts and appear, holding real plants, in the images of the institution's showrooms. Most likely these are not the same items—the ones in the play have a more rudimentary, satirical aspect—but they are clearly linked.

---

54 Gheorghe Dinu, "Teatrul Central. Înscenări moderne," *Integral*, no. 10 (January 1927), 5.
55 Scarlat Froda, "Cronica dramatică. Omul, bestia și virtutea," *Rampa*, 16 December 1926.

Figure 8: The Vilna Troupe in *Man, Beast and Virtue*, Act II, 1926 (Courtesy of National Art Museum of Romania)

Furthermore, the interaction between Signora Perella and the potted flowers advanced the action of the play in a physical sense: her movements and by extension that of the plants signalled a change both in the spatial relationships between the objects on stage, as well as in the psychological relationship between the characters of the play. This recalls a concept that we have previously encountered in Maxy's writings in *Integral*, namely that in a successful scenic construction the sets and the actors merge together, becoming part of the same dynamic mechanism that conveys the drama.[56] According to an article in *Rampa* that outlined preparations for the production, the props used to furnish the play's interiors were not there simply for ambiance but purposely re-enforced the dramatic action and constituted a "continuation" of the actors' hands.[57] The article, reporting a conversation between the writer and Maxy, also revealed that wooden beams were used to construct the see-through structures. These would ensure that "the movement of the actors is visible to the public at all times, and the room resembles a bird cage in which the

---

56 Maxy. "Regia scenică—decor—costum."
57 "O piesă de Pirandello la Teatrul Central."

poor beings move according to Piradello's plan and sense of irony."[58] A later review in *Integral*, although largely a paean devoted to Pirandello, made some further comments concerning Maxy's decor. Emphasising their spatial innovation, the reviewer observed that the on-stage rooms "do not have 3 walls, but 4" which being "schematic, transvisible" are not an obstacle to the spectator who becomes privy to Maxy's "Roentgen eye."[59] The constructions so plastically described were illustrated by two photographs which demonstrated how the play's environments were present on stage only through their outlines, so that the actors operated inside transparent structures populated by equally sketchy and geometric props. The Vilna Troupe, concluded the article, was the only ensemble experimenting locally with the new trends in stage design.[60]

In a second version of the sketch for Act II, which exists only in an undated archival photograph, the sloping table and the anchor-topped chairs are placed on a circular carpet that exhibits the markings of a compass. The illusory space of the theatrical stage thus expands outwards to encompass a limitless geographical space, in the same way that the collaborations between Maxy and the Vilna Troupe exist in a nation-blurring cultural context. In December 1926, Maxy observed that "the expanding field of scenic possibilities is gradually transforming the use of the stage" and one might add that the expanding geographies of the theatrical avant-gardes did likewise.[61]

Conclusion

The productions staged by the Vilna Troupe with Maxy as scenographer brought theatrical experimentation to Bucharest in many ways, from multi-functional sets to intense physicality of performance, to a blurring of the boundaries between modern life and the stage. At its most extreme, that which was termed Maxy's "Roentgen eye" dissolved barriers by literally removing walls and replacing them with transparent structures that furthermore suggested the even vaster landscapes stretching outside the theatrical realm. Gathering photographs, artworks, and documents from international sources has made it possible to reconstruct the outputs of this richly innovative collaboration. The lack of recognition afforded to these productions within the Romanian avant-garde historiography is

---

58   Ibid.
59   Dinu, "Teatrul Central. Înscenări moderne."
60   Ibid.
61   "O piesă de Pirandello la Teatrul Central."

thus even more indicative of the very real risk that practices and practitioners that do not fit a particular national narrative are resigned to a scholarly no-man's land.

To return to the original argument, this article demonstrates that a theatrical revolution did take place in Bucharest, but its existence was obscured by the ephemerality of the performative and by its unwieldy transnational trajectory. The productions discussed in this essay defy national categorisation, posing challenges not only of the theoretical kind (where do they fit into the discipline) but also of the practical kind (materials are dispersed geographically and come in many different languages). Despite, or perhaps because of, this recovering these narratives is a challenge worth undertaking and one that may ultimately open the door towards a more inclusive history of avant-garde performance.

Compulsory Primary Education and State Building in Rural Bessarabia (1918–1940)

Petru Negură

Abstract: *This article examines the way in which public primary education was established in rural Bessarabia during 1918–1940. The imposition of mass compulsory education resulted from an unequal relationship of power between the state education authorities and the village population, which at times conflicted and at other times negotiated with each other. This process was crucial for the expansion of the state in rural areas and the development of citizenship among the civilian population of what was at the time a new Romanian province. Yet, primary schooling did not succeed entirely, due to the resistance of the rural population, the indetermination of state agents, and the lack of institutional infrastructure.*

Introduction

This article examines the way in which general public primary education was established in rural areas of Bessarabia in 1918–1940 under the Romanian administration. This process is studied from the perspective of the implementation of compulsory schooling, assessed on the basis of indicators such as school attendance and statements of key stakeholders. In this peripheral region, the establishment and expansion of mass public education were central components of a wider project of nation and state building, as in other countries undergoing modernization.[1] The population of Bessarabia was subject to ambitious schooling policies in

---

1 On the role of education in nation-building, see Ernest Gellner, *Thought and Change* (Chicago: University of Chicago Press, 1965); Ernest Gellner, *Nations and Nationalism* (Ithaca, NY: Cornell University Press, 1983); Anthony Smith, *Nationalism and Modernism: A Critical Survey of Recent Theories of Nations and Nationalism* (London: Routledge, 1998); Stephen J. Heathorn, *For Home, Country and Race: Constructing Gender, Class and Englishness in the Elementary School 1880–1914* (Toronto: University of Toronto Press, 2000); Eugen Weber, *Peasants into Frenchmen. The Modernization of Rural France 1870–1914* (Stanford: Stanford University Press, 1976); Andy Green, *Education and State Formation. Europe, East Asia and the USA* (London: Palgrave Macmillan, 2013). For the role of literacy and schooling in the development of modern nation in Romania, see Alex Drace-Francis, *The Making of Modern Romanian Culture. Literacy and the Development of National Identity* (London: I.B. Tauris, 2006).

view of facilitating the province's rapid integration into Romania. Implementation of this project faced difficulties and encountered resistance from the local population.

Through school state authorities wanted to mold enlightened, disciplined, and loyal citizens, but the process was ambiguous, contradictory, and often disappointing. The primary school remained in Bessarabia, and to a large extent in other Romanian regions after World War I, the only education program attended by most literate persons.[2] By 1930, the latter accounted for slightly more than half of the total population,[3] but such a wide intervention left the province changed. Beyond the official discourse and ambitions of the Romanian authorities, the primary school catalyzed an ample, although initially difficult and contradictory, process of negotiation and cooperation between the state authorities and the civilian population, adults, and children alike.

This study focuses on the rural population without neglecting the development of primary education in urban areas. This limitation is motivated by differences in establishing general public education observed in rural areas where the literacy rate and the schooling rate were much lower than in cities.[4] By virtue of modernization and the nationalizing ambitions of the Romanian state, the level of coercion applied by the authorities and the intensity of the population's response to this project were higher in villages than in cities where the school had been an established institution for nearly half a century.[5] At the same time, the conflicting nature of this process in villages reveals *in extremis* the relation between the state and the civilian population during intense modernization. Note also that the rural population was an overwhelming majority in interwar Romania (79 percent in 1930), especially in Bessarabia (87 percent).[6] Therefore, at least statistically, the rural population prevailed

---

2   In Romania, 85.1 percent of literate people had only an elementary education. In Bessarabia, the percentage was 87.3 in rural and 57.9 in urban areas. See Dumitru Şandru, *Populaţia rurală a României între cele două războaie* (Iaşi: Ed. Academiei Române, 1980), 182, and Nicolae Enciu, *Populaţia rurală a Basarabiei (1918–1940)* (Chişinău: Epigraf, 2002), 214.

3   Literate people represented 57 percent of Romania's population in 1930. Şandru, *Populaţia rurală a României*, 180–2.

4   In 1930, literate people accounted for 39 percent of the population in rural Bessarabia, and 72.2 percent in its cities. See Enciu, *Populaţia rurală a Basarabiei*, 212.

5   Drace-Francis, *Geneza culturii române*, 113–21, 123–6, 162–4; Mirela-Luminiţa Murgescu, *Între bunul creştin şi bravul român. Rolul şcolii primare în construirea identităţii naţionale româneşti (1831–1878)* (Iaşi: Editura A'92, 1999), 31–9.

6   Şandru, *Populaţia rurală a României*, 180 and Enciu, *Populaţia rurală a Basarabiei*, 14.

in this province. Despite populist speeches exalting peasant virtues, the Romanian administration perceived this dominant rurality as a challenge to the modernization project announced after 1918.[7]

Romanian authorities criticized the Tsarist administration's achievements in mass education.[8] The 1897 census, the only one carried out in the Empire prior to its dissolution in 1917, revealed an extremely low literacy rate throughout the Empire. Bessarabia registered only 19.4 percent literacy (22 percent among males and 8.8 percent among females[9]). To legitimize their program, the new authorities neglected the significant efforts made by Russian central (Ministry of Education) and local authorities (the so-called *zemstva*) to boost mass schooling in the region at the beginning of the 20th century. In 1900–1914 primary schooling in the Empire knew an unprecedented expansion measured by schooling indicators and the number of schools.[10] These indicators were outstripped by the new regional administration in 1928, but during the economic crisis of 1929–1933 the schooling rate in the region was lower. By exaggerating the "negative legacy" left by the Tsarist administration in the schooling of the masses, the Romanian administration legitimized itself. By denying the efforts of the Tsarist authorities in public education, the Romanian administration offered a credible excuse for the schools' poor performance which after 1918 rested on the unacknowledged bases of the previous efforts of mass schooling.

A guiding hypothesis of this study is that establishment and strengthening of primary education in rural Bessarabia under the Romanian administration were conducted along with recognition of this institution's legitimacy by the population of the region. This difficult and sinuous process involved the gradual imposition and recognition of the

---

7   Irina Livezeanu, *Cultură și naționalism în România Mare* (Bucharest: Humanitas, 1995), 111, Charles King, *Moldovenii, România, Rusia și politica culturală* (Chișinău: Arc, 2002), 41–2.
8   The Romanian Minister of Education Constantin Angelescu underplayed literacy and schooling rates in pre-1918 Bessarabia: Constantin Angelescu, *Activitatea Ministerului Instrucțiunii. 1922–1926* (Bucharest: Imprimeria Națională, 1926), 10, Constantin Angelescu, *Evoluția învățământului primar și secundar în ultimii 20 de ani* (Bucharest: Imprimeria Centrală, 1936), 19.
9   Enciu, *Populația rurală a Basarabiei*, 204.
10 On the expansion of mass public education in Bessarabia under Russian domination, see Ludmila Coadă, *Zemstva Basarabiei. Aspecte istorico-juridice* (Chișinău: Pontos, 2009), 92–102; Onufrii G. Andrus, *Ocherki po istorii shkol Bessarabii i Moldavskoi SSR pervoi poloviny XX veka* [Essays on the history of education in Bessarabia and Moldovan RSS in the first half of the 20th century] (Chișinău: Școala sovietică, 1952), 28. On the expansion of primary education in the Russian Empire, see Ben Eklof, *Russian Peasant Schools: Officialdom, Village Culture, and Popular Pedagogy, 1861–1914* (Berkeley: University of California Press, 1986).

pedagogical authority of the state.[11] From this perspective, mass primary education was a transmission belt through which the rural inhabitants adopted, by communicating and negotiating with the school agents of the state, their status as conscious citizens, endowed with rights, freedoms, and decision-making capacity, not only as subjects of the state. In Romanian Bessarabia a pluralistic and democratic system began to function after 1918, and local residents enjoyed a significant degree of influence on the state's decisions (male citizens had the right to vote for one party or another, thus influencing the state's policy in the region since the parties were dependent on citizens' votes).[12]

The institutionalization of the public school in rural communities and the transformation of subjects into citizens were part of a troublesome nation-state building process. During this interwar process the attitudes and strategies of the population towards the schools underwent significant changes. Between flat refusal and unreserved recognition, there was a wide range of accommodation tactics and negotiation strategies, from bottom to top and top to bottom, through which the state and the local population defined their authority and decision-making power. The balance of forces between the two was unequal, as the Romanian administration made use *in extremis* of physical violence against the civilian population; for instance, during the popular uprisings in Hotin (1919) and Tatar-Bunar (1924).[13] Thus, the authorities saw the imposition and recognition of mass public education as central to state expansion and state building, with political, economic and cultural dimensions. This process was not linear and univocal, but often manifested itself as a genuine cultural and 'class' struggle, with clear political implications.[14] As in other countries that underwent modernization in

---

11 Pierre Bourdieu and Jean-Claude Passeron, *La Reproduction. Eléments pour une théorie du système d'enseignement* (Paris: Minuit, 1970), 32.
12 Ioan Scurtu, *Istoria contemporană a României (1918–2005)* (Bucharest: Ed. Fundaţiei România de Mâine, 2005); Svetlana Suveică, *Basarabia în primul deceniu interbelic (1918–1928). Modernizare prin reforme* (Chişinău: Pontos, 2010), 52–104. For a critical view on the political and electoral system in interwar Romania, see Sergiu Gherghina and Mihail Chiru, "Cât de departe era România interbelică de democraţie? Un exemplu de manipulare a procedurilor electorale," in *România interbelică: Istorie şi istoriografie*, ed. by Ovidiu Pecican (Bucharest: Limes, 2010).
13 On the uprisings, see Ludmila Rotari, *Mişcarea subversivă în Basarabia, 1918–1924* (Bucharest: Editura Enciclopedică, 2004) and Alberto Basciani, *La difficile unione. La Bessarabia e la Grande Romania, 1918–1940* (Rome: Aracne, 2005), 122–45, 206–19.
14 School education was involved in the Soviet "cultural revolution" in 1929–33. See Sheila Fitzpatrick, *Education and Social Mobility in the Soviet Union, 1921–1934* (Cambridge: Cambridge University Press, 1979), 159.

the 19th and 20th centuries, in Bessarabia the establishment of mass schooling faced the reluctance of the population, including "passive resistance" tactics in relation to the cultural space dominated by the school and other cultural and administrative institutions.[15] This article shows the equivocal power relations that state authorities used in establishing monopoly over legitimate physical (and symbolic) violence in rural Bessarabia, a province perceived and administered as a 'borderland' territory.[16]

This article sheds light on the establishment of compulsory public education in a region with very low schooling and literacy rates, by means of the unequal balance of forces between state agents and the local population. To this end, I regard the school as a "contact zone"[17] between two previously distinct social worlds: the state authorities represented by the institutions involved in and responsible for the schools (school inspectorates, directorates, the School House, the Ministry of Education) and the rural population, subject to schooling and literacy campaigns, represented by school-age children, their parents, and the village communities as a whole. This "contact zone" reveals disputes between these two parties on divisive issues such as mass public education, compulsory school attendance, the language and content of education for ethnic minorities and women, and the use of corporal punishment in school. In examining these controversial issues, I consider the position of state authorities overseeing education, teachers implementing this project, and the population involved in the schooling process.

To this end, this article relies on official and unofficial sources, both published and unpublished, of public institutions and officials of various ranks, books and reports published by the Ministry of Public In-

---

15 I use 'tactics', not 'strategy', to refer to the reaction of subjects in a space dominated by a group or institution. Michel de Certeau, *Practice of Everyday Life* (Berkeley: California University Press, 1984), xi–xxiv, 34, and James C. Scott, *Weapons of the Weak. Everyday Forms of Peasant Resistance* (New Haven: Yale University Press, 1985).

16 On border areas in Europe, see Rogers Brubaker, *Nationalism Reframed. Nationhood and the National Question in the New Europe* (Cambridge: Cambridge University Press, 1996), 84–93, Kate Brown, *A Biography of No Place. From Ethnic Borderland to Soviet Heartland* (Cambridge: Harvard University Press, 2003), Florin Țurcanu, "Roumanie, Bessarabie, Transnistrie. Les représentations d'une frontière contestée," in *Frontières du communisme. Mythologies et réalités de la division de l'Europe de la révolution d'Octobre au mur de Berlin*, ed. by Sophie Coeuré and Sabine Dullin (Paris: La Découverte, 2007).

17 A "contact zone" refers to "social spaces where cultures meet, clash, and grapple with each other, often in contexts of highly asymmetrical relations of power, such as colonialism, slavery, or their aftermaths lived out in many parts of the world today." See Mary-Louise Pratt, "Arts of the Contact Zone," *Profession* (1 January 1991): 33–40.

struction, and periodicals supported by the Ministry and county associations of teachers. To highlight the bureaucratic subtleties of this process, I studied a large number of archival documents of public institutions engaged in the implementation of compulsory education, particularly the archives of the Ministry of Public Instruction and of the regional and county inspectorates.[18] These sources allow us to reconstitute the way in which important issues were addressed in requests, complaints, and petitions submitted to the Ministry by representatives of rural communities. Finally, for this study, I also have interviewed sixty individuals, recruited by the snowball sampling technique, born in the 1920s–1930s in five rural areas of Bessarabia and two areas in Transnistria. Thirty-eight subjects were interviewed at their homes in the seven villages and twenty-two subjects were interviewed in two homes for the elderly (in Chisinau and Transnistria).[19] These oral sources reveal the daily experience of schooling, or lack of such experience in the case of unschooled children.

The social history of education has a long academic tradition in the West.[20] In Eastern European and Soviet studies, this area gained attention more recently. Due to limits of academic autonomy in the communist bloc, research in this field was marked by political and ideological positions. The history of education and culture in the region gained renewed interest after the fall of communism and the opening of government and party archives.[21] Several researchers elaborated funda-

---

18 These archival funds have been consulted in the National Archives of Romania in Bucharest and in the County Directorate of the National Archives of Ilfov (Bucharest).
19 The interviews have been conducted during the winter of 2007, January 2008 and February 2009.
20 Jurgen Herbst, "The History of Education: State of the Art at the Turn of the Century in Europe and North America," *Paedagogica Historica: International Journal of the History of Education* 35, 3 (1999): 737–47, Laurence Brockliss and Nicola Sheldon, "Introduction," in *Mass Education and the Limits of State Building*, ed. by Laurence Brockliss and Nicola Sheldon (Basingstoke: Palgrave MacMillan, 2012), 13–20.
21 Eklof, *Russian Peasant Schools*; Sheila Fitzpatrick, ed., *Cultural Revolution in Russia, 1928–1931* (Bloomington: Indiana University Press, 1978); Sheila Fitzpatrick, *Education and Social Mobility in the Soviet Union, 1921–1934* (Cambridge: Cambridge University Press, 1979); Wladimir Berelowitch, *La soviétisation de l'École russe, 1917–1931* (Lausanne: L'Age d'or, 1990); Thomas Ewing, *The Teachers of Stalinism: Policy, Practice, and Power in Soviet Schools of the 1930s* (New York: Peter Lang, 2002); Thomas Ewing, *Separate Schools: Gender, Policy and Practice in Postwar Soviet Education* (Illinois: Northern Illinois University Press, 2010); Larry E. Holmes *The Kremlin and the Schoolhouse. Reforming Education in Soviet Russia, 1917–1931* (Bloomington: Indiana University Press, 1991); Catriona Kelly, *Children's World: Growing Up in Russia, 1890–1991* (Lancaster: Yale University Press, 2007).

mental works in this area and interpreted primary sources. Researchers studied in a thorough and balanced way the history of public education in Romania (including interwar Bessarabia) and Soviet Moldova (including Transnistria). The works of Irina Livezeanu and Alex Drace-Francis[22] on the role of public education in the nation-building of Romania (and Bessarabia) are pioneering. A small number of Romanian and Moldovan historians developed comprehensive studies of the history of education in the region based on recently discovered archival documents. Some of them focused on the study of primary education in the first half of the 20th century.[23]

Primary Education in Bessarabia: National Integration and "Spiritual Unification"

Immediately after Bessarabia was incorporated into Romania in December 1918, the Romanian political elites sought to unify their school education systems to effect "national integration."[24] Cultural unification was indispensable and imperative because the province was believed to be, according to the Russian census of 1897, the most backward in terms of literacy in a country that itself lagged behind Europe in this respect.[25] The cultural unification of Bessarabia with Romania sought to harmonize the province with an economic and administrative system that was believed to be more advanced.[26] On official occasions, this project was

---

22 Livezeanu, *Cultură și naționalism*; Drace-Francis, *Geneza culturii române moderne*.
23 On the beginnings of mass public education in Bessarabia, see Cătălina Michalache, *Copilărie, familie, școală: politici educaționale și receptări sociale* (Iași: Ed. Universității "Al. I. Cuza", 2016). On the history of school education in Romania and Bessarabia, see Nicolae Adăniloaie, *Istoria învățămîntului primar (1859–1918)* (Bucharest: Cris Book Universal, 1998); Murgescu, *Între "bunul creștin" și "bravul român"*; Ioana-Aurelia Axentii, *Gândirea Pedagogică în Basarabia (1918–1940). Studiu istorico-pedagogic* (Chișinău: Civitas, 2006); Enciu, *Populația rurală a Basarabiei*; Nicolae Bargari, *Evoluția învățământului școlar în RSS Moldovenească (1956–1990)* (Chișinău: Evrica, 2005); Sergiu Musteață and Petru Negură, "Îndoctrinare, sovietizare și rusificare prin învățământ în RSSM," in *Fără termen de prescripție. Aspecte ale investigării crimelor comunismului în Europa*, edited by Sergiu Musteață and Igor Cașu (Chișinău: Cartier, 2011).
24 Livezeanu, *Cultură și naționalism*, 111–56, and Mihalache, *Copilărie*, 171–276.
25 The literacy rate in Bessarabia was 19.4 percent in 1897 and 38 percent in 1930. In Romania as a whole, it reached 57 percent in 1930. See Enciu, *Populația rurală*, 204, and Șandru, *Populația rurală a României*, 177 and 180.
26 On national integration and modernization in the province after 1918, see Basciani, *La difficile unione* and Suveică, *Basarabia în primul deceniu interbelic*. "Nowhere were the state of siege and censorship more rigorous, nowhere gendarmes and policemen were more brutal. As for officials, they went beyond any limits.

presented by senior officials of the Ministry of Public Instruction as an eminently idealistic endeavor, a "call of the soul."[27] Constantin Angelescu, who served intermittently as Minister between 1919 and 1937, claimed that this cultural unification achieved "the unification of the soul of the whole nation, directed to the same goal, the same aspirations, the same ideal."[28] This ideal was understood as building a strong, united nation, capable of facing its enemies. As Angelescu wrote, the school "must ensure the unity of the soul of all Romanians with Romanian culture and life and increase the power of life and resistance of the nation to all assaults from outside and inside, thus ensuring the durability of our rule within the new borders of Romania."[29] Enemies were those who opposed this "spiritual unification," and the school was the most appropriate tool—as the experience of more advanced nations confirmed—to achieve that idealistic goal given the difficulties lying ahead in the newly annexed province.[30]

The start in 1917 was very energetic. In 1922, the nationalization and Romanianization of Bessarabian schools were declared accomplished,[31] but this pronouncement should be treated with caution. Nationalization implied transforming Russian language schools into Romanian language schools or, to a lesser extent, "minority" (non-Russian) language schools according to a statistical proportion of the Romanian population that was inaccurately estimated at 70 percent.[32] The process

---

Their abuses of power and venality were so obvious that a senator thought that he had to denounce them in the plenary of the Parliament." "Report of the general Pétin of 6 October 1920," cited in Basciani, *La difficile unione*, 154.
27 Angelescu, *Activitatea Ministerului Instrucțiunii*, 4.
28 Ibid, 4.
29 Ibid, 6.
30 Reference to Western countries was frequent in the speeches of political and intellectual elites in Romania at that time. See Iosif Gabrea, *Școala românească. Structura și politica ei. 1921–1932* (Bucharest: Tipografia Bucovina, 1933), 9, 76; Angelescu, *Activitatea Ministerului*, 11; Constantin Angelescu, *Evoluția învățământului primar și secundar în ultimii 20 de ani* (Bucharest: Imprimeria Centrală, 1936), 21; Dimitrie Gusti, "Cuvânt înainte," in *Un an de activitate la Ministerul Instrucției, Culturii și Artelor. 1932–1933*, ed. by Dimitrie Gusti (Bucharest: Tipografia Bucovina, 1934), xvii–xviii. Policies aimed at transforming minority schools into schools teaching in the state (national) language were extensively used in the establishment of the European nation-states. See Weber, *Peasants into Frenchmen*, 67–104; Marjorie Lamberti, *State, Society, & the Elementary School in Imperial Germany* (New York: Oxford University Press, 1989); Agoszton Berecz, *The Politics of Early Language Teaching: Hungarian in the primary schools of the late Dual Monarchy* (Budapest: Pasts Inc., Central European University, 2013).
31 Livezeanu, *Cultură și naționalism*, 144.
32 The other ethnicities were: Ukrainians (10 percent), Jewish (8.6 percent), Russians (4.4 percent), Bulgarians (3.3 percent). See Mihalache, *Copilărie*, 211.

continued for many years. The goal, as some school inspectors suggested, was an entirely Romanian school system, including private schools and confessional education.[33] In reality, the transformation was much slower and more problematic than what the Romanian authorities desired.[34]

Momentum and Fatigue of a "Cultural Offensive"

Between 1917 and 1922, 300 new primary schools were opened, reaching a total of 1,680.[35] The number was considered insufficient, as enrollment in primary schools amounted to only 34 percent of all school-age children (compared to 60 percent throughout Romania), and school attendance was even lower.[36] Three years after unification, enrollment in primary schools was lower than in 1906, when Bessarabia was a Russian *guberniia* and primary education was in full swing in the entire Empire without being declared compulsory.[37]

Unhappy with the poor schooling results in Bessarabia, some school inspectors suggested a more determined intervention, especially since the Paris Peace Conference enshrined the recognition of Bessarabia's unification with Romania by the international community.[38] The laws on primary education of 1921 and 1924 had to unify the primary education system of the new and old provinces of Romania in an effort

---

33 This perception is shared by inspectors visiting the new schools. In Briceni county, the Ukrainian schools were turned into Romanian-Ukrainian schools and then into "purely Romanian" schools: Arhivele Naționale Române (ANR), Fondul Ministerului Instrucțiunii Publice (FMIP), inventory no. 710 (1922), file no. 11, p. 125 (hereafter: ANR, FMI, 710 (1922)/11/125), FMIP, 710(1922)/11/105, and Mihalache, *Copilărie*, 215, 217.
34 In several German schools, inspectors found that teachers and students "do not know Romanian at all": ANR, FMIP, 907(1933)/33/82; ANR, FMIP, 909(1935)/15/283. In Cetatea-Albă, a school inspector concluded that "the 20 years of Romanian rule [...] and the nationalization of minority villages through school did not bear any fruit." See Livezeanu, *Cultură și naționalism*, 145.
35 Enciu, *Populația rurală a Basarabiei*, 205, 207, Livezeanu, *Cultură și naționalism*, 133.
36 In the Old Kingdom, primary school enrollment accounted for 61.6 percent of all school enrolment. Attendance was half that rate. In the 1931/32 school year primary school attendance was only 54 percent in Bessarabia, and 72.3 percent across the country. See Gusti, *Un an de activitate*, 576, and Angelescu, *Activitatea Ministerului*, 5.
37 A bill on free and compulsory public education was proposed in 1907, before the Duma was dissolved on 3 June. See Coadă, *Zemstva Basarabiei*, 102–3, Ben Eklof, *Russian Peasant Schools*, 283–6.
38 Mihalache, *Copilărie*, 231, note 3. About the contested status of Bessarabia before the Paris Peace Conference, which recognized its annexation, see King, *Moldovenii*, 35–40.

declared imperative by the Minister of Public Instruction, Constantin Angelescu. A 1921 decree introduced compulsory primary education of four classes for all children, boys and girls alike, aged 7 to 16 in Bessarabia.[39] A 1924 decree imposed seven classes (four years of primary school and three of upper primary education) for children of both sexes aged 5–18 years.[40]

The year 1922 gave a new impetus to schooling. The number of "normal schools" (pedagogical colleges) increased from 20 in 1920 to 113 in 1929 across the country, training 3,500 graduates annually (many of whom were sent to work in the annexed provinces). In Bessarabia, the number of primary schools increased from 1,564 in 1921/22 to 2,224 (of which 2,038 were in rural areas) in 1931/32, while the number of teachers increased from 2,938 in 1921/22 to 6,217 (5,422 in rural schools) in 1931/32. The state budget for education increased from 9.5 percent in 1921/22 to 15.7 percent in 1928. The number of enrolled children increased from 34.16 percent of all children in 1921/22 to 63.93 percent in 1931/32.[41] The inspection reports coming from the regions overstated the efforts of those charged with implementing these sustained, but fragile, reforms. [42] This "cultural offensive," as the schooling project was named at that time, drew criticism.[43] The increase in the number of normal schools of over 500 percent and in the number of their students and graduates, most of them from rural areas (73 percent in Bessarabia and 79.6 percent in the Old Kingdom in 1933), concealed

---

39 Compulsory primary education was introduced in the Romanian principalities by the Law of Public Instruction of 1864. See Adăniloaie, *Istoria învăţămîntului primar*, 83. It was adopted in Bessarabia in 1921, by ministerial decree, but came into effect once the Law on Primary and Normal Education of 1924 was passed. See ANR, FMIP, 2553(1921)/420/215.

40 The law required children aged 5–7 to attend kindergartens, and young people aged 16–18 to attend primary courses for adults. See *Legea învăţământului primar*, 1–1, 8–9; ANR, FMIP, 712(1924)/146/10.

41 In 1922–26, 74 new schools (with 152 classrooms) were opened in Cetatea-Albă County, 32 schools (65 classrooms) in Cahul, seven schools (26 classrooms) in Bălţi, 115 schools (193 classrooms) in Iaşi, nine schools (24 classrooms) in Tighina. Most of them were constructed with public funds. Anton Golopenţia, "Date statistice asupra situaţiei de fapt," in Gusti, *Un an de activitate*, 48, 64, 80, 149–51, Angelescu, *Activitatea Ministerului*, 5, 6, 8, 11, and Gabrea, *Şcoala românească*, 9.

42 In the 1920s, many reports from Bessarabia had a slightly triumphalist tone, referring to "amazing progress," "beautiful results," "schools are well populated," "school attendance is regular," "the law applied strictly at the beginning achieves results." See ANR, FMIP, 713(1925)/17/19; FMIP, 713(1925)/18/154; FMIP, 713 (1925)/256/96; FMIP, 713(1925)/257/179, 197, and 216.

43 Mihail Popovici, "Ofensiva culturală şi corpul didactic primar," *Buletinul Asociaţiei Învăţătorilor Judeţului Bălţi* (September 1928), 1.

the poor theoretical and pedagogical training of the teachers.[44] Schools were hastily built or opened in rented premises that did not meet minimal requirements. They hardly coped with the massive flow of children enrolled at the beginning of the year.[45] This "offensive" schooling policy became the victim of its own success. By 1927 the considerably expanded education system showed signs of fatigue.

The Great Depression: Coup de Grâce to a Fragile Construction

The economic crisis of 1929–1933 hit Romania violently and delivered a *coup de grâce* to its fragile education system. As stated by sociologist Dimitrie Gusti, Minister of Education in 1933–1934, the economic crisis and the government change reinstated realism in an endeavor that previously was guided only by idealism.[46] The first signs of disappointment appeared in 1930. In a report submitted to the Minister in April 1930, the school inspector of Tighina County noted desperately that "based on an analysis of the monthly situation and the findings of inspections, in almost all villages attendance is so poor that the public school simply does not exist."[47]

At the country level, enrollment increased steadily in both rural and urban areas until 1931/32, due to the increase in the number of school-age children and the population's involvement in the schooling process, but attendance in rural schools increased only by 1.76 percent compared to 25 percent in urban schools across the country. A more

---

44   Golopenția, "Date statistice," 147.
45   According to a 1925 report on primary schools in Cetatea-Albă, Arciz constituency, 8,669 of the 27,229 school-age children did not attend school for lack of institutions and teachers. Shortage of schools and improper sanitary conditions were reported in Hotin and Cahul, Bălți, Iași, Vaslui, Soroca, Hotin, Dorohoi, Suceava and Botoșani Counties. In 1931, in Cetatea-Albă school buildings were still few and inadequate. Across the Prut "they can welcome everybody." See Alexandru Vasilescu, "Localurile școlilor primare din Cetatea-Albă," *Cetatea-Albă* (March 1932), 39; ANR, FMIP, 713(1925)/18/39; FMIP, 713 (1925)/16; FMIP, 812 (1928)/23; ANR, 812(1928)/24/4–6; FMIP, 713(1925)/16, FMIP, 811(1927)/6.
46   Golopenția, "Date statistice," 151, 156. On the austerity policies of previous governments, see Gusti, *Un an de activitate*, IX. After the parliamentary elections of December 1928, the National Peasants' Party (PNȚ) replaced the National Liberal Party (PNL) in the government and ruled until June 1931; PNȚ returned to the government from July 1932 to 1933. The PNȚ thus administered the Ministry of Public Instruction during a period of crisis. See Vasile Pușcaș and Marcel Știrban, "Perfecționare și atitudini critice în sistemul politic al României interbelice," in *Dezvoltare și modernizare în România interbelică, 1919–1939. Culegere de studii* (Bucharest: Ed. Politică, 1988), 28.
47   ANR, FMIP, 814 (1930)/115/8.

negative development was seen in Bessarabia. According to an investigation initiated by Gusti, in the 1931/32 school year only 53.1 percent of children enrolled and only 33.7 percent of all school-age children attended primary rural schools there. After thirteen years of Romanian public education in Bessarabia, only a third of all children enrolled in public schools attended them.[48] This was less than in 1906.[49]

Due to cuts in the education budget in 1929–30 and 1932–33, the number of schools stalled in 1928, even decreasing slightly in 1931/32. The number of teachers fell slightly in 1931/32 compared to 1928/29.[50] The 10 percent increase in the number of enrolled children and the decrease in the number of teachers aggravated the resource scarcity and poor school infrastructure. The state lacked resources (that is, the schools, classrooms and teachers needed for the ever-larger number of children subject to compulsory public education). This shortage worsened during times of economic crisis. In 1931/32, there were 55.6 enrolled children for every teacher in the rural primary schools in Bessarabia, while the appropriate ratio was considered to be 40–45 children per teacher. The number of children attending rural primary schools in Bessarabia (29.5 pupils for every teacher) was significantly lower than the teacher capacity.[51]

Attendance in primary schools can also be assessed by looking at the promotion rate. To be promoted to a higher grade, the pupil had to possess a minimum level of knowledge of subjects learned, be tested through exams, and miss no more than 50–70 classes. The promotion rate reflected the pupils' attendance rate.[52] In primary school that rate also revealed a characteristic of primary education in interwar Romania, especially in Bessarabia, Moldova and Wallachia (and to a lesser extent Transylvania and Bucovina): the concentration of pupils in the first classes of the primary school, in Bessarabia mostly in the first class. According to Gusti's investigation, the huge number of pupils in the first class in

---

48 Golopenția, "Date statistice," 117 and 85.
49 In 1906, 44 percent of all school-age children attended primary school. See "O vvedenii vseobshchego obucheniia v Bessarabii," in *Doklad gubernskoi zemskoi upravy* (Chisinau: no press, 1907), 36. In 1911, the percentage went up to 40.3 in Bessarabia. See Eklof, *Russian Peasant Schools*, 285.
50 Golopenția, "Date statistice," 114–6.
51 Ibid, 90–3.
52 *Law on Primary Education of the State*, article 58, *Școala Noastră* 10 (supplement) (September 1924), 11, P. Antohi și M. Ispir, "Concluzii la Monografia Plătăreștitilor," *Cetatea-Albă* (September 1932), 20, D. Barbu, "Raporturile etnice dintre Români și Ruși. Starea culturală la Copanca," excerpt from *Buletinul de Cercetări Sociale al României. Regionala Chișinău* II, 1938 (Chișinău: Tiparul moldovenesc, 1939), 48–52.

Bessarabian primary schools and the decreasing number of pupils in grades 2–4 was largely due to low promotion rates. In 1931/32 only 30.2 percent of grade 1 pupils were promoted and 47.4 percent of grades 2 and 3 pupils; 50.9 percent finished grade 4. The ratio between those promoted to grade 4 in state schools in rural Bessarabia in 1931/32 and those enrolled in grade 1 in 1928/29 (the same series after four years) was 15.7 percent.[53] Thus, ten years after the unification, less than a quarter of those enrolled in grade 1 in 1928 reached grade 4 in 1931. The share of pupils reaching grades 5–6 was even lower. Few finished the seven primary classes, despite compulsory primary education. This finding characterized primary education throughout interwar Romania, especially Bessarabia and its rural areas.

A survey conducted by teacher D. Barbu, based on data from three schools in a village in central Bessarabia, suggests that the promotion rate was closely linked to the economic crisis. The promotion rate was the lowest in 1929–33, followed by the halving of the budget for primary education in 1931–34.[54] The school committees that collected community funds and managed them for the school also reported a sharp decrease of resources during the crisis since they depended on town hall's contributions (14 percent of the annual income) and school fines. During the crisis, both revenue sources dropped sharply and affected the budget of school committees.[55] The accompanying decrease in attendance and promotion rates reflected the low capacity of Bessarabian peasants to cope with school expenditures in times of crisis.[56]

---

53   Golopenția, "Date statistice," 110, 131.
54   Barbu, "Raporturile entice," 49–50, and Golopenția, "Date statistice," 139–40.
55   School committees constantly reported insufficient funds, to the discontent of teachers and school directors. These complaints intensified in 1929–32. See N.S., "Comitetele școlare de pe lângă școlile primare și grădinile de copii," *Buletinul Asociației Învățătorilor din județul Bălți* (January–April 1929), 1; P. Soltinschi, "Comitetele școlare," *Buletinul Asociației Învățătorilor din județul Bălți* (January–February 1930), 27–9; "Adunarea generală a membrilor Asociației învățătorilor din jud. Ismail, 30–31 august 1931, orașul Bolgrad," *Buletinul Asociației Învățătorilor din județul Ismail* (January–February 1933), 20–1; Barbu, "Starea culturală la Copanca," 40–4; Gheorghe Palade, "Comitetele școlare din Basarabia interbelică: contribuții la dezvoltarea învățământului," *Studia Universitatis Moldaviae* 4, 84 (2015), 138–45.
56   The income and living standards of Bessarabian and Romanian peasants sharply declined during the Great Depression. The droughts of 1928–1934 hit central and southern Bessarabia, affecting living standards and the diet of the population. See Enciu, *Populația rurală din Basarabia*, 173–4.

School Absenteeism: Who Is to Blame?

In the 1920s and the 1930s, school attendance was a constant concern for education authorities and employees in Romania. Hundreds of reports, written by the Ministry's oversight staff, monitored school attendance in Bessarabia. The Bessarabian pedagogical journals debated the issue.[57] Intellectuals, inspectors, and teachers tried to explain the phenomenon and asked why villagers did not take their children to school. Who was to blame? Some observers proposed a cultural explanation.[58] Others blamed the education system for being too theoretical and not practical enough.[59] In 1921, an author proposed two sets of explanations for poor attendance:

> The external factor (...) is the state of the school, the means at its disposal, which it uses according to its needs: 1) the school building, 2) the classroom, 3) its size, the light, the hygienic state, 4) the furniture, 5) the didactic material, and 6) the economic situation of the pupil's family ... The internal factor is the power and quality of the source from which the pupil quenches the thirst of the soul and heart.[60]

---

57 "Frequentarea [sic] obligatorie," *Şcoala. Organ al Corpului Didactic din Basarabia* (1921), 99; P. Lupaşco, "Relativ la chestia obligativității învățământului primar," *Şcoala* (1922), 34–5; "Despre obligativitate, gratuitate şi durata şcolii obligatorii, despre misiunea socială a şcolii," *Şcoala Basarabiei* (January–February 1923), 39; Teodor Balmuş, "Despre obligativitate," *Şcoala Basarabeană. Revistă de cultură pedagogică şi de apărare a drepturilor învățătoreşti* 2, 1 (May 1933), 13–4; "Frecvența şcolară," *Cetatea Albă* (September 1931), 27; Gheorghe Biciuşcă, "Obligativitatea în învățământul primar," *Buletinul Asociației Învățătorilor din jud. Bălți* (July–August 1930), 72–4; "Aplicarea obligativității şcolare," *Buletinul Asociației Învățătorilor din jud. Ismail* (January–February 1933), 19; "Un cuvânt de îmbărbătare. Cu ocazia începutului noului an şcolar, d. Ministru d-r Angelescu vorbeşte învățătorimei despre problemele ce interesează şcoala românească," *Şcoala Basarabeană* (September–October 1936), 7; Ilie Isbăşescu, "Frecvența şcolară în lumina realității," *Şcoala basarabeană* (September–October 1938), 36–8.
58 On 8 December 1932, deputy D.V. Țoni blamed poor school attendance on the fact that "our people do not sufficiently understand the benefits of education." Şandru, *Populația rurală a României*, 175. D. Barbu explained the differences in school attendance between three neighboring villages by the fact that *Mazils* (rural dwellers of noble origins) sent their children to school. See D. Barbu, "Probleme şcolare în satele Nişcani, Iurceni şi Stolniceni din jud. Lăpuşna," *Buletinul Institutului Social din România* I (1937), 10–11.
59 Barbu, *Probleme şcolare*, 17; D. Barbu, "O organizare rațională a învățământului rural" (Chişinău: Tiparul moldovenesc, 1938) advocates a separation of rural and urban primary schools with the same profile. Minister Gusti criticized the primary school system in Romania, before the reform he initiated in 1932–33, for being disconnected from the practical interests of rural inhabitants and the theoretical content of school curricula. See Gusti, *Un an de activitate*, 588–91. This criticism was voiced by C. Rădulescu-Motru, "Şcoala satului," *Revista Fundației Regale* 8 (1934), discussed by N. Țane, *Cetatea-Albă* (September–October 1936), 1–4.
60 P. Lupaşco, "Relativ la chestia obligativității învățământului primar," *Şcoala. Organ al Corpului Didactic din Basarabia* (Chişinău: Tipografia Societății Anonime "Glasul Țării," 1922), 34–5.

If the "external" factor was fulfilled, the author claimed, then the "internal" factor would boost attendance. This explanation idealized the "thirst for knowledge" of peasant children and their parents and underestimated their agency. The "external" factor was far from being ensured at the time. School inspectors complained until the late 1930s of the lack of "proper" school facilities, insufficient classrooms, and premises not roomy enough given the steady increase in enrollment and attendance.[61] Appropriate furniture and didactic material were missing from many rural schools, even in the 1930s.[62] The peasants' economic situation and living standards were dire, while drought and hunger periodically ravaged rural Bessarabia, even after the agrarian reform of 1921.[63] These were all reasons why Bessarabian peasants did not send their children to school.[64] Several petitions signed by villagers justified their refusal to send children to school, citing the brutal behavior of teachers, particularly the use of corporal punishment "harshly" or "out of revenge."[65] The number of pupils who attended school (on average 30 children per grade in 1931/32) remained lower than classroom capacity (40 seats).

---

61 Minister Angelescu said that over 11,000 schools were built in Romania during his mandates (1922–28, 1933–36), but there was still "a need for at least 20,000 schools so that all school age children subject to compulsory education could attend school, have the necessary premises, hygienic premises." See Angelescu, "Un cuvânt de îmbărbătare," Școala Basarabeană (September–October 1936), 7.

62 The author of an article in the pedagogical journal of Lăpușna County, after noticing that 76 percent of all school-age children were not in school in 1937/38, added that the existing school premises were insufficient in the county: "Overall, there are in Lăpușna county and Chișinău 297 primary schools. 251 have their own premises, the rest being situated in rented premises. In rural areas, out of 268 schools, only 145 have the necessary furniture, 123 schools use improvised furniture, and students are kneeling by the windows or on the floor." See "The situation of primary schools in Lăpușna County," Școala Basarabeană (January–February 1939), 65.

63 Enciu, Populația rurală din Basarabia, 173–4.

64 School inspectors referred to "poverty and famine" as impediments to attendance: ANR, FMIP, 714(1926)/212/16); 713(1925)/16/10. Several localities requested the suspension of the collection of fines, on grounds of hardship and poverty: FMIP, 714(1926)/74. In 1925, school inspectors blamed poor attendance on the drought: FMIP, 713(1925)/18/154; 713(1925)/257/110. See Tatiana Suflery, "Considerații reale asupra foametei din Basarabia," Cetatea-Albă 8–9, 3 (April–May 1936), 18–9. Ilie P., born in 1921 (village Bălănești), Maria B., b. 1931 (v. Petroasa), Maria P., b. 1923 (v. Bălănești), Agafia C., b. 1926 (v. Bălănești).

65 ANR, FMIP, 712(1924)/273/381; 712(1924)/275/150–151; 811(1927)/274/127; 815(1931)221/272; 908(1934)/251/48; 908(1934)/251/48; 909(1935)/214/210; 910(1936)/299/190; 910(1936)/333/30. See Petru Negură, "De la punition corporelle à violence symbolique. L'enseignement primaire rurale en Bessarabie de l'entre-deux guerres," Education et Sociétés 24 (2009/2), 159–79.

As for the economic conditions in Bessarabian villages, even wealthier peasants found credible excuses for their children not to attend school, including heavy workload in the household.[66] Thus, the cultural factor was not entirely irrelevant, as many teachers and civil servants claimed at the time.[67]

Although the education laws of 1921, 1924, and later years provided for compulsory education for girls and boys alike, attendance in primary schools was lower among girls across the country, while girls' absenteeism was the most marked in primary schools in Bessarabia. The discrepancy between the share of boys and girls enrolled in rural schools was the largest in this province: 61 percent of boys versus 39 percent of girls (in cities, 51.7 percent of boys versus 48.3 percent of girls).[68] School inspectors explained girls' absenteeism by "objective" factors, as a rule, also invoked in case of boys' absenteeism: nonpayment of fines, annulment of fines, abusive behavior of the teacher, and inadequate premises.[69] Reports further suggested that poor attendance of girls stemmed from the villagers' gender stereotypes, according to which girls would not need to study or at least not as much as the boys. The explanations were again cultural, blaming the "stubbornness of villagers" and "refractoriness of parents."[70] This perception is also found in a number of interviews with people educated during the interwar period.[71] Other documents show that gender stereotypes of girls' education were shared and even tolerated by some teachers or school

---

66   Some wealthy parents did not send their children to school because the children helped with their work: ANR, 1938/362/237–238; Interviews: Alexandru Ț., b. 1924 (v. Grigorovca), Vera F., b. 1930 (v. Dănceni), Marina C., b. 1924 (v. Bălănești). Among those interviewed were persons from wealthy families who attended school willingly or were even encouraged by parents: Minadora A., 1925 (v. Arionești), Vasile N., b. 1929 (v. Petrești).
67   See note 57. On 2 April 1930, a school inspector in Tighina County considered that villagers showed "criminal recklessness" towards the school (ANR, FMIP, 814 (1930)/115/8); other reports mention the "stubbornness of villagers" (FMIP, 714(1926)/212/45) and "refractoriness of parents" (FMIP, 812 (1928)/282/52).
68   Golopenția, "Date statistice," in Gusti, Un an de activitate, 65, 82.
69   See ANR, FMIP, 811(1927)/6/18; FMIP, 812(1928)/282/52; FMIP, 714(1926)/212/46; FMIP, 812(1928)/282/73; FMIP, 909(1935)/214/211.
70   ANR, FMIP, 2552(1919)/182/8; FMIP, 714(1926)/12/45; FMIP, 812(1928)/282/52.
71   Interviews with: Agafia C, 1926, v. Bălănești; Maria P., 1923, v. Milești; Ecaterina C., 1922, v. Bălănești; Ilie P., 1921, v. Bălănești; Alexandra G., 1920, v. Bocani; Alexandru C., 1918, v. Bocani; Maria B., 1931, v. Petroasa; Nina C., 1927, v. Petroasa; Paraschiva R., 1918, v. Petroasa; Ion C., 1924, v. Petroasa; Maria B., 1931, v. Petroasa.

inspectors.[72] Yet the laws on education allowed for such discrimination, providing for compulsory education "especially for boys," when school premises did not allow education for all children.[73] At the same time, the lack of women's right to vote prior to 1938 (when literate women gained the right to vote in Romania) and women's exclusion from the army and many public institutions further legitimized and enhanced these gender stereotypes.[74]

Compulsory Schooling and Systemic Limits

All measures were considered appropriate to encourage peasants to honor their obligations to the state and school. When mild measures did not achieve the desired effect, school authorities called for legally provided coercive mechanisms to force peasants to fulfill their duty to the state.[75] The 1921 decree and the 1924 law provided for fines on parents who did not allow their children to attend primary school.[76] Fines were used especially after the promulgation of the 1924 law. After sporadic but sometimes energetic manifestations of dissatisfaction, attendance exceeded the critical threshold of 50 percent in several Bessarabian counties in 1924 and 1925.[77] Given the zeal to establish schools and create new jobs for teachers in villages, this positive development was perceived as definitive and irreversible at all levels. However, the periodic worsening of the peasants' material situation, as after the drought that affected the province in 1925,[78] and the incessant frustration in areas

---

72 Barbu, "Probleme școlare," 9.
73 *Lege pentru învățământul primar al statului*, art. 39, 7.
74 Doina Bordeianu, "Evoluția constituțională a drepturilor electorale ale femeilor în România," *Sfera Politicii* 149 (2010), 53–57 On women's education in Romania in 1880–1930, see Theodora-Eliza Văcărescu, "Contexte de gen. Educația femeilor din România între anii 1880 și 1930," *Sfera Politicii* 175 (2013), 13–23.
75 ANR, FMIP, 713(1925)/257/110, 812(1928)/278/17, 813(1929)/218, 816(1932)/187/32, and Ilie Isbășescu, "Frecvența școlară," 36–38.
76 Article 21 of the 1924 law stipulated: "Parents, tutors and those referred to in art. 6, that do not enroll their children, as provided for by article 19, shall be fined by the Ministry of Instruction with a fine of 100–300 *lei*, while the children will be enrolled ex officio." See "The Law on Primary Education of the State," *Școala Noastră* 10 (supplement) (September 1924), 4. On the application of fines, see Article 27 of the law. Article 28 provided for imprisonment, up to five days monthly, "in case of obvious bad faith of parents."
77 After visiting 22 schools in Soroca County, in February 1925, the inspector said with joy: "Pupils have attended school regularly. The consequences of applying the new law are very good." Reports with similar content: ANR, FMIP, 713 (1925)/257/176 and 197; 714(1926)/212/11, 42.
78 ANR, FMIP, 713(1925)/18/39 and FMIP, 713(1925)/257/110.

inhabited by "minorities" (especially Ukrainians), prompted by the contemptuous attitude and restrictive, often abusive, behavior of the authorities towards a population always perceived as hostile "to all that is Romanian,"[79] imposed flexibility on the Ministry and its agents responsible for enforcing compulsory education. A "tactful" application of the "compulsory education" requirement (euphemism for the application of fines) was recommended, while arbitrary or "passionate" application of fines was sanctioned by harsh administrative punishment.[80]

Teachers and oversight bodies tolerated absenteeism in some situations (during autumn and spring agriculture work, old style religious holidays, bad weather conditions, epidemics)[81] and for various categories (orphans, disabled parents, sometimes girls). Such flexibility was partly ensured by laws on education.[82] Between the consistent application of fines for massive and persistent absenteeism, provided by the law, and the recommendation to apply them "tactfully," suggested by local school authorities and control bodies, a duplicitous discourse and double normativity were articulated in the daily practice of schooling. Teachers and inspectors used sensitivity and flexibility and did not apply the letter of the law.

The system, supposedly open to cooperation with local communities, sometimes worked against itself. School committees—intermediary bodies drawing on both the national model of school ephors and the zemstvo school committees of the late Tsarist period—linked the school

---

79 On the behavior of Romanian officials towards Bessarabians, especially "minorities," see Cristina Petrescu, "Construcția națională în Basarabia," in *Stat slab, cetățenie incertă. Studii despre Republica Moldova*, ed. by Monica Heintz (Bucharest: Curtea Veche, 2007), 127–53; Basciani, *La difficile unione*, 140–5, 154, 206–19.

80 ANR, FMIP, 713(1925)/257/216; FMIP, 812(1928)/24/209; FMIP, 813(1929)/203/244; FMIP, 908(1934)/90/229; 909(1935)/214/210.

81 ANR, FMIP, 713(1925)/256/98–99; FMIP, 714(1926)/74/189; FMIP, 812(1928)/279/156; FMIP, 812(1928)/283/375; FMIP, 813(1929)/7/179; FMIP, 813(1929)/293/11 and 70; FMIP, 816(1932)/187/126; FMIP, 908(1934)/8/14; FMIP, 908(1934)/108/200; FMIP, 908(1934)/228/56; FMIP, 909(1935)/15/28, 283, 305, 328; FMIP, 909(1935)/214/211, 218, 219, 243 and 245; FMIP, 910(1936)/299/18; FMIP, 913(1939)/15; FMIP, 914(1940)/24/341; FMIP, 2552(1919)/182/6; FMIP, 2553(1920)/107/49; Golopenția, "Date statistice," 94; and Suflery, "Considerații reale," 18–9.

82 On cases in which the Ministry exempted (or not) disabled individuals, orphans and war widows from school fines, at their request, see: ANR, FMIP, 2552(1919)/182/37, 54; FMIP, 714(1926)/74/106; FMIP, 2553(1920)/107/17. Articles 12–15 of the 1924 law exempted from compulsory schooling persons with no "stable housing," "children affected by any physical or intellectual disability" or "by illness or infirmity, who could adversely affect others," and "sickly, weak, dull-witted children." It recommended the creation of special classes or schools for the latter. "Law on primary education," 2–3.

to local communities through local leaders (usually the mayor, the priest, the village leaders).[83] School committees, set up in 1919 by a special decree, collected local funds from the town hall and the community, approved fines suggested by school teachers and principals, and administered them for the benefit of the school. Compelled by strong pressures from the community and driven by their own local "political" interests, many school committees unilaterally delayed or suspended the application of fines, violating the law on compulsory school attendance.[84] In turn, tax collectors often shunned responsibility to collect fines, violating the law while providing various excuses.[85] Teachers constantly complained about the passivity of school committees, the inaction, sometimes described as 'criminal', of collectors, and the lack of support from the village hall and gendarmerie. In October 1933, a Ministry order made it possible to avoid the bottlenecks caused by the refusal of school committees to cooperate with teachers and school administrators in applying fines.[86] This provision pitted teachers against rural communities.

The "big" politics interfered on several occasions with the good intention of avoiding "turmoil," with disastrous effects on school attendance at the local level. The minister periodically ordered school inspections to suspend the "application of fines" temporarily.[87] Observers explained such gestures of "generosity" by the struggles preceding parliamentary elections, held every second year, and even more often by the endless crises that marked the Romanian political environment during

---

[83] N.S., "Comitetele școlare," 1; Soltinschi, "Comitetele școlare"; "Adunarea generală a membrilor Asociației învățătorilor din jud. Ismail"; Barbu, "Starea culturală la Copanca," 40–4; Palade, "Comitetele școlare din Basarabia interbelică"; Mihalache, *Copilărie, familie, școală*, 206, 229.

[84] On school committees unwilling to apply school fines proposed by school teachers and principals, see: ANR, FMIP, 713(1925)/257/58; FMIP, 713(1925)/16/71; FMIP, 812(1928)/24/5, 154; FMIP, 812(1928)/275/170; FMIP, 813(1929)/7/110, 211–212; FMIP, 815(1931)/218/53; FMIP, 909(1935)/15/28.

[85] On collectors and other officials accused of not cooperating sufficiently with schools and school committees to collect fines: ANR, FMIP, 713(1925)/16/85; FMIP, 812(1928)/23/37, 52; FMIP, 812(1928)/24/367; FMIP, 812(1928)/278/1; FMIP, 812(1928)/281/29, 34; FMIP, 813(1929)/7/166; FMIP, 813(1929)/293/5; FMIP, 814(1930)/115; FMIP, 908(1934)/90/56; FMIP, 909(1935)/15/28; FMIP, 914(1940)/24/368; FMIP, 2552(1919)/182/57; FMIP, 2553(1920)/107/44, 46.

[86] ANR/FMIP, 908(1934)/59/62.

[87] On cases of collective suspension of fines at the request or in agreement with the Ministry, see: ANR, FMIP, 2552(1919)/182-26; FMIP, 713(1925)/136/80; FMIP, 713(1925)/257/222; FMIP, 714(1926)/212/46; FMIP, 813(1929)/293/11; FMIP, 816(1932)/187/32; FMIP, 908(1934)/108/200.

the interwar period.[88] These *ad hoc* decisions had a double negative effect on the process of establishing primary schools in rural Bessarabia (and other predominantly rural provinces of Romania). On the one hand, they raised the expectation of imminent abolition of compulsory schooling among certain segments of the rural population, an expectation that teachers and inspectors struggled to disprove by encouraging school attendance.[89] On the other hand, the suspension of compulsory schooling undermined the moral and institutional authority of school teachers and principals regarding the constantly controversial decision on the application of fines.[90]

Reform Attempts and Quantitative Leaps

As a result of the primary education reform laws of 1934, 1937, and 1939, the Ministry partially renounced the centralization and unification provided by the 1924 law and introduced new provisions that catered to rural communities by increasing the practical content of primary education according to residence—agricultural in villages and handicraft in cities.[91] After the 1937 and 1939 reforms, primary education acquired a practical emphasis by recommending "intuitive," "active" teaching methods based on "centers of interest" under the influence of the innovative pedagogies of J. Dewey and O. Decroly.[92] The 1934 law regional-

---

88 FMIP, 908(1934)/108/200.
89 ANR, FMIP, 714(1926)/212/16; FMIP, 811(1927)/16/42; FMIP, 812(1928)/23/97; FMIP, 812(1928)/24/230; FMIP, 812(1928)/281/46.
90 On claims that suspension of fines undermined the authority of school teachers and principals, see ANR, FMIP, 812(1928)/275/170; FMIP, 812(1928)/282/240; FMIP, 813(1929)/281/34; FMIP, 813(1929)/281/46.
91 On reforms in primary education that gave it a stronger practical profile, see: Gusti, "Obligativitate și frecvență școlară," 588–91; "Un cuvânt de îmbărbătare," *Școala Basarabeană* (September–October 1936), 7; Iosif Gabrea, "3/4 teoreticieni și 1/4 practicieni," *Școala Basarabeană* (January 1938), 24–31; Teodor Iacobescu, "Noua lege de organizare a învățământului primar," *Cultura poporului* 4-5-6 (April-May-June 1939), 1–3; Panait Antohi, "Legea Învățământului primar-normal," *Cultura Poporului* 10 (December 1939), 17–9.
92 On pedagogical methods introduced in primary schools in 1934, see A. Dupin, "Metoda centrelor de interes," *Cultura Poporului* (January–February 1934), 14–6; D. Antohi, "Metoda activă," *Cultura Poporului* (January–February 1934), 27–30; "Personalitatea creatoare a învățătorului," *Cultura Poporului* 10 (December 1939), 23; Ion Bădărău, "Noua lege a învățământului primar," *Școala Basarabeană* (September–October 1938), 1–8; N. Dragomir, "Noua programă analitică," *Școala basarabeană* (November 1938), 4–5; Vasile Chicu, "Considerațiuni asupra noii programe analitice," *Școala Basarabeană* (March 1939), 20–31; Teodor Iacobescu, "Un mare pedagog și gânditor: John Dewey," *Cultura Poporului* 11-14 (January–April 1940), 3–7.

ized education by setting up regional councils, empowered to tailor school curricula to local and regional needs.[93] These reforms sought to meet demands of the provinces' residents for an education adjusted to the practical needs of rural life.

The 1934 reform of primary education, initiated by Minister Gusti, and the subsequent reforms emphasized the need for a school assistance service, responsible for subsidizing the purchase of books, clothes and shoes for the children of needy families, very numerous in villages, a fact that was well-known and periodically acknowledged by the control bodies.[94] In 1936, Minister Angelescu recommended the opening of school canteens in villages, not only cities. The expense was to be borne by school assistance committees that collected the necessary funds from the community and local authorities.[95] Finally, in 1939 Minister Petre Andrei set funds aside to open canteens in villages as part of a new educational program that emphasized community strengthening and group solidarity.[96] Money was set aside to open canteens in drought-stricken villages of Bessarabia.[97] These initiatives, like those on school assistance that aimed at bringing the peasant closer to school and boosting school attendance, remained ineffective in rural areas due to lack of funds.[98]

---

[93] Article 71 of the Law of 27 May 1939 recommended the establishment of county and regional councils to adjust primary education to local and regional life. Antohi, "Legea învățământului primar," 18. On the regionalization project of normal primary education, see Gusti, "Obligativitate și frecvență școlară," 586–7.

[94] The problem of social assistance to pupils in poor environments was addressed more firmly in the second half of the 1930s by teachers, school inspectors and senior officials. See ANR, FMIP, 912(1938)/28/86, 87; Mihail Ciumacov, "Asistența medicală în școală," Cetatea-Albă (November 1935), 20. School assistance became the subject of legislative initiatives starting in 1934: Gusti, "Cuvânt înainte," xvii; Gusti, "Obligativitate și frecvență școlară," 588; "Un cuvânt de îmbărbătare," Școala Basarabeană (September–October 1936), 9–11; N. Olaru, "Asistența materială a copiilor în timpul școlarității," Școala Basarabeană (September–October 1936), 39; Iacobescu, "Noua lege," 1; Vladimir Dascălu, "Serviciul social," Școala busarabeană (November 1938), 36–7.

[95] "Un cuvânt de îmbărbătare," Școala Basarabeană (September–October 1936), 9–10.
[96] Iacobescu, "Noua lege," 1–3.
[97] Suflery, "Considerații reale," 18–9.
[98] In October 1941 (four months after Romanian administration was restored in Bessarabia), the inspector concluded after visiting a primary school in Lăpușna: "There is no school canteen. The patronage committee of the canteen has to be established, composed of intellectuals and leading peasants, to collect the necessary food for the poor and needy pupils." See Direcția Județeană a Arhivelor Naționale Ilfov (DJANI), Fondul Inspectoratului Școlar al Regiunii Lăpușna (FIȘRL), 206(1922–1943)/1/64.

The annexation of Bessarabia by the Soviet Union and World War II further impeded the implementation of these initiatives.[99]

After the Romanian economy recovered from the Great Depression and budget allocations to primary education increased, the school building campaign was re-launched. Minister Angelescu enhanced supervision over compulsory schooling.[100] School inspectors recommended compliance with the letter of the law by applying fines and reported a remarkable improvement in school attendance where fines were applied.[101] In the late 1930s, inspectors noted that attendance was "very good," sometimes "100 percent" although "fines were not applied."[102] Attendance requirements became more stringent. Based on wishful thinking, the Minister declared that attendance in primary school reached 95 percent across the country in 1935/36.[103] Such enthusiasm was shared by some of the inspectors who visited Bessarabia, although there were less optimistic signs. In 1939 the journal *Școala Basarabeană* read that: "During the school year 1937–8 in the Lăpușna county and Chișinău, 27,669 pupils attended the school out of 44,962 pupils enrolled. There were 115,882 children of school age. Thus, 88,013 students were out of school, that is, 76 percent. It is an alarming figure and authorities must give thought to this matter."[104]

In 1940, twenty-two years after the Union, indicators seemed impressive: the number of schools increased from 1,747 to 2,718, of teachers from 2,746 to 7,581, and of enrolled school children from 136,172 to 346,747.[105] These figures show indisputable progress, although 53.4 percent of Bessarabia's population was still illiterate in 1941.[106] The il-

---

99 In May 1940, in the inspection report of the school in the commune Slobozia-Mare, Ismail county, the inspector noted that "a school canteen was opened for 60 schoolchildren and 2 old persons. The canteen worked for a month and a half"—until the annexation of the province by the Soviets. See ANR, FMIP, 914 (1940)/24/368.
100 "Un cuvânt de îmbărbătare," 7. In October 1933, the minister ordered that "compulsory schooling will be applied in all communes with all due strictness but also with due understanding." See ANR/FMIP, 908(1934)/59/62.
101 ANR, FMIP, 909(1935)/15/305; FMIP, 913(1939)/15/311; FMIP, 913(1939)/30/309.
102 See ANR, FMIP, 908(1934)/242/17; FMIP, 909(1935)/15/294; FMIP, 909(1935)/211/40; FMIP, 909(1935)/15/330; FMIP, 909(1935)/211/32; FMIP, 909(1935)/211/34; FMIP, 910(1936)/12/167; FMIP, 913(1939)/30/201.
103 "Un cuvânt de îmbărbătare," 7.
104 "Situația școalei primare în județul Lăpușna," *Școala Basarabeană* (January–February 1939), 65.
105 Enciu, *Populația rurală a Basarabiei*, 207.
106 Extrapolating data from the inventory of assets of the Government of Bessarabia in summer 1941, in five counties (Bălți, Soroca, Orhei, Cahul, Ismail), the rate of

literacy rate in 1940 was lower than in 1930 (61.9 percent),[107] showing the slow penetration of primary school in rural areas. This process was reversible since most literate people had only attended grades 1 or 2 of primary school.

In Lieu of Conclusions

The establishment and expansion of mass primary education in rural Bessarabia faced a range of impediments that slowed it down and made it troublesome. These impediments related partly to the villagers' resistance to schooling, which was not only cultural in nature. Rural children's low enrollment and attendance rates reflected the social and economic interests of peasants who employed their own children on agricultural farms and in households. In addition, the school was seen as an institution that alienated children from parents socially (due to social mobility) and culturally (by loosening attachment to established norms and values), thus dividing the traditional family home. Despite the investment in schooling the population of Bessarabia, the Romanian education system had limitations and shortcomings. The schooling process that boomed in the 1920s led to increased school enrollment and attendance rates but was constrained by limited resources and inadequate school infrastructure by 1927–28. The economic crisis of 1929–33 aggravated the situation. In addition, the Ministry of Instruction and schooling agents in the province failed to manage the available resources efficiently, and classes remained small. School committees did not apply school fines rigorously, and fiscal collectors did not always collect them, while the ministry regularly suspended the application of fines, undermining the authority of teachers and school committees in rural communities.

The attitude of the Ministry and school authorities towards minority schools was also inconsistent. On the one hand, by law the state guaranteed the right to education in the mother tongue of citizens who were not Romanian speakers. On the other hand, it implemented an intensive program of Romanianization of schools, forcing legal provisions based on incomplete or distorted statistical data on the minorities. Lower enrollment and attendance rates for girls was due to gender stereotypes shared by the rural population, teachers, and school inspectors. These

---

literate people in Bessarabia, in 1941, was 46.6 percent (Enciu, *Populația rurală a Basarabiei*, 219).
107 Enciu, *Populația rurală a Basarabiei*, 210.

discriminatory attitudes relied on the law on education, which gave priority to the schooling of boys. In addition to school fines, the Ministry and the regional school authorities failed to encourage attendance by opening school canteens, providing free textbooks and school supplies, and offering clothing and footwear to students from poor families. In 1934 and 1939, the Ministry of Education resolved to make municipalities responsible for establishing School Assistance Funds, but this decision remained a dead letter since local authorities and the Ministry lacked the necessary funds.

In conclusion, the Romanian government made great efforts to school the civilian population of Bessarabia, particularly the least educated, rural residents, as demonstrated by the number of schools, teachers, and children. However, material and institutional limitations related to school infrastructure and inconsistency in applying school fines led to a slow increase (even decrease during times of economic crisis) in school enrollment and attendance rates.

Record Weak: Romanian Judiciary in Occupied Transnistria

Vladimir Solonari

Abstract: *This article explores the role of the Romanian judiciary in occupied Transnistria in 1940–1944. Based on a wide array of sources from American, Israeli, Romanian, Ukrainian, and Moldovan archives, the article focuses on the role of the judiciary in the fight against official corruption and administrative abuse, enforcement of legal norms in the fight against pro-Soviet guerrilla groups, and curtailment of violence against Jews. In these areas the Romanian judiciary had a weak record. Not only did they fail to fight official corruption and administrative abuse effectively, but Romanian prosecutors and courts were notoriously corrupt themselves. While military magistrates on duty in Transnistria refrained from imposing harsh sentences on suspected partisans, they looked another way when gendarmes murdered partisans under the pretense of attempted escape. Romanian prosecutors sometimes investigated the illegal appropriation of Jewish possessions by the guards, they never concerned themselves with their mass murder.*

Scholarship on the Romanian occupation of Transnistria, a territory in south-western Ukraine between the Dniester and South Buh rivers centered in Odessa, has recently made considerable progress.[1] Most scholarly attention has focused on the Romanian persecution of local Jews and

---

1 In 1941–1944, Transnistria had a territory of 40,000 square kilometers and a population of about 2.3 million people; its major urban center was the Black Sea port city of Odessa. Transnistria was somewhat of an anomaly in the wartime organization of occupied Soviet territories, almost all of the rest of which was ruled directly by the Nazi German occupiers. In 1957, Alexander Dallin published the first English-language scholarly book on wartime Transnistria, *Odessa, 1941–1944: A Case Study of Soviet Territory under Foreign Rule* (Santa Monica, CA: Rand, 1957). After a hiatus of decades, scholars turned their attention to this subject again in the 1990s, e.g., Ekkehard Völkl, *Transnistrien und Odessa (1941–1944)*, Schriftenreihe des Osteuropainstituts Regensburg-Passau; Bd. 14 (Kallmünz: Lassleben, 1996). The latest book on Transnistrian war-time history is Herwig Baum, *Varianten des Terrors: Ein Vergleich zwischen der deutschen und rumänischen Besatzungsverwaltung in der Sowjetunion 1941–1944* (Berlin: Metropol, 2011). I addressed this topic in Vladimir Solonari, "Nationalist Utopianism, Orientalist Imagination, and Economic Exploitation: Romanian Aims and Policies in Transnistria, 1941–1944," *Slavic Review*, 75, no. 3 (2016), 583–605.

Roma.[2] Scholars tend to agree that Romanian rule in the area was harsh and oppressive, especially since 270,000 to 310,000 Jews and 11,000 Roma perished there.[3] Still, considerably higher numbers of Jews survived in Transnistria and the treatment of local Christians was somewhat more lenient in Transnistria than in Nazi Germany-occupied Ukraine. The contradictory record of Romanian occupation policy in Transnistria begs some important questions about the local role of the Romanian judiciary. While German occupation policy in the Soviet territories was generally based on administrative arbitrariness and disregard for law in the relationship with the occupied, could the same be said about Romanian rule in Transnistria? Did the Romanian judiciary consider itself as a guardian of legality? If yes, in what spheres and to what extent? Did they try to enforce the law? If yes, even if only sporadically, could they had been more successful in that endeavor?

This article explores these interrelated but under-researched questions. They have been overlooked because of the inaccessibility of the files

---

2   Among the most important books on persecution of Jews and Roma in the areas under the control of the Romanian state, among which Transnistria occupies the most prominent place as the site with the greatest number of victims, are the International Commission on the Holocaust in Romania (hereinafter ICHR), *Final Report* (Iași: Polirom, 2005); Radu Ioanid, *The Holocaust in Romania: The Destruction of Jews and Gypsies under the Antonescu Regime, 1940–1944* (Chicago: Ivan R Dee, 2000); Jean Ancel, *Transnistria, 1941–1942: The Romanian Mass Murder Campaigns*, vol. 1, *History and Document Summaries*, trans. by Rachel Garfinkel and Karen Gold (Tel Aviv: Tel Aviv University, 2003); Jean Ancel, *The History of the Holocaust in Romania*, trans. by Yaffah Murciano (Lincoln, NE: Nebraska University Press and Jerusalem: Yad Vashem, 2011); Wolfgang Benz and Brigitte Mihok, eds., *Holocaust an der Peripherie: Judenpolitik und Judenmord in Rumänien und Transnisrien 1940–1944* (Berlin: Metropol Verlag, 2009); Viorel Achim and Constantin Iordache, eds., *România și Transnistria: Problema Holocaustului* (Bucharest: Curtea Veche, 2004); Dennis Deletant, *Hitler's Forgotten Ally: Ion Antonescu and His Regime, Romania, 1940–1944* (New York: Palgrave Macmillan, 2006); Diana Dumitru, *The State, Antisemitism, and Collaboration in the Holocaust: The Borderlands of Romanian and the Soviet Union* (Cambridge: Cambridge University Press, 2016); Simon Geissbühler, *Romania and the Holocaust: Events-Contexts-Aftermath* (Stuttgart: ibidem-Verlag, 2016); and Armin Heinen, *Rumänien, der Holocaust und die Logik der Gewalt* (Munich: R. Oldenbourg Verlag, 2007). My interpretation of some of the relevant questions can be found in Vladimir Solonari, "A Conspiracy to Murder: Explaining the Dynamics of Romanian 'Policy' towards Jews in Transnistria," *Journal of Genocide Research*, 19, no. 1 (2017), 1–21; Vladimir Solonari, "Hating Soviets—Killing Jews: How Antisemitic Were Local Perpetrators in Southern Ukraine, 1941–42?," *Kritika: Explorations in Russian and Eurasian History*, 15, no. 3 (2014), 505–33.

3   See ICHR, *Final Report*, 178–9 and 236.

created by the Romanian military courts.⁴ However, other archival collections now kept in Chișinău, Moldova and Odessa, Ukraine, of both Romanian and Soviet origin, combined with the published memoirs of some Romanian officials, offer important insights into the Romanian judiciary, its institutional setting, culture, and overall record in various spheres. Here, I first examine the international and domestic legal norms that defined the nature of the Romanian occupation, its institutional structure, and the place of the judiciary within it. Then I explore and assess their records in such areas as the prevention and punishment of corruption and embezzlement, the fight against Soviet partisans, and the murder of Jews. I focus not only on what the Romanian magistrates did do but also on what they were manifestly obligated but failed to do.

The Legal Nature of the Romanian Occupation and Military Justice in Transnistria

On 19 August 1941, Prime Minister and State *Conducător* (Leader), General (and within three days Marshal) Ion Antonescu, who at the time led military operations against the Red Army from his temporary headquarters in the Bessarabian town of Tighina, issued a decree establishing the Romanian administration in the territory between the Dniester and (southern) Buh Rivers.⁵ By that time, the Romanian troops had besieged the Soviet port city of Odessa, the most coveted prize in that territory, for two weeks. Two more months of heavy battles and the loss of 90,000 dead and wounded Romanian soldiers ultimately ensued the fall of Odessa and Romanian control over what would become known as Transnistria.⁶ Antonescu signed this decree in his capacity as Commander-in-chief of the Romanian armed forces, not as head of state. This way, Transnistria became an occupied territory, not part of Romania. Its status was designated as *occupatio bellica*, with the occupier enjoying the rights and duties defined in international law. Although during the war the Romanian government

---

4 According to Ottmar Trașcă, these files are kept at the Romanian Military Archive in Pitești but are not inventoried or released to researchers. In summer 2018, I was denied access to this archive.
5 See the decree in the National Archive of the Republic of Moldova (Arhiva Națională a Republicii Moldova or ANRM), F. 706 Inventar 1 dosar 556 f. 84 United States Holocaust Memorial Museum (USHMM) RG-52.004M reel 10.
6 According to the official count, Romanian losses in the battle of Odessa reached 92,545, of whom 17,729 were dead, 63,345 wounded, and 11,471 missing in action. Dinu C. Giurescu, *Romania in the Second World War (1939–1945)* (Boulder: East European Monographs, 2000), 145.

considered annexing Transnistria—an illegal act—it ultimately refrained from doing so, for reasons that should not detain us here.[7]

The status of Transnistria thus defined, Romania assumed rights and obligations as the occupying power under international law. The main legal instrument in force at the time was the 1907 Hague Convention that committed signatory powers to "Regulations Respecting the Laws and Customs of War on Land," whose third section was entirely devoted to the problem at hand. Article XLIII provided that the occupying power was under obligation "to restore and ensure, as far as possible, public order and safety, while respecting, unless absolutely prevented, the laws in force in the country."[8] This provision, together with Article XLVI on the obligation to respect the lives and private property of the local residents, limited the occupiers' freedom of action, despite numerous qualifications (for example, "as far as possible," Article XLIII quoted above). Crucially, these provisions implied that the occupying power was obligated to uphold the rule of law in the occupied territory. Even reprisals against local residents engaged in the acts of sabotage, although permitted, could generally not be "inflicted on the population on account of acts of individuals for which they cannot be regarded as jointly or severely responsible" (Article L).[9] Moreover, Romanians had to refrain from imposing their laws on the local population and see to it that Soviet legal norms remained in force during the occupation, unless circumstances "absolutely prevented" them from doing so.

Although the authority of the Convention was shattered by Germany's numerous violations of its provisions during World War I and lack of punishment after the end of hostilities of the German officials responsible for war crimes, the Convention remained in force and binding upon its signatories, Romania among them.[10] In 1916–1918, most of the Romanian territory was occupied by the Central Powers (Austria-Hungary, Ger-

---

7   On debates in the government on the status of occupied Transnistria and Mihai Antonescu's explanation as to why the government decided against formally annexing it, see Marcel-Dumitru Ciucă and Maria Ignat, eds., *Stenogramele ședințelor Consiului de Miniştri. Guvernarea Ion Antonescu* (Bucharest: Arhivele Naționale ale României, 2000), vol. 4, 342–5 (20 August 1941), vol. 5, 490–1 (16 December 1941) and vol. 5, 716–7 (23 January 1942).
8   Leon Friedman, ed., *The Law of War: A Documentary History*. Vol. 1 (New York: Random House, 1972), 321.
9   Ibid, 322.
10 On the quick abandonment of the project, see Isabel V. Hull, *A Scrap of Paper: Breaking and Making International Law during the Great War* (Ithaca: Cornell University Press, 2014), 1–16.

many, and Bulgaria) and in the inter-war period the Romanian government bitterly complained about the numerous abuses of international law committed by the occupiers, demanding compensation, mostly without effect.[11] At that time, the Romanian legal experts participating in the interwar debates on international law, often insisted on imposing further limitations on the use of force and demanded the extension of criminal liability over the officials guilty of violating international norms. One such expert was Mihai Antonescu who before the war taught international law at the University of Bucharest and advocated strict observance of the Versailles treaties as the surest guarantee of international peace.[12] However, during the war Mihai Antonescu was the closest collaborator of Marshal Ion Antonescu, whose distant relative and erstwhile personal lawyer he was. Mihai Antonescu served as both the Vice-Chairman of the Council of Ministers and the Foreign Minister and was the greatest government authority on legal matters. As such, he gave an extremely wide interpretation of the international law of military occupation, explicitly referencing German impunity for their violations after World War I.[13]

Upon occupying Transnistria, the Romanians found it impossible to enforce Soviet law. As Soviet judges and attorneys (*prokurory*) left the territory, only the Romanian military justice was available to the local residents and the Romanian officials. It was based on the 1941 Romanian Code of Military Justice.[14] Although its jurisdiction normally was limited to the military personnel, art. 119 of the Code allowed its extension over "all those [who may be subjected to it] by a special law." Let us examine its place within the Romanian occupation apparatus and organization more closely.

---

11   Grigore Antipa, *L'Occupation ennemie de la Roumanie et ses consequences économiques et sociales* (New Haven: Yale University Press, 1929); David Mitrany, *The Effect of the War in South-Eastern Europe* (New York: Howard Fertig, 1973), 138–54. The Romanian position was complicated by their own record of abuses in occupied Hungary. Keith Hitchins, *Rumania 1866–1947* (Oxford: Clarendon Press, 1994), 287–8.
12   Mihai A. Antonescu, *Organizarea păcii și Societatea Națiunilor*, 2 vols. (Bucharest: Tipografia Munca Grafică, 1932); and Mihai A. Antonescu, *Qu'est-ce que la révision des traités internationaux?* (Bucharest: Marvan, 1937)
13   Mihai Antonescu explaining the international law's implications to his ministers in Ciucă and Ignat, eds., *Stenogramele*, vol. 6, 712–5 (23 January 1942) and vol. 8, 112 (28 August 1942).
14   V. Pantilimonescu, ed., *Codul justiției militare "Regele Mihai I" (cu ultimele modificări). Legislație, trimiteri și modificări* (Bucharest: Universul, 1941).

The Institution of Occupation and "Repressive Justice" in Transnistria

Although Transnistria was under *occupatio bellica*, the Romanian government opted to create a civilian administration there. In that, it probably followed the example of the Nazis, who established a civil administration in the occupied Polish and Soviet territories.[15] The said decree appointed Gheorghe Alexianu as Antonescu's Plenipotentiary (*Împutenicit*) in Transnistria. Alexianu was a professor of administrative law at the University of Cernăuți and, in 1938–1939 during the royal dictatorship of King Carol II, served as Governor (*Rezidentul Regal*) of Suceava Region (*Ținut*, which roughly coincided with the historic province of Bukovina. By decree #3 of 4 October 1941, Alexianu was granted the title of "civil governor," routinely abbreviated afterwards to "governor" (or *guvernător*). On 17 October 1941, the day after the Romanian troops' entry into Odessa, this city was designated as the seat of the governor and the provincial administration subordinated to him.[16] Alexianu and his administration were entrusted with responsibilities over communications, economy and finance, religious affairs, education, culture, and propaganda. The governor was empowered to "issue ordinances he considered necessary for the functioning of the administration and continuation of activity in all spheres", and to appoint prefects, who in turn had to appoint *pretor* in *raioane* (sing. raion, equivalent to *plasă*) and mayors (*primari*) assisted by their staff constituting primării (sing. primăria) in towns and villages (*comune*).[17] The Odessa police *prefectura* was subordinated to the mayor; the gendarmerie legions, which included bureaus of *Siguranța* or political police, to the prefects. Transnistria also had offices and informers recruited and run by the SSI, the Secret Information Service—the Romanian intelligence and counter-intelligence agency, as well as various units of the occupation army, which were deployed there while not taking part in military actions at the front. Neither the SSI nor the army were subordinated to the governor but were expected to and did cooperate with him and his office.

---

15   On the Nazi ways of ruling over occupied European territories, see Mark Mazower, *Hitler's Empire: How the Nazis Ruled Europe* (New York: Penguin, 2008), 245–6. On the influence of Nazi administrative thinking over the design of provincial institutions in Bessarabia, Bukovina, and Transnistria, see Hildrun Glass, *Deutschland un die Verfolgung der Juden im rumänischen Machtbereich 1940–1944* (Munich: Oldenburg, 2014), 33–7, 96–147.
16   See the decree in ANRM F. 706 Inventar 1 dosar 556 f. 87–8 USHMM RG-52.004M reel 10.
17   Ibid.

The administration of a province with a population of 2.3 to 2.5 million required substantial bureaucracy, which during Alexianu's tenure as a governor grew to thirty departments (*direcții*) in his administration or *guvernământ*.[18] This was before Alexianu was sacked on 29 January 1944, when he was replaced by General Gheorghe Potopeanu, thus making the shift from a civilian to a military administration, which lasted until 16 March 1944. There were thirteen counties (*județe*) overseen by prefects, assisted by their own offices or *prefecture*, each *județ* consisting of three to eight *raioane* headed by *pretori* assisted by their offices, *preture*. Gendarmerie companies or Legions were placed in every *județ* and subordinated to the prefects.

The problem of adjudicating disputes between Transnistria's residents and limiting abuses of various officials inevitably arose. Ion Antonescu wanted to run Transnistria as his own personal fiefdom, sealed from the oversight of the Bucharest bureaucrats, accountants, and comptrollers, and was not at all keen on ensuring the rule of law there but had to provide a veneer of legality for his administration. He made it clear that Alexianu was subordinated exclusively to himself. Tellingly, all ordinances and other regulations in the occupied region were issued by the governor in Antonescu's name. On several occasions, the *Conducător* encouraged the governor to keep double accountancy to conceal the amount of goods extracted from the occupied region, some of which he then distributed to veterans and other socially-vulnerable groups of Romanians, in his own name. For example, in the Council of Ministers meeting of 17 March 1943, he turned down the request of the Minister of Finance Alexandru Neagu that rules of public accountancy be followed in Transnistria, a request that Alexianu vehemently opposed.[19] The registration of all requisitions from the region was undesirable, intoned Antonescu, because they could strengthen Moscow's claims that Romanians were indiscriminatedly plundering the region. "We have to take as much as we can

---

18 On Alexianu's replacement with Potopeanu, see Archive of Romanian Intelligence Service (Arhiva Serviciului Român de Informații or ASRI), dosar 40013, vol. 6, f. 440, USHMM RG-25.004M, reel 29. On Potopeanu's order to withdraw from Transnistria and transfer its administration over to the Germans, see Potopeanu's 15 March 1944 order in ASRI, dosar 40013, vol. 6, 339, USHMM Rg-25.004M, reel 30. On the structure of *guvernământ* see activity reports of various departments in ANRM Fond 706, dosar 518 vol. 1. No exact number of civil servants (*funcționari publici*) is mentioned in the activity reports generated by the governor's office (*guvernământ*) except the department of railways, which mentioned 19,499 local employees and 3,746 from Romania (Ibid., f. 355).

19 For Ion Antonescu's order to replace Alexianu with Potopeanu, see ASRI, dosar 40013, vol. 6, f. 440, USHMM RG-25.004M, reel 29.

from Transnistria," Ion Antonescu expounded, "but without receipts since otherwise the Russians will pick these documents up tomorrow and bring them to the Green Table [of the peace conference]."[20] Thus, the application of legal regulations to public accountancy in Transnistria had to be avoided.[21] In this context, Alexianu's malpractices gradually became so severe that they prompted Neagu's accusations—probably incorrect, since Neagu had no way of knowing all the ways in which Transnistrian resources were exploited for the benefit of his country—that Transnistria was a drag on the country's resources. Eventually, Antonescu scapegoated his governor blaming him for those same abuses he encouraged and even demanded him to implement.

Romanian citizens on duty in Transnistria and local residents who committed crimes against the occupying authorities were under the jurisdiction of military courts which exercised what Romanian lawyers defined as "repressive justice, prompt and severe."[22] There were two levels of military courts: pretorial courts at county (*județ*) level and two martial courts, in Odessa for southern Transnistria and in Tiraspol for its northern part. Gendarmerie legion commanders, usually in the rank of major, performed the functions of pretorial courts, serving as prosecutors, grand jurors, and deciding judges. They were guided by the provisions of the Romanian Code of Military Justice, the decrees on the organization of Transnistria, together with the governor's ordinances and other regulations. They also imposed sentences for breaches of their own county-wide regulations. Initially, according to Alexianu's Ordinance 37 of 20 December 1943, military *pretori* (otherwise known as legion commanders) could impose sentences of up to two prison years, a 20,000 *lei* fine, or a combination thereof. Ordinance 10 of 4 January 1944 lengthened these sentences to 12 years in prison and/or equivalent fines.[23] The martial courts, presided over by military magistrates, imposed stiffer sentences going up to the death penalty for crimes outlined in the Military Justice

---

20 Ciucă and Ignat, eds., *Stenogramele*, vol. 9, 157–8.
21 Ibid, 156.
22 See legal opinions and draft decrees and ordinances, mostly unsigned and undated, in State Archive of Odessa *Oblast'* (Derzhavnyi arkhiv Odes'koi oblasti or DAOO) F. 2242 Opis' 1, spr. 1a, without pagination, apparently 1941–3.
23 Ordinance #37, in DAOO F. 2242 Op. 1 spr. 1 ark. 49–50 USHMM RG-31.004 reel 1. I was unable to find Ordinance #10, but detailed instructions on its application signed by the Head of the Division of Justice and Administrative Litigation of the Military Administration of the Territory between the Dniester and Buh Rivers (successor to *guvernământ*) can be found in DAOO F. 2242 Op. 1 spr. 1569 ark. 624–627 USHMM RG-31.004M reel 6.

Code in all matters pertaining to state security and by the governor's ordinances. There was no legal recourse for such sentences, save petitions for their suspension, with probation. Local residents could request suspension in the court that sentenced them, while Romanian citizens sentenced by military *pretori* could request suspension from martial courts. Decisions pronounced on requests for suspension were definitive, and no further appeal was allowed.

Alexianu's Ordinance 133 of 9 September 1943 established an unprecedented procedure for the prosecution of civil servants, recruited both from Romania and from among local residents. Their administrative bosses could initiate an investigation into their supposed wrongdoing, both on their own volition and following a denunciatory lead. For sentencing, they then sent the cases to the military courts, depending on the rank, obviating prosecutors.[24] Needless to say, such provisions ensured the full dependence of local civil servants on their prefects, who could both initiate their prosecution and sentence them at will as judges in the pretorial courts. The Governor's powers over employees of the central office of *guvernământ* were also increased but not as drastically since sentencing depended on magistrates in the martial courts who were supposedly independent from him.

Legal disputes between Soviet citizens who resided in Transnistria were resolved on the basis of Soviet law. Given the non-existence of Soviet courts of law in Transnistria and the inability of Romanian judges to apply Soviet law, the application of Soviet private law (in Soviet legal parlance, this referred to a substantial part of the Penal, Civil, and Administrative codes that were not available in Romanian translation) inevitably caused difficulty. Perhaps tellingly, Romanian archival sources contain no information on how this task was performed. According to noted Odessa lawyer Iakov Borisovich Brodskii, a surviving member the of liberal-minded and cosmopolitan local upper-middle class and a lawyer with a record of service stretching back to pre-revolutionary Russia, there were no courts to adjudicate civil cases, but "interested parties could resort to the services of mediators whom Romanians quasi-recognized; that is, one could obtain enforcement of their decisions."[25] Brodskii failed to provide further information as to who these mediators were, but another Odessa

---

24 This ordinance is available in DAOO F. 2242 Op. 1 spr. 1a, no pagination. Instructions on the implementation of Ordinance #10/944 referred to in the previous note (DAOO F. 2242 Op. 1 spr. 1569 ark. 624–627 USHMM RG-31.004M reel 6) contain an informative discussion of legal difficulties arising from these provisions.
25 State Archive of the Russian Federation (Gosudarstvennyi arkhiv Rossiiskoi Federatsii or GARF) F. P-7021 Op. 69 delo 343 ll. 17–22ob. YV JM 19.969. Brodskii was

lawyer named Lukashev, who also spent the war years under occupation, noted in his deposition to the Soviet Extraordinary State Commission to Investigate Nazis and Their Allies and Collaborators' Crimes (ChGK) that in Odessa "civil cases were litigated either in the legal *direcția* of *primăria* or in the board of arbitration (*arbitrazh*)." Lukashev added that the "process of law in arbitration boards was extremely simplified; procedural norms were not followed. All proceedings were held in Romanian."[26] This strongly suggests that arbitration functions were performed in Odessa, and probably elsewhere in Transnistria, by Romanian officials who were not necessarily lawyers, and the application of Soviet legal norms was rather "theoretical."

Corruption Outside and Inside the Judiciary

All Romanian, German, Soviet, and Jewish sources which provide accounts of life under occupation agree on the ubiquity of official corruption at all levels and in various forms—black trafficking of goods, extortion and taking of bribes, and embezzlement of public goods. Enumeration of individual cases can cover dozens of pages, so I will provide several pieces of evidence informative for the scale and ubiquity of corruption.

There was massive speculation in goods and currency brought from Romania by military and civil servants, who were the only people with permission to cross the Dniester River into Transnistria. In March 1943, the Second bureau of the Third Army Corps (intelligence) deployed in Transnistria reported that "on the occasion of one single search in a Bucharest-Odessa passenger train on February 7, 1943, we found 14,000 *lei* in cash, 62 meters of silk, 23 pairs of female stockings, 490 reels of thread, 60 bottles of lamp gas, 1500 boxes of matches," all articles of great value strictly banned from importation into the province.[27] On 9 February 1943, Alexianu issued Ordinance 9, instituting severe customs control at the borders and ordering the internment of contrabandists in concentration

---

a Christian Orthodox Jew. Although imprisoned for several months as an undisclosed Jew—a capital offense in occupied Odessa—Brodskii was released and practiced under Romanian law. This account comes from his deposition with the Soviet Extraordinary State Commission for Ascertaining and Investigating Crimes Perpetrated by the German-Fascist Invaders and Their Accomplices known by its Russian acronym ChGK. For more on this person, see the memoirs of his son, Mikhail Brodskii, *Mama, nas ne ub'iut ... Vospominaniia*, no date, available at http://bookscafe.net/read/brodskiy_mihail-mama_nas_ne_ubyut_vospominaniya-2391 21.html#p1, accessed on 8 October 2015.

26   GARF F. P-7021 Op. 69 delo 343 ll. 24–24ob. YV JM 19.969.
27   ANRM F. 706 Inventar 1 dosar 8 vol. 2, ff. 455–456.

camps.[28] By August 1943, the authorities confiscated contraband merchandise valued at 292,340 RKKS.[29] In November 1943, Colonel-in-reserve (a rank in the Romanian military, even during active duty) Mihai Botez, the Prefect of Ovidopol *judeƫ*, was under investigation for contraband, and Ion Antonescu ordered him court-martialed.[30] This was just a drop in the bucket since many basic necessities such as clothes and shoes could be procured only on the black market as contraband merchandise from Romania because local industries were working almost exclusively for Romanian troops.[31] Alexander Werth, a BBC correspondent in Russia, visited Odessa days after its liberation by the Red Army in April 1944. He noted that one could still buy "German pencils, Hungarian cigarettes, German cigarettes, and even bottles of scent and some stockings," on the black market. Werth attributed this bounty to the legacy of Romanian domination since, as he remarked probably based on rumors collected from the locals, "Romanian generals used to bring whole truckloads of ladies' underwear and stockings from Bucharest, and get their orderlies to sell them on the market."[32] According to Werth's local informer, Romanian soldiers, too, "always had a variety of things to sell."[33]

Bribery was endemic. As Werth's informer put it, "with a little money [one] could buy anything from the Romanians, even a passport in the name of Richelieu."[34] Among the materials the ChGK collected after Odessa's liberation were testimonies on atrocities in the Odessa *oblast'*, most of which came from the Odessa intelligentsia, often Jews who survived by bribing Romanian officials. As lawyer Lukashev (no first name and patronymic provided) put it: "Every Romanian functionary, from the lowest to the highest, took bribes ... They arrested a lower-level employee of the mayor's office and put him in front of the city hall with a sign, 'bribe-taker,' while at that very same time every employee of the mayor's office was accepting bribes."[35] In September 1943, the SSI reported from

---

28   DAOO F. 2242 Op. 1 spr. 1 ark. 186–187 USHMM RG-31.004M reel 1.
29   ANRM F. 706 Inventar 1 dosar 518 vol. 1 ff. 150–151, activity report of the Department of Domestic Commerce for 17 August 1941–1 August 1943.
30   ANRM F. 706 Inventar 1 dosar 52, f. 9. CBBT summary of this case, with Ion Antonescu's order.
31   Transnistrian General Inspectorate of Gendarmerie report for March 1943 in National Archives of Romania (Arhivele Naƫionale ale României or ANR) Fond IGJ dosar 80/1943, f. 90 USHMM RG-25.101m reel 26; Odessa Inspectorate of Gendarmerie report for October 1943, in ANR F. IGJ dosar 84/1943 f. 142 USHMM RG-25.010M reel 27.
32   Alexander Werth, *Russia at War, 1941–1945* (New York: E.P. Dutton, 1964), 818.
33   Ibid, 820.
34   Ibid.
35   GARF F. R- 7021 Op. 69 delo 343, l. 25ob. YV JM-19.969.

Ananiev that "bribery is accepted by absolutely all authorities" and "is considered customary."³⁶

Embezzlement of public funds, goods considered "war booty," and things belonging to murdered Jews or other victims was another widely reported practice. According to Pretor Pădure, his boss Golta *judeţ* prefect Isopescu used to smuggle farm animals from Transnistria into Romania, indicating addresses of other Transnistrian officials' farms with whom he was in cahoots. According to the same source, Isopescu "once traveled to Kiev to procure spare parts there and returned with Persian rugs, saying that he needed them as a memento."³⁷ Persian rugs as coveted objects of illegal appropriation are mentioned in other depositions, including that of Alexianu, who asserted that after one (unnamed) *Siguranţa* commissar had been "caught with Persian rugs," he was tried. Tellingly, Alexianu failed to indicate the verdict.³⁸ As already mentioned, the Odessa mayor's office (*primăria*) was often seen as extremely corrupt, and among its officials the most infamous was Gherman Pântea's deputy Constantin Vidraşcu.³⁹ According to his brother-in-law's deposition, Vidraşcu occupied a ten-room apartment in Odessa, and when he left the city, he brought with him two railcars filled with furniture.⁴⁰ During his stay in office Alexianu resolutely defended his administration's reputation by refuting most accusations of wrongdoing, but he changed his tune during the 1945 pretrial investigations and acknowledged that despite his best efforts he failed to prevent massive pillaging of murdered Jews' movable properties. "They used to ship [into Romania, former Jewish] pianos in military trucks," he said. Defending his record in fighting corruption, he cited only the case of an unnamed prefect colonel (likely Mihai Botez, mentioned above) who was involved in contraband, caught, tried, and sentenced to eight years in prison.⁴¹

Sentencing just one official while corruption flourished under his very nose for three years condemns Alexianu's leadership and shows how ineffectual the Romanian justice system was in this regard. Not only did it not help the fight against corrupt practices, it facilitated and normalized

---

36 Cited in Pavel Moraru, *România şi bătălia informaţiilor între Prut şi Bug (1940–1944)* (Bucharest: Editura Militară, 2011), 193.
37 Pădure's deposition in ASRI dosar 40010 vol. 20 f. 67 USHMM RG-21.004M reel 21.
38 Alexianu's deposition in ASRI dosar 40010 vol. 45 f. 243 USHMM RG-25.004M reel 34.
39 Cf. Ion Antonescu's marginal note on Alexianu's report on the increased number of unauthorized persons from Romania showing up in Transnistria: "Unverified but increasingly numerous reports indicate the Odessa's mayor's office as the nest of illegal commercial activity" ANRM F. 706 Op. 1 dosar 52 f. 78, August 1942.
40 Dosar 21401 vol. 2 f. 254–254v. USHMM RG-25.004M reel 30.
41 ASRI dosar 40010 vol. 45 ff. 227–228 USHMM RG-25.004M reel 34.

them by setting up a negative example. All lawyers who lived in occupied Odessa and deposited their testimonies to the ChGK after liberation unanimously condemned the Romanian judiciary in Transnistria for its abuses and insatiable, insolent, and shameless venality. According to Brodskii, the most eloquent, informative, and surprisingly nuanced eyewitness, "Bribery thrived everywhere ... among Martial Court magistrates and employees, all but three persons used to take bribes, including stenographers and guards." Brodskii told the story of another lawyer, Baranovskaia (with whom he fathered a son), who was denounced as a Jewess hiding under an assumed name. Following her arrest, she managed to send negotiated bribes to *Siguranța* chief Porumbescu and prosecutor Gavrilovich via Romanian lawyer Sârbu. The latter failed to deliver the bribe (presumably appropriating it), and therefore on 20 April 1942 Baranovskaia was executed by firing squad. Another Jewish lawyer, Kaidman, was also denounced and arrested and paid a bribe to Gavrilovich. When Gavrilovich requested additional payment, Kaidman was unable to gather the funds and then he was sentenced to death and executed. Still another Jewish lawyer, Bogopol'skii, while interned in a ghetto together with other Jews, sent a bribe to Odessa *Siguranța* chief Răzvan. The latter did nothing for his release. Bogopol'skii then submitted a complaint to Prosecutor Ionescu, whom Brodskii characterized as a decent man of liberal views. Ionescu summoned both Bogopol'skii and Răzvan to his office where they negotiated a price for the Jew's release in Ionescu's presence. According to Brodskii, the majority of Romanian prosecutors were liberals, Anglophiles, and Russophiles (this latter assertion seems unlikely, added to divert probable NKVD attention to Brodskii's ties to pro-Western Romanians); they did not believe in the Axis powers' victory, considered the war a mistake, and despised "Antonescu's men." When confronted with evidence of abuses in Romanian law-enforcement bodies, they explained that they resulted from a war-time shortage of trained personnel, so that Bucharest authorities assigned the worst cadres to Transnistria.[42] Whether "liberal" or not, Ionescu was mentioned by at least one other eyewitness as a brutal and cynical bribe-taker.[43]

Some of Romanian judiciary were defense lawyers, both local and from Romania, who needed each other. While Romanians knew Romanian law and could argue cases in court, local lawyers knew local layers

---

42   GARF F. R-7021 Op. 69 delo 343 ll. 18ob.-20 YV JM 19.969.
43   Alexandr Nikolaevich Lebedinskii, identified in the ChGK file as "a scientist," asserted that Ionescu arrested him because a group of unidentified "Ukrainian nationalists" paid him a bribe for this arrest, half of which Ionescu transferred to his boss prosecutor Soltan. GARF F. P-7021 Op. 69 delo 434 l. 1ob YV JM 19.971.

and were familiar with local realities, being able to function as interpreters between defendants and their defense lawyers from Romania. Soviet lawyers who decided to remain in occupied Transnistria were seemingly those with pre-revolutionary education and experience since only these testified before the Soviet Extraordinary State Commission after liberation. Their knowledge of French, which was also part of higher education in Romania, served as a means of communication with their Romanian counterparts.

According to eyewitness Aleksandr Nikolaevich Lebedinskii, the main function of Romanian lawyers was to take bribes (probably from their Russian counterparts—a detail that Lebedinskii did not mention explicitly) and then to give part of them to prosecutors and presiding magistrates: "One could bribe his way out of jail even after having committed the heaviest crime ... The court trial had no significance whatsoever, being a simple formality."[44] Another defense lawyer, Lukashev, testified that Romanian lawyers did not even acquaint themselves with materials from the files before the court sittings. Punishment and mistreatment of inmates, including torture by prison guards, policemen, and gendarmerie, could be avoided by paying bribes on time.[45] Former members of the pro-Soviet resistance, commonly known as partisans after the war, also mention cases of "ransoming out" (*vykupili*) their comrades from the Romanian gendarmerie.[46]

Reliability of these and many other accounts of bribe-taking by Romanian magistrates may be questioned on the grounds that eyewitnesses were speaking to Soviet authorities interested in gathering solely negative information on the occupation. Furthermore, some of the eyewitnesses were under investigation for their role during the occupation or had other good reasons to expect arrest by the NKVD in the near future.[47] Thus, they had great incentive to demonstrate their "Sovietness" by besmirching the occupiers. Still, the sheer frequency with which bribery in

---

44 GARF F. R. 7021 Opis' 69 delo 434 l. 1v YV JM-19.971.
45 GARF F. R. 7021 Opis' 69 delo 343 l. 24v.
46 See the summary report on partisan activity in Vynnitsia *oblast'*, shortly after November 1942. This *oblast'* was divided during the occupation: the northern part belonged to the German zone of occupation, the southern to Romania. The report mentions that these persons were ransomed out from the Romanians. (TsDAGOU, F. 1 Opis' 62 spr. 156 ark. 71–2). Also Serafim Bedniazhevslii's mention of ransoming out his sister from gendarmerie arrest "for five thousand marks." Those marks were *Reichskassenkreditscheinen* (RKKS), the German quasi-currency used in the occupied territories and served as legal tender in Transnistria. (TsDAGOU, F. 1 Opis' 62 spr. 452 ark. 5–6.)
47 Such was the fate of lawyer Brodskii. See Brodskii, *Mama, nas ne ub'iut ... Vospominaniia*.

the Romanian judiciary was mentioned—less so than in accounts of events in the German zones, where the unbridled brutality of the former masters was prevalent—suggests that these accounts reflect an important aspect of Transnistrian reality during the war. Given how corrupt the Romanian judiciary in Transnistria was, it is small wonder that it was an inadequate tool in the fight against administrative corruption.

The Romanian Judiciary and the Fight against the Soviet Partisans

The Partisan movement in Transnistria never gained as much strength as in other occupied Soviet territories, mostly due to the preponderance of open-steppe spaces offering little cover for armed groups.[48] Nevertheless, during his May 1946 interrogation Alexianu insisted that partisans and saboteurs were practically "nonexistent" in Transnistria, but he exaggerated.[49] Odessa sat on a labyrinthine maze of stone quarries, which had been created during the decades of economic boom prior to the Bolshevik Revolution. Chaotic mining resulted in multiple meandering tunnels, known as catacombs, some of which were interconnected, while others led into dead ends. Its overall length reached 1,400 kilometers under the city and much more under the outlying villages. Since the early twentieth century, they presented an increasing problem for the authorities, initially tsarist and later Soviet, as a refuge for violent gangs terrorizing local residents.[50] In the weeks before the final Soviet withdrawal, the Soviets decided to use the catacombs as a base for their own terrorist groups that were to operate behind enemy lines.

Most catacomb groups were created and commanded by NKVD officers, others by the Communist Party. Groups were supplied with ammunition and provisions. They were also supposed to benefit from a network of spies and liaisons in the city. Although after the war the Soviet propagandists worked hard to create the myth of catacomb guerrillas' exploits, a myth that has survived to date (in the museum of "Partisan Glory" in the

---

48　Forests occupied only six per cent of Transnistrian territory, mostly in its northern part closer to the Buh River. See the activity report of the department of forestry of the *guvernământ* for the period August 19, 1941–August 1, 1943 in ANRM F. 706 Inventar 1 dosar 518 vol. 1 f. 228.
49　See Alexianu's statement in ASRI dosar 40010 vol. 45 ff. 242–243 USHMM RG-25.004M reel 34.
50　On the catacombs' history as a nest of criminal gangs before World War II, see Viktor Anatol'evich Savchenko, *Neofitsial'naia Odessa epochi nepa (mart 1921–sentiabr' 1929)* (Moscow: ROSPEN, 2012), p. 270.

village of Usatovo, a suburb of Odessa, this myth is still "supported" by fake exhibits) was that their military efficiency was low and the human cost of their operations very high. The only somewhat successful group was led by Vladimir Aleksandrovich Badaev (real name Molodtsov), Captain of State Security (rank equivalent to that of colonel in the Red Army) sent from Moscow.[51] According to Soviet and Romanian accounts, his group performed acts of sabotage on the railways and transmitted valuable military information to Moscow high command.[52] In January 1942, Badaev was arrested during a meeting with his liaison, after which the group fell apart. In September that year, the Odessa Martial Court heard the cases of forty guerilla members, most of them from the Badaev group. Twenty-five were sentenced to death and executed, including Badaev; others received up to twenty-five years of hard labor. Of the latter, few survived the end of the war.[53]

By spring of 1942, the Romanians had completely destroyed the catacomb groups; in the rest of Transnistria, where guerrilla groups were also created by the retreating Soviets, they fell apart even earlier—during the first days of occupation—mostly due to the mass surrender or flight of putative "partisans." The anti-Soviet feelings of the local residents, who massively supported Romanian efforts to squash the guerrillas, were another reason for the quick destruction of these groups.[54] Throughout 1942, the Romanians registered no signs of the pro-Soviet groups' activity, being more concerned with the Ukrainian nationalist underground than with the communist one. The latter's activity was largely reduced to educational and cultural spheres and presented no immediate danger.[55]

---

51 On the NKVD ranks, see Aleksandr Nikolaevich Iakovlev, Alksandr Ivanovich Kokurin, Nikolai Vasil'evich Petrov, eds., *Lubianka: Organy VChK-OGPU-NKRB-MGB-MVD-KGB. 1917–1991. Spravochnik* (Moscow: MFD, 2003), 61. Some Romanian sources identify Badaev's rank as major (SSI note of 14 December 1942 ANR F. IGJ dosar/1942 f. 91 USHMM RG-25.010M reel 22).

52 See Romanian summary of their activity in Tsentral'nyi derzhanyi arkhiv hromadskykh ob'ednan' Ukrainy (Central State Archive of the Social Organizations of Ukraine or TSDAHOU) Fond 57, Opis' 4, Delo 103, ll. 9, 79. For the Soviet summary, see TSDAHOU F. 1 Op. 22 spr. 444, ark. 18–21, recto and verso. Soviet accounts are exaggerated. For example, a train crash in December 1941 which supposedly killed Romanian and German top brass and which the Soviets attributed to this group is never mentioned in Romanian documents.

53 See Romanian sources cited in note 37 above.

54 Summary of the partisan activity complied by the Odessa Regional party committee (*obkom*) in May 1946 based on information collected by the party district committees in the region, in TSDAHOU F. 1 Op. 42 spr.450 ark. 47–49.

55 See SSI note on the mood of the Odessan population dated 29 September 1942 in ANRM F. 706 Inventar 1 dosar 8 ff. 318–320 USHMM RG-54.002M reel 1and reports of gendarmerie legions in Tulcin (ANR F. ICJ dosar 125/1942 f. 155–156

After the German-Romanian defeat at Stalingrad, Romanians registered the activity of newly created pro-Soviet groups which, they believed, were stockpiling arms and other munitions in preparation for an armed uprising. The Romanian counter-intelligence service, the SSI, penetrated the underground network and in March 1943 delivered a crushing blow to the burgeoning armed resistance.[56]

Despite the continuing repression in summer 1942 additional underground cells reappeared, and in fall 1943 they started attacking individual gendarme posts, railway and telegraph lines, and columns of horse-drawn and auto vehicles in rural areas, especially in northern Transnistria. According to SSI sober reports, by early 1944 Romanians had lost control over northern *județe*, where numerous bands, some of them consisting of hundreds of armed men led by parachuted Red Army commanders, operated.[57] In February 1944, the Romanian and the Germans had to divert a serious military force, including German tanks and Stuka bombers, to suppress a partisan detachment of 500 men in the Spicov forest in Tulcin *județ*. Despite heavy losses on both sides, the partisan force escaped to the east, across the frontline.[58]

In the final months of the occupation, fighting Soviet partisans was the single most important preoccupation of the Romanian gendarmerie, including the *Siguranța*, police, and the SSI. The army troops also became heavily involved. Arrested suspects were often tried in martial courts and condemned to various extreme sentences, including death. Sometimes they were executed in an extrajudicial manner by the gendarmes. Romanian and Soviet sources allow for a better understanding of how these methods of punishing the wrongdoers were interlinked.

Preliminary investigations conducted by the police, gendarmerie, and lower-ranking military prosecutors routinely mentioned cruel methods such as beatings (with fists and rubber hoses); wrapping in wire; breaking fingers by squashing them between doors and doorframes;

USHMM RG-25.010M reel 17; August 1942) and Iampol' (ANR F. IJG dosar 147/1942 f. 68v. USHMM RG-25.010M reel 20; September 1942).

56 A massive gendarmerie, police, and SSI operation on March 12–13, 1943 resulted in the arrest of 295 "bandits" all over Transnistria, with further arrests soon to follow. See Russian translation of SSI report in TSDAHOU F. 57, op. 4 spr. 103, ark. 59, 69, 88.

57 See SSI report on the developments all over Transnistria from January 23, 1944 in AMAP F. Fond Armata a 3-a Inventar N S/6776 din 1976 dosar 2208 f. 170–171 USHMM RG-25.101M reel 20.

58 See German and Romanian daily military, gendarmerie and SSI reports to that effect in AMAP F. Fond Armata a 3-a Inventar N S/6776 din 1976 dosar 2208 f. 286–313 USHMM RG-25.101M reel 20.

burning heels with flaming coals; and even a local invention, the "electric chair," which, according to Brodskii, did not kill but caused serious burns. Its inventor was Răzvan, and the chair was reportedly so popular among Romanian investigators that they borrowed it from the Odessa office for use elsewhere in Transnistria (they called its use "scientific treatment").[59] Still, the same source argued that these methods were not practiced by prosecutors in the "highest" martial court (probably meaning Odessa). According to many Soviet resisters who survived arrest and investigation, some defendants renounced their depositions during the trial and claimed they made them under duress, resulting in the invalidation of such depositions.[60] Former SSI investigator Constantin Hariton independently confirmed such accounts during his interrogation in April 1945.[61]

That the Romanian version of "repressive justice" was not the same as complete lawlessness and the arbitrary application of lethal violence against anybody suspected of hostile attitudes is further confirmed by the release of individual resisters when martial courts concluded that the prosecution had failed to prove their guilt. Summarizing the findings of SMERSH on the Soviet resistance in Transnistria and the Romanian fight against them, the Deputy Head of the Organizational-instructional Section of the Central Committee of the Communist Party of Ukraine (CC CP(B)U), Viktor Ivanovich Alidin, related to Nikita Sergeevich Khrushchev, the CC CP(B)U first secretary, in April 1945, that after a transfer of cases to martial courts, "they would accept defendants' complaints about torture, treat them with respect during interrogations, and even release some of the less active members of the underground." Perplexed by this practice and the rather lenient sentences that some of the leaders of Soviet underground received (various prison terms or forced labor, *katorga*, instead of the death penalty), Alidin explained them away as the Romanians' "cunning" (*ukhishchreniie*).[62]

In fact, the record of the martial court in Transnistria leaves no doubt that the judges did try to distinguish graver proven cases from those in which the guilt of defendants appeared as minor or unproven.

---

59   GARF F. R-7021 Op. 69 delo 343 l. 21 Yad Vashem (YV) JM 19.969, Brodskii's testimony. Practically all members of Soviet resistance "processed" by SSI or *Siguranța* mention torture in their recollections.

60   For example, Vladimir Il'ich Trofimovskii, who was editor of an underground pro-Soviet bulletin in Odessa, mentioned such a fact in his autobiography, submitted to the Odessa obkom in 1967. DAOO F. 92 Op. 1 spr. 18, ark. 25. Another resistance member, Pantelei Nikolaevich Kozyrev, mentions a similar episode; see the transcript of his interview in DAOO F. 92 Op. 1 spr. 135, ark. 9–10.

61   See transcript of his interrogation in DAOO F. 92 Op. 1 ark. 10–11.

62   TSDAHOU F. 1 Op. 22 spr. 450 ark. 30.

Perhaps the strongest support for this conclusion comes, paradoxically, from the well-documented practice of Romanian police and gendarmerie putting to death suspected partisans who were released by the martial court or sentenced to punishment deemed by the officers as too light. In such actions, the police and gendarme officers were empowered by Ion Antonescu himself. According to his memoirs, General Ion Lissievici, who headed an SSI echelon on the Eastern Front, received an order to that effect from the *Conducător* in response to a proposal to modify the moderate punitive policy towards suspected partisans in Transnistria. Lissievici failed to provide the date, but most probably he was referring to fall 1941. According to his account, the initiative came from the Odessa Martial Court magistrates who due to the high number of arrested suspects were unable to process all their cases while the city prison had no capacity to house them. As such, the magistrates suggested that from then on only "active partisans would be tried by the Martial Court." The "proven simple accomplices" were to be interned in a concentration camp in Romania. When this proposal reached Ion Antonescu in a report submitted by the SSI Information Center in Odessa, he turned it down, adding that "all partisans—those active and their accomplices—had to be shot. This order will be also transmitted to the *governors* of Bessarabia and Bukovina." Lissievici claimed that he decided not to implement this order. Although he did inform the military commandant of Odessa of its existence, he recommended that all partisans continue to be tried by the Martial Court.[63]

Whether Lissievici concealed the order or not is less important than its issuance. The gendarmerie commander was undoubtedly aware of its existence and acted accordingly, even if not with respect to each and every suspect. Soviet sources mention numerous instances of extra-judicial killings of suspected resistance members by the gendarmes. To cite a notorious case, in February 1943, the gendarmes arrested thirty members of an underground Komsomol cell in the village of Krymka, Golta *județ*. This cell had failed to achieve much of anything except killing one of their own for obscure reasons and carrying out a failed raid on the gendarme post, but all of the arrested were escorted to the jail in Golta, where they were beaten and tortured. Shortly afterwards, twenty-three of them were sent back to the village and shot *en route* by the escort, in close vicinity to the village. The remaining seven made their way to the Tiraspol martial court, which found no evidence of their subversive activity, and

---

63 Ion Lissievici, "Amintirile unui fost lucrător în serviciul de informații al statului," in *Glorie și tragedii. Momente din istoria Serviciilor de informații și contrainformații pe Frontul de Est (1941–1944)*, ed. Cristian Troncotă (Bucharest: Nemira, 2003), 158–9.

sent them back to reside in the village under gendarme surveillance. The gendarmes shot and killed this group, too, under the same pretext.[64]

Romanian sources also abound with evidence of extrajudicial killings committed by gendarmes, before or after the trials. For example, in the quarterly activity report by Transnistria Gendarmerie Inspector Colonel Mihail Iliescu, probably drafted in June 1942, on 25 March 1942 nine suspected Soviet guerrillas from Odessa tried to escape during their transportation to a prison; gendarmes opened fire and shot all of them to death.[65] According to an information note from Tulcin Gendarmerie Legion, on November 1942, gendarmes transferred four suspected partisans to the village of Trostianeț. When they attempted to escape, the escort opened fire and killed them.[66] Such killings continued into the next year, even when the withdrawal from Transnistria became inevitable, as an activity report of Odessa Gendarmerie Inspector Colonel V. Grosu made clear: when three "bandits" who were escorted to the crime scene for forensic reconstruction attempted to escape, they were shot to death.[67] The matter-of-fact manner in which gendarme officials reported such "events" (the category under which these killings were reported) strongly suggests that they knew that no punishment for the murderers would ensue.

In 1948–1949, while investigating crimes of the Romanian gendarmerie and police in occupied Transnistria, the communist authorities interrogated former magistrates who had served in the region, some of whom claimed that they tried to put a stop to the illegal practices committed. For example, Chirilă Zoltan (also known as Soltan) served as the main public attorney (*prim-procuror*) at the Odessa Martial Court in 1942–1944. He declared that the attorneys (*parchet*) were aware of numerous "illegalities" such as "mistreatments, plunder, and even acts of extermination." Referencing the murder of suspected partisans in February or March 1943 (probably the Krymka case mentioned above), he testified that attorney Lieutenant-in-reserve Dumitru Leșeanu, "a courageous

---

64 See the summary of the Soviet investigation in TSDAHOU fond 1 op. 22 spr. 472. Romanians investigated the gendarmes who perpetrated this crime in 1955. Some materials from this investigative file were then transferred to the archive of the Mykalev *oblast'* of Ukraine; they are summarized in Mykola Mykolaiovych Shytiuk, "Pidpil'na organizatsiia 'Partizans'ka iskra' v svitli novykh istorychnykh dzherel i dokumentiv," in *Mykolaïvshchyna v roky Velykoï Vitchyznianoï viiny: 1941–1944: do 60-richchia vyzvolennia oblasti vid nimets'ko-rumuns'kykh okupantiv*, ed. O. M. Harkusha (Mykolaïv: Vyd-vo ta drukarnia "Kvit", 2004), 92–102.
65 ANR F. IGJ dosar 184/1942 ff. 38–39USHMM RG-25.010 reel 22.
66 ANR F. IGJ dosar 199/1942 f. 213 USHMM RG-25.010M reel 22.
67 ANR F. IGJ dosar 84/1943 f. 445 USHMM RG-25.010M reel 27.

man," suspected foul play and started an investigation. In another case, the unnamed attorneys ordered the arrest of several policemen suspected of similar crimes during investigations of the communist underground in Odessa. Zoltan presented many reports on such illegalities to the chairmen of the Odessa Martial Court, but the only outcome was harassment from Governor Alexianu and Gendarmerie Inspector Colonel Mihail Iliescu, who threatened to redeploy him to the front in Crimea.[68]

During his own interrogation, Leșeanu confirmed that he protested the extralegal murder of suspected partisans in Krymka, "saying that he was unable to work in such conditions." If this was a threat of resignation, Leșeanu did not follow up on it. He remained in this position until the end of the Romanian occupation, while criminal practices continued. In January 1944, forty-seven arrested suspects arrived at the court in Oceacov *judeţ* bearing "signs of horrible torture." Leșeanu claimed that he opened an investigation into the abuse by gendarmes but was unable to complete it due to his recall to Romania (he reportedly released all suspects before departing). According to him, "all of those so-called cases of escape from under escort were nothing but a systematic cover-up by the police and gendarmerie of their own acts of extermination."[69] This is a damning assessment, but the magistrates' protestations against the abuses were rare (Zoltan could cite only one episode), feeble, and easily squashed by vague threats of transfer to the front. As long as gendarmerie and police bosses were set on the physical extermination of individual partisans, they murdered them regardless of the sentences imposed by the judges and used torture on the arrestees irrespective of the judges' decisions.

Only when the police, gendarme, and the SSI were not interested in the fate of the "small fish" suspects could they escape death, and the less stringent martial court decisions were applied. After the Red Army liberated Transnistria, some former partisans testified to the incredulous Soviet authorities about such cases. One such case is quoted in the activity report of a group of partisans from the town of Zhmerinka (1944). Following arrests of dozens of the group's members in July 1943, they were tried in the Tiraspol Martial Court, which sentenced twenty defendants to death (the sentences were carried out) and forty-four to hard labor.[70] Given the report's silence about the fate of the latter, it is likely that they survived the occupation. Serafim Grigori'evich Bedniazhevskii declared in his 1944 testimony that the Romanians arrested his sister for spreading

---

68 ASRI dosar 38891 vol. 14 ff. 205–205v. USHMM RG-25.004 reel 26.
69 ASRI dosar 38891 vol. 14 ff. 323–323v. USHMM RG-25.004 reel 26.
70 DAHOU F. 1 Op. 2 spr.156 ark. 91.

leaflets with Soviet news from the front but released her after they paid "6,000 marks via lawyers."[71] It remains unclear whether this payment constituted the lawyer's fee or a bribe, and for whom was the money intended. The great majority of former partisans' accounts of surviving arrest during the occupation attribute survival to the payment of bribes. The bribery likely occurred in the early stages of the investigation, before the case reached the court hearing. Bribes were paid to police and gendarmerie officers. Bribing them was a more secure way to escape death than relying on the professionalism and impartiality of the magistrates.

A separate category includes cases of high-ranking leaders of the Odessa communist underground, to whom the Odessa Martial Court demonstrated an unusual leniency by sentencing them to imprisonment, not death. Such were the fates of Odessa underground *Obkom* first secretary Aleksandr Pavlovich Petrovskii and his immediate underling, first secretary of Il'ichevskii underground *raikom* (*raion* committee), Ivan Emil'ianovich Platov. The court's leniency resulted either from the defendants' history of double-dealing, which led to the *Obkom* exposure and arrests of hundreds, or the SSI intentions to recruit them for espionage if Transnistria were abandoned.[72] Legal and humanitarian considerations were unlikely to have intervened, especially in view of harsher sentences meted out for lesser offenses.

The Romanian Judiciary and the Murder of Jews

By far the greatest failure of Romanian magistrates in Transnistria was their non-prosecution of Romanian officials who authorized, facilitated, and carried out the mass murder of Jews. In one particularly egregious case, the Bogdanovca *raion*, Golta *judeţ* Pretor Vasile Mânescu was prosecuted for embezzling valuables that he, and other local officials, had taken from Jewish inmates of Bogdanovca camp, who shortly afterwards (late December 1941–January 1942) were summarily shot by local policemen subordinated to the *judeţ* gendarmerie.[73] Mânescu's and others' role in

---

71 DAHOU F. 1 Op. 2 spr. 452 ark. 5–6. Bedniazhevskii likely meant the RKKS.
72 See the summary of the Odessa region *obkom*'s investigation into the activity of underground *obkom* in DAOO [Derzhavnyi arhiv Odes'koi oblasti] F. 92 Op. 1 spr. 10.
73 On the Bogdanovca Massacre, see Jean Ancel, *The History of the Holocaust in Romania* (Lincoln, NE: University of Nebraska Press, 2011), 334–52. Ancel fails to mention participation in this operation of the local ethnic German militia who were under orders of SS Sonderkommando R officers. Eric Steinhart, *The Holocaust and the Germanization of Ukraine* (Washington, DC: German Historical Institute, 2015), 114, 122, 129, 146, 150, 162.

the mass murder of Jewish inmates was not a subject of investigation. According to the post-war trial deposition of Plutonier Nicolae Melinescu, who in December 1941–January 1942 was chief of gendarmerie post in the Bogdanovca sector, when he testified in Tiraspol Martial Court about the massacre the Court Chairman Colonel Constantin "adjoined the sitting saying that this affair is an old case and the Martial Court has been aware of it." Constantin closed the case and refused to follow on the available evidence.[74] By turning away from this and similar violations of Romanian and international law, Romanian magistrates enabled war criminals. They themselves were guilty of criminal negligence.

Evidently, Romanian magistrates caved in under political and administrative pressure and acquiesced in what they themselves called abuses by the police and gendarmerie against suspected partisans. At the same time, Romanian magistrates, as a rule, refused to impose the death penalty on Jews arrested for violating the ban on leaving their concentration camps and ghettoes, a "crime" for which the notorious Ordinance 23 meted out punishment. This follows from the post-war prosecution of Dionisie Fotino, who in 1942 served as commander of a gendarmerie legion and military pretor in Iampol *judeţ*. Fotino interpreted the ordinance to mean that the sentencing and execution of Jews who escaped from designated areas had to be carried out by him. Consequently, he both sentenced and personally executed tens of victims, evidently deriving pleasure from such actions.[75] In his defense, Fotino claimed that his actions followed directly from the ordinance text. Unwilling to execute it, he initially sent arrested Jews to the martial court, which refused to try the accused and sent them back to him. He then requested interpretation from the Grand Pretor (prosecutor) of the Romanian Army, General Ioan Topor, who responded that the ordinance had to be applied on the spot, without trial by the Martial Court. Thus, Fotino claimed, he simply followed the ordinance's provisions, which left him no room to maneuver.[76] These arguments were turned down by the prosecution and the presiding judge on grounds that Fotino's was an exceptional case among other pretors and his successors did not interpret the ordinance in this way. The executions stopped as soon as he was transferred to another post.

---

74 See Melinescu's deposition in ASRI dosar 40011 vol. 20 f. 54. USHMM RG-25.004M reel 21.
75 See his bill of indictment and sentence in ASRI dosar 40013 vol. 6, ff. 72–73 (USHMM RG-25.004M Reel 29) and f. 335 (USHMM RG-25.004M reel 30), respectively.
76 See his defense in ASRI vol. 40013 vol. 4, ff. 284–287 USHMM RG-25.004M reel 29.

Conclusion

The Romanian repressive justice failed to ensure legality in occupied Transnistria. While not a complete sham, it was institutionally weak and morally muddled. Only sporadically did magistrates provide protection to the victims of military and administrative authorities' arbitrariness and brutality. Glaring was the judiciary's failure to punish perpetrators of lethal violence against Jews and suspected Soviet partisans. So malleable were magistrates to political pressure that only in cases when demonstrative lenience was deemed in Romania's best interest (such as trials of leaders of the party underground) or, conversely, when defenders were such small fish that gendarmes had no interest in their fate, was magistrates' inclination to mete out sentences roughly proportionate to the defendants' proven guilt.

While less inclined to apply lethal violence than gendarmerie and military officers, magistrates looked another way when faced with the latter's *faites accomplis*. Perhaps the long history of extra-legal violence against alleged enemies of the inter-war Romanian state conditioned Romanian magistrates to selectively apply legal protective norms in Transnistria.[77] As to the role played by the Romanian magistrates vis-à-vis official corruption, they mostly enabled it. Not only did they fail to prosecute and punish official bribe-takers and embezzlers, they themselves were notoriously corrupt, thus setting a very low bar to other institutions of occupation.

---

77 On the blurred boundaries between criminal law and political repression in interwar Romania, see Cosmin S. Cercel, "The Enemy Within: Criminal Law and Ideology in Interwar Romania," in *Fascism and Criminal Law: History, Theory, Continuity*, ed. Stephen Skinner (Portland, Oregon: Hart Publishers, 2015), 102–26.

A Political Palimpsest:
Nationalism and Faith in Petre Țuțea's Thinking

Delia Popescu

Abstract: *This article examines the political thinking of Petre Țuțea, a noteworthy public figure in post-1989 Romania. I develop Țuțea's views as a significant instance of a reconstructive nationalist imaginary "for all seasons": a radical religious ethno-nationalism that both transcends its pre-communist roots and conceals its continuity during communism in order to be recast as a suitable post-communist alternative. Țuțea samples radicalism on both sides of the political spectrum and ultimately embraces the mystical, elitist, nationalist ideology that distills the protochronic nuance of much of Romanian political life.*

In one of his last essays on the topic of ethnic nationalism, Romanian sociologist Andrei Roth asks "who are the nationalists of Romania after 1989?" and resolutely answers: "the same who represented this ideology before 1989."[1] Roth's response encompasses both the communist and the interwar eras, and gestures toward what George Ekiert and Daniel Ziblatt call the "long durée" understanding of Romanian politics. Adapting Fernard Braudel's notion of developing historical "mentalities," Ekiert and Ziblatt argue that socio-political discontinuity is fundamentally encased in continuity,[2] which makes rupture comprehensible and provides a mechanism for "filling in the blank" of a crisis moment with the effusion of past political mythologies.[3] When the socio-political fabric rips at the seams, we can peer at the makeup of substantial and long-running identity-making strands. The foundational strand is, as Roth argues, a nationalism that "comprised the whole Romanian social-political spectrum."[4] The enduring nationalist character of Romanian politics resulted in a

---

1   Andrei Roth, "Ethno-Nationalism: The Romanian Version," *Anthropological Journal of European Cultures*, 4, no. 2 (1995): 30.
2   George Ekiert and Daniel Ziblatt, "Democracy in Central and Eastern Europe One Hundred Years On," *East European Politics and Societies and Cultures*, 27, no. 1 (2013): 96.
3   Vladimir Tismăneanu, *Fantasies of Salvation: Democracy, Nationalism, and Myth in Post-Communist Europe* (Princeton: Princeton University Press, 1998).
4   Roth, "Ethno-Nationalism: The Romanian Version," 30.

post-1989 "battlefield between different, often incompatible myths"[5] grafted onto a revolutionary moment that had a much more pronounced anti-liberal character than that proclaimed by the triumphalist Western interpretation. Vladimir Tismăneanu argues that in post-communist Romanian politics, "we cannot make real sense of the old-fashion distinctions between Left and Right," which have been replaced by different flavors of what he calls "fantasies of salvation."[6] He echoes Roth's commentary on the post-communist resurrection of so-called "historical parties" that initially populated the interwar political scene (such as the Peasant Party and the Liberal Party) and their invigorated anachronistic nationalism. Roth agrees with Adam Michnik's view that post-communist politics is a "qualitatively new phenomenon" reflected by a "mixture of ideas" that combines populism and ethnocentrism in mainstream political parties.[7] "None of the parties belonging to the democratic opposition ... are free from the nationalist orientation (which some of them insistently and consistently promoted in the inter-war period)," Roth writes. He further specifies that "this state of affairs contributes to the non-crystallization of the pro- and anti-democratic positions" which further obscures traditional Western-type political alignments, because Left and Right are not clearly delineated, and "an important part of the Left is more nationalistic than the democratic Right."[8] The dialectic of continuity and change, nationalism and democratic politics plagues current attempts to make sense of Romanian politics. I adopt Ekiert's "long durée" perspective, and I analyze the particular case of Petre Țuțea in the Romanian ideological revival that followed the 1989 revolution by drawing on Tismăneanu's commentary on the resurrection of political mythology.

Țuțea was an important part of this discussion for several reasons: his political biography was in tune with the times and registered a radical shift from far left to far right; he never left Romania (as did Cioran and Eliade); he languished in communist prisons for thirteen years; and he openly invited public discussion after 1989. Although he claimed cultural allegiance to a number of expats who made a name outside of Romania, Țuțea was a case of staunch nationalism and longevity and had the will to shape post-communist political and cultural life. Not widely known be-

---

5   Tismăneanu, *Fantasies of Salvation*, 15.
6   Ibid., 11.
7   Adam Michnik, quoted in Roth, "Ethno-Nationalism: The Romanian Version," 8.
8   Roth, "Ethno-Nationalism: The Romanian Version," 30.

fore 1989, Țuțea became a prominent public intellectual in post-communist Romania, and he was frequently (if perhaps inaccurately) called the Socratic spirit of Romanian politics.[9]

I develop Țuțea's views as an example of the reconstruction of a nationalist imaginary "for all seasons," to use Tismăneanu's phrase: a radical religious nationalism that both transcends its pre-communist roots and conceals its continuity during communism in order to be recast as a suitable post-communist alternative—an updated political recipe for the new political circumstances. Țuțea samples radicalism on both sides of the political spectrum and ultimately embraces the mystical, elitist, nationalist ideology that in many ways distills the Romanian experience of the twentieth century. Roth, Tismăneanu, and especially Ekiert comment on the fact that the post-1989 political environment in Romania was circumscribed by past political choices and understandings, and the rise of nationalism was not unexpected. But it was less obvious what form the reimagined nationalism would take, and an analysis of Țuțea's views reveals both the protean character of ideological thinking and its particular appeal.

Țuțea's arguments after 1989 expose a set of symptoms that reflects what Marci Shore diagnosed as the "politics of excesses" in Romania.[10] Țuțea's ideological views, which are a variant of Roth's "proto-chronic" orientation, advance a post-communist mythology of Romanian spiritual and national primacy with deep roots in the Romanian imaginary. A term developed most explicitly by literary critic Edgar Papu, protochronism proposes a socio-political thesis that roots some major European trends (like Romanticism, Existentialism, and the development of sociology) in Romanian cultural foundations, thereby emphasizing the privileged place of Romanian cultural identity in world history.[11] For Roth, proto-chronism is symptomatic of "a group of former nationalist opponents of the

---

9   Gabriel Klimowicz, "Explanation," in *Petre Țuțea: Între Dumnezeu și Neamul Meu* (Bucharest: Anastasia, 1992), 7; and Aurel Ion Brumaru, "Introduction," in Țuțea's *Proiectul de Tratat: Eros* [*A Treatise Project. Eros*] (Brașov: Pronto, 1992), 7. The label "Romanian Socrates" seems to narrowly rely on Tutea's willingness to entertain a variety of interlocutors, but Tutea was certainly not modest about his claims, and epistemological modesty arguably is a central trait of Socratism.
10 Marci Shore, *The Taste of Ashes: The Afterlife of Totalitarianism in Eastern Europe* (New York: Random House, 2013).
11 Edgar Papu, "Protocronismul Românesc" [The Romanian Protochronism], *Secolul 20*, nos. 5–6, 1947, 8–11. The protochronist ideas, which were developed by Romanian intellectual Bogdan Petriceicu-Hașdeu and historian Nicolae Densușianu, form the foundation of the Romanian right-wing Iron Guard. The Nicolae Ceaușescu regime continued to extol the pioneering virtues of the Romanian people, merging the cults of leadership and of the nation with communist values. See

communist regime" who "sustained the priority of Romanian achievements in relation to the West in all—or almost all—important domains of spiritual creation, together with an accentuated ethnocentrism and xenophobia."[12]

The point of turning to Țuțea's political thinking is twofold: first, it seeks to close a particular gap in a literature that mentions Țuțea as an example of controversial political thinking but does not address the root of that conclusion. Țuțea's name features prominently but briefly in virtually every analysis of the so-called "great generation" of the late 1920s and the 1930s, but not much space is devoted to what Țuțea actually said. Second, the purpose of this analysis is to show the need to adopt a more critical attitude toward Țuțea's political stance. Much of his post-1989 popular reception was framed by his torment in Romanian communist prisons, yet looking beyond his biography, his public outlook reveals a xenophobic, ethno-Christian nationalism that is elitist, exclusionary, and generally anti-liberal.

I start by laying out Țuțea's political evolution, from his early publication "The Left" to right-leaning Iron Guard sympathies, and his eventual dedication to Orthodox Christianity. The point is to highlight both the radical shift in his political allegiances as well as briefly anchor his thinking in the broader context of Romanian politics. I then analyze Țuțea's work with an emphasis on his post-communist commentary. I argue that Țuțea's "orality" harbors radical and anti-liberal ideological frames: the fundamental connection between faith and nationalism, elitism, anti-Semitism, and a general ethno-nationalism grounded in a privileged position for the historical existence of the Romanian people. Țuțea's logic of national redemption repurposes the old themes of Iron Guard ideology and combines them with novel elements, such as an affinity for American-style capitalism. I argue that Țuțea's broad appeal as the "Romanian Socrates" rests precisely on his ability to articulate the continuity of old and new Romania under the umbrella of a charismatic "fantasy of salvation."

Katherine Verdery, *National Ideology under Socialism. Identity and Cultural Politics in Ceaușescu's Romania* (Berkeley: University of California Press, 1991); Lucian Boia, *Istorie si Mit in Conștiința Românească* [Myth and History in the Romanian Consciousness] (Bucharest: Humanitas, 2011); and Lucian Boia, *Două Secole de Mitologie Națională* [Two Centuries of National Mythology] (Bucharest: Humanitas, 2012).

12 Roth, "Ethno-Nationalism: The Romanian Version," 16.

Political Shifts

As he frequently reminded his listeners, Țuțea was the son of a priest and an illiterate peasant, one of nine children from a humble Romanian village (Boteni, Argeș County).[13] The details of his biography are a matter of debate, especially among various hagiographers,[14] but it is generally agreed that he was bright and pursued studies away from his native village in the city of Cluj, a hotbed of intellectual activity in inter-war Romania. He expressed early sympathies for the National Peasant Party, which he eventually joined, and penned articles for party newspapers like *The Homeland* (Patria). His initial political inclinations favored public education, social democracy, and greater political involvement for the rural class. After receiving his Ph.D. in Administrative Law in 1929 at the University of Cluj, he worked as a magistrate's clerk in Pui, a Transylvanian town where, according to one of Țuțea's sympathetic commentators, he was disturbed by the legal charade of the old magistrate's court at the expense of poor people.[15] He continued to write on public corruption and political abuses in another Peasant Party publication, *The Calling*. In 1932, Țuțea moved to Bucharest where he co-founded *The Left*, a newspaper in which he advocated communist principles like the revolutionary abolition of private property and deep socio-economic centralization (including a state effort to increase the population).[16]

In 1933, Țuțea had the chance to study political science in Germany, at the Friedrich Wilhelm University. His German studies brought him in contact with the rhetoric of a strong nationalist state and marked the beginning of his shift away from the left. He reportedly attended some of Carl Schmitt's lectures and read the work of economists like Werner Sombart and Othmar Spann challenging Karl Marx. At this time, Țuțea's thinking suffered two major "corrections" toward nationalism and Christianity. His early statism was enhanced by a strong nationalism that subsumed the state to a greater, organic, communitarian, national cause. He adopted Schmitt's notion of the state as not merely the expression of legal order, and extended this thinking by turning toward a Christian, transcendent interpretation of the sovereign source as God-given.

---

13   Alexandru Popescu, *Petre Țuțea: Between Sacrifice and Suicide* (London: Ashgate, 2004).
14   For side-by-side biographical disputes, see Gabriel Gheorghe, "Petre Țuțea, Între Legendă și Adevăr," *Gândirea*, no date, available at: http://gandirea.ro/petre-tutea-intre-legenda-si-adevar/, accessed on 20 February 2019.
15   Popescu, *Petre Țuțea: Between Sacrifice and Suicide*, 10.
16   Ibid.

Țuțea's shift to the right aligned with the general Romanian political scene at the time. The rise of Hitler found fertile ideological ground among Romanian intellectuals.[17] The Legion of Archangel Michael, the fascist flagbearer of the Romanian right, was created in 1927 around Corneliu Zelea Codreanu as a "movement of national awakening."[18] The Legion was dedicated to solving Romania's problems, including the "Jewish problem."[19] In contrast to German fascism, the Legion had strong Christian Orthodox leanings (a distinctive trait that attracted many Romanian thinkers). Prayer, the myth of the fatherland (deliberately masculine), as well as a propensity for mysticism, elitism, xenophobia, and anti-Semitism were all grounded in a cult of Romanian exceptionalism, self-abnegation, and heroic death in the service of a "New Man" and a new ethno-nation.[20]

Noteworthy Romanian public intellectuals like Vasile Marin, Nichifor Crainic, and Nae Ionescu helped shape what was initially an underspecified ideology into a philosophical call appealing to the young, interwar intellectual generation.[21] Nae Ionescu, the influential right-wing philosopher and professor at the University of Bucharest, was especially important to the ideological evolution of the Legion, since he acted as a catalyst for his young disciples, including Cioran, Eliade, Noica, and Țuțea who "converted" to Legion doctrine. In 1933, while in Germany, Cioran wrote to Eliade "I am absolutely enthralled by the political order they've set up here,"[22] and elsewhere he wrote "I firmly believe that a dictatorship could stifle for good the imposture plaguing our society. Only terror, bru-

---

17   Right-wing leanings have a long history in Romanian political development, starting from the early formation of the modern Romanian state under Alexandru I. Cuza. See Marta Petreu, *An Infamous Past: E.M. Cioran and the Rise of Fascism in Romania* (Chicago: Ivan R. Dee, 2005).
18   Ibid.
19   Marta Petreu, *De la Junimea la Noica: Studii de Cultură Românească* [From Junimea to Noica: Studies in Romanian Culture] (Iași: Polirom, 2011).
20   For an overview of the Legion's ideology, see Marta Petreu, "An Infamous Past. The history of the Legion's assassinations of political opponents is well documented: Petre Pandrea," *Garda de Fier. Jurnal de Filosofie Politică: Memorii Penitenciare* [The Iron Guard. Journal of Political Philosophy: Memoirs from the Penitenciary] (Bucharest: Vremea, 2001); Zaharia Boilă, *Amintiri și Considerații asupra Mișcării Legionare* [Memories and Considerations Regarding the Legionnaire Movement] (Cluj-Napoca: Apostrof, 2002); and Renee De Weck, *Jurnalul Unui Diplomat Elvețian în România: 1939–1945* [The Journal of a Swiss Diplomat in Romania: 1939–1945] (Bucharest: Editura Fundației Culturale Române, 2000).
21   Petreu, *An Infamous Past*, 58–76.
22   Cioran to Eliade, 15 November 1933, in *Scrisori* (Letters), 269.

tality, and endless anxiety are likely to bring about a change in Romania."[23] Nichifor Crainic described the ideological underpinnings of the Legion as ultra-nationalist and concerned with the "rabbinical aggression against the Christian world" through "unexpected 'protean forms': freemasonry, Freudianism, homosexuality, atheism, Bolshevism."[24] As both Țuțea and the historian Radu Ioanid remarked, the Legion had an unusual profile among right-wing movements, because it "willingly inserted strong elements of Orthodox Christianity into its political doctrine to the point of becoming one of the rare modern European political movements with a religious ideological structure."[25]

Upon his return to Bucharest, Țuțea co-authored *The National Revolution Manifesto*, an expression of his rightist shift to the notion of a divinely inspired nationalist revolution. He also started writing for pro-Legion publications such as Cuvântul (*The Word*), along with Eliade and Cioran. Persuaded by Nae Ionescu, Țuțea allegedly joined the Iron Guard (*Garda de Fier*), the Legion's paramilitary wing, in 1940.[26] While the certainty of his official appurtenance to the Iron Guard is debated, his Legion sympathies are well-documented and based on his own declarations and articles, both in the 1930s and later in life. Țuțea frequently argued that support for the Iron Guard was largely motivated by "their radical position against the harmful influence of Russian Bolshevism," which Țuțea and many of his contemporaries considered "controlled by Jews."[27] Thus, a combination of anti-communism and anti-Semitism shaped Țuțea's allegiance to the Romanian right.

The popularity of the Legion (which became synonymous with the Iron Guard) increased throughout the 1930s, but it was cut short by King Carol II's ascension to the Romanian throne. Carol eagerly disposed of political opponents and arrested prominent Iron Guard members, which triggered a Guard campaign of political assassinations. The history of the Romanian monarchy is well-known: caught between communist Russia and Nazi Germany, Romanian socio-political conditions fuelled the rise of

---

23 Cioran to Nicolae Tatu, 1 December 1933, in *Scrisori* (Letters), 313.
24 Nichifor Crainic, *Ortodoxie și Etnocrație* [Orthodoxy and Ethnocracy] (Bucharest: Cugetarea, 1938), 162–164.
25 Radu Ioanid, "The Sacralized Politics of the Romanian Iron Guard," *Totalitarian Movements & Political Religions*, 5, No. 3 (2004): 419–453, and Radu Ioanid, *The Sword of the Archangel* (New York: Columbia University Press, 1990).
26 There is a debate about whether or not he formally belonged to the Iron Guard. See Popescu, *Petre Țuțea: Between Sacrifice and Suicide*, 10, and Pandrea, *Garda de Fier*.
27 Țuțea, *Între Dumnezeu și Neamul meu*, 287.

a strong Nazi ally, Marshall Ion Antonescu, who forced the King to abdicate and leave the country. Antonescu and the Legion briefly collaborated when many Legionnaires (*legionari*), including Țuțea, were given cabinet positions. The collaboration ended with political disagreements that led to a Legion rebellion against Antonescu. The Legion fell into disfavor, and when Antonescu (at Hitler's urging) sent the Romanian army into Russia, many Legion members were sent to die on the Eastern front. Țuțea reportedly asked to join Legion soldiers, but his request was denied. He maintained his position as Director of the Office of Economic Publications and Propaganda and then Director of the Research Office within the Ministry of Foreign Trade.[28]

In 1944, the Russian army occupied Romania and imposed a leftist regime with virtually no local support. King Michael abdicated in 1947, and the ensuing political "restructuring" was marked by public kangaroo courts. Țuțea was arrested in 1949 and sent, without trial, to several prisons including Ocnele Mari where he was to be "re-educated" through torture by "New Men" (re-educated fellow prisoners).[29] His traumatic experience in Ocnele Mari paved the way to his ultra-religious attitude. He was rearrested in 1956 for "conspiracy against the State" and convicted to eighteen years. He served eight years in various prisons, including four years at Aiud, an infamous communist prison, where he was subjected to a second "re-education." In Aiud, Țuțea met several theologians and Christian thinkers, including Nichifor Crainic who had taught a course on Orthodox Mystical Theology at the University of Bucharest, and Father Dumitru Stanilaoe, a Theology Professor in Sibiu and at the Bucharest Theological Institute. The prisoners reportedly created a secret university of sorts, teaching Bible lessons in Morse code and sharing philosophical lessons about the Classics.[30] Prison sharpened Țuțea's mystical Orthodox thinking, and his belief in the primacy of God and revelation as the source of all knowledge. His carceral experience was formative not only for his own mystical beliefs but also for his later public image. A well-known story recounts that philosopher Constantin Noica's interrogator, in a moment of exasperation, told Noica "You listen here, I'm the one who interrogated Țuțea!"[31] boasting his brutality through the prominence of his victim. In his

---

28 Popescu, *Petre Țuțea: Between Sacrifice and Suicide*, 22.
29 For a detailed account of this "reeducation system" see Monica Ciobanu, "Pitești: A Project in Re-education and its Post-1989 Interpretation in Romania," *Nationalities Papers*, 43, no. 4 (2015): 615–33.
30 Popescu, *Petre Țuțea: Between Sacrifice and Suicide*, 23.
31 Andrei Pleșu, "Petre Țuțea—A Kingly Peasant," *România Liberă*, 21 January 1990. Constantin Noica is a famous Romanian philosopher and logician who is credited

later speeches, Țuțea frequently referenced the beatings and humiliations he suffered in prison and explained prison life as the catalyst for his understanding of liberating prayer and his view of life as *imitatio Christi*.

In 1964, Ceaușescu's predecessor, Gheorghe Gheorghiu-Dej, granted a general amnesty and Țuțea was released, placed under house arrest, and then continuously monitored by the secret police, the Securitate, until the end of communism in 1989. Poor and marginalized, Țuțea survived on a subsistence-level state pension. In 1968 he was granted a Writers' Union pension, which allowed him to eat at the Writer's Union restaurant, where he met many of those who would gradually become his circle of close friends and self-proclaimed followers.

Țuțea's Work and Words after 1989

Tutea's involvement with Nae Ionescu's group sharpened his philosophical interests. He was encouraged by his friends: Emil Cioran[32] frequently said that if Țuțea had been born in Paris, he would have been one of the most celebrated figures of his time. Cioran called Țuțea the only genius he had ever met,[33] although he counted Mircea Eliade, Eugene Ionescu, Paul Celan, and Samuel Beckett among his close friends. Eliade, the philosopher and historian of religion, wrote in his autobiography that Țuțea was "perhaps the liveliest intelligence" he had ever encountered, and about their generation, that it "emerged from Țuțea's overcoat, just as the great Russian writers came out of Gogol's Overcoat."[34]

---

with the intellectual formation of many in the contemporary generation of Romanian philosophers, like Andrei Pleșu, Gabriel Liiceanu and H. R. Patapievici.

32 Emil Cioran (1911–1995) was a renowned Romanian essayist and philosopher who wrote in Romanian and French. He lived most of his life in France where he wrote the majority of his works, which generally align with philosophical nihilism. Early on, he expressed deep sympathy for the extreme right, including Hitler, a stance that he later regretted. For a discussion of Cioran's far right leanings, see Marta Petreu, *An Infamous Past; and Zigu Ornea, Anii Treizeci. Extrema Dreaptă Românească* [The Thirties: The Romanian Far Right] (Bucharest: Editura Fundației Culturale Române, 1995).

33 Although clearly flattered, Țuțea frequently brought up the compliment and insisted he was embarrassed by it. He wrote letters urging Cioran to stop telling others that he was a genius and mentioned it when he was interviewed, as a message to Cioran who lived in France at the time.

34 Reported to Alexandru Popescu by Christinel Eliade and Ioan Alexandru, in Popescu, *Petre Țuțea: Between Sacrifice and Suicide*, vi. In a 1941 letter, Eliade calls Țuțea "the most annotated man in Romania," Mircea Eliade, Private Correspondence to Țuțea from Lisbon, 26 December 1947. The full text can be found at http://www.marturisitorii.ro/2014/01/28/inedit-mircea-eliade-despre-fenomenul-spiritual-petre-tutea-omul-cel-mai-adnotat-din-romania-scrisoare-olografa-confisca

Many of Țuțea's pre-1989 writings were confiscated by the Securitate, but he continued to write in order to produce a magnum opus titled *Man: A Treatise of Christian Anthropology*, a five-volume work he never finished. Between December 1989 and December 1991, Țuțea's notoriety saw a meteoric rise. He was "rediscovered" through a series of televised conversations, and his penchant for dialogic allocution earned him the repute of a "Romanian Socrates." Essays were published in newspapers, and interviews and informal discussions were broadcast on national TV. Andrei Pleșu, the Minister of Culture, wrote about him in a major periodical, and Gabriel Liiceanu, a prominent intellectual, staged a video-recorded conversation between Țuțea and Emil Cioran, who was still in Paris. Important politicians, members of the post-communist intelligentsia, and some of the young revolutionaries who had spearheaded the 1989 events came to visit and converse with him.[35] Many of their exchanges were transcribed or recorded. Țuțea did not stand on decorum, and he received his guests willingly, even enthusiastically, up to his last day on the hospital death bed.[36] His frailty was belied by his perorations, peppered with humor and pithy phrases that were widely quoted. The combination of informality (he frequently sported a knitted nightcap) and hubristic pronouncements, philosophical and theological references, and occasional coarse language rendered Țuțea a public figure perceived as both approachable and admirable. Commentary on Țuțea's place in Romanian culture soon followed. A slew of devotees referred to him with the agoraeic "Master Țuțea,"[37] while others deemed him a saintly exemplar of Christian life through suffering and asked for spiritual guidance.[38] Marian Munteanu, one of the student leaders of the 1989 revolution said that in Țuțea one could find "the meeting point of the

---

ta-de-securitate-si-redata-de-petru-voda-ro-si-marturisitorii-ro/, accessed on 18 September 2018.

35 The 1990 anti-government student protests were said to have been inspired by Țuțea. See Petre Țuțea, "Omul este un animal care poate fi mișcat din loc de iluzie" [Man is an animal which can be moved along by illusion], interview by Marius Costineanu, *Tinerama*, 16–23 November 1990.

36 He was frequently interviewed simply sitting on his bed and wearing his signature beanie hat. See *"Cuvântul care Zidește"* [The Word That Builds], interview with journalist Vartan Arachelian, TVR Cultural, 1990.

37 Cassian Maria Spiridon, *Petre Țuțea: Între Filosofie si Teologie* [Petre Țuțea: Between Philosophy and Theology] (Iași: Doxologia, 2013); and Marian Muntean, ed., "Conversations with the Master," *Cuvântul Studențesc*, 1, no. 2 (1993), 9.

38 According to Popescu, one prominent example is Dumitru Mazilu, the vice-president of the first post-revolutionary party in power, the National Salvation Front, who went to Țuțea for spiritual counsel, Popescu, *Petre Țuțea: Between Sacrifice and Suicide*, 27. At a time when the political was imbued with a search for spiritual meaning, transitional politics in Romania encouraged Christianity as the source of political legitimacy.

apostle with the patriarch," a man who acted as proxy for "whole state institutions" throughout the century. To be Țuțea's disciple, Munteanu argues, you had to be "an absolute Romanian."[39]

At the same time, Țuțea's written work started to be widely circulated. Several of his essays were serialized and published in literary and cultural magazines.[40] Some of his manuscripts were retrieved from Securitate archives and released for publication. Many of his writings were finally printed, including a book-length essay on Mircea Eliade's work,[41] a few edited volumes with interviews and shorter essays,[42] and the first two volumes together with the very last of what will remain his unfinished *Treatise on Christian Anthropology*,[43] although much of his book-length work was published posthumously. The initial commentary on his most serious attempts at philosophy and theology was unfavorable. Writing about the book on Eliade, literary critic Alexandru Ștefănescu confessed that he was confused by Țuțea's writing style, which amounted to a "frenetic exchange between two encyclopedic spirits."[44] In the 1993 preface to *322 Memorable Words from Petre Țuțea*, philosopher Gabriel Liiceanu remarked that Țuțea's "oeuvre seems to be constituted out of a book he never wrote, while the many pages that he did write will never constitute

---

39 Marian Munteanu, "Introducere," in *Petre Țuțea: Între Dumnezeu si Neamul Meu* [Petre Țuțea: Between God and My People] (Bucharest: Anastasia, 1992), 6.
40 "Mircea Eliade," I–VIII, *Familia*, February–September 1990; "Filosofia Nuanțelor" [The Philosophy of Nuances], *Baricada*, I–V (March–May 1990).
41 Petre Țuțea, *Mircea Eliade* (Oradea: Biblioteca Revistei Familia, 1992).
42 Petre Țuțea, *Bătranețea și Alte Texte Filosofice* [Old Age and Other Philosophical Texts] (Bucharest: Viitorul Românesc, 1992); Radu Preda, *Jurnal cu Petre Țuțea* [Journal with Petre Țuțea] (Bucharest: Humanitas, 1992); Petre Țuțea, *Philosophia Perennis, Essays* (Bucharest: Icar, 1992); Petre Țuțea, *Reflecții Religioase Asupra Cunoașterii* [Religious Reflections on Knowledge], part I (Bucharest: Nemira, 1992); Oana Barna and Vlad Zografi, eds., *322 de vorbe memorabile ale lui Petre Țuțea* [322 Memorable Words from Petre Țuțea] (Bucharest: Humanitas, 1993); Petre Tutea, *Neliniști metafizice* [Metaphysical Angst] (Bucharest: Eros, 1994).
43 Omul, Tratat de Antropologie Creștină, Vol. I, Problemele sau Cartea Întrebărilor [Man, A Treatise of Christian Anthropology, Problems or the Book of Questions] (Iași: Timpul, 1992); Omul, Tratat de Antropologie Creștină, vol. 2, Sistemele sau Cartea Întregirilor Logice, Autonom-Matematice, Paralele cu Întregirile Ontice [Man, A Treatise of Christian Anthropology, Systems or The Book of Logical Wholes, Autonomously-Mathematical, Parallel with Ontic Wholes] (Iași: Timpul, 1993); Omul, Tratat de Antropologie Creștină, Dogmele sau Primirea Certitudinii [Man, A Treatise of Christian Anthroplogy, Dogmas or the Receiving of Certainty] (Iași: Timpul, 2000); also Omul, Tratat de Antropologie Creștină, Addenda: Filosofie și Teologie [Man, A Treatise of Christian Anthropology, Addenda: Philosophy and Theology] (Iași: Timpul, 2001); and Proiectul de Tratat. Eros (Brașov: Pronto, 1992).
44 Alexandru Ștefănescu, "La o Nouă Lectură: Petre Țuțea" [Reading It Anew: Petre Țuțea], *România Literară*, no. 40 (8 October 2003).

an oeuvre."[45] He added that the proverbial "gods never stood in the corner of Țuțea's room" while he was writing, and that it was hard to explain how this lucid "genius of orality" produced thousands of "hard to digest and useless pages."[46] He concluded that one needed no treatise to produce a "system of thinking," thus effectively putting aside what Țuțea himself called his *Treatise*, and praised Țuțea as a "folkloric" author.[47] In a televised interview, Liiceanu restated his opinion that Țuțea's "teologal" (Tutea's word) work did not represent an analytical contribution, and that his writing style was tremendously tedious and downright boring. Another commentator noted that the value of Țuțea's *Treatise* was "nonexistent" and that if the editor had truly respected Țuțea, he would have never published his work.[48] Even Tudor Munteanu's sympathetic commentary in the introduction to the Eliade essay stated that Țuțea "had no intention of writing a monograph, and is not interested in ideas and references, but rather in finding the truth, in the light of which people, things, and deeds can be seen as they are."[49] Țuțea, Munteanu added, did not write fiction "nor did he write academic works,"[50] shelving the question whether or not Țuțea's self-chosen "treatise" style amounted to a scholarly work.

Liiceanu's opening volley provoked a series of responses meant to "clarify" Țuțea's style authored by writers personally sympathetic to his beliefs. Tudor Munteanu argued that virtually nobody in contemporary philosophy has written in the "hieratic style of early philosophy."[51] Cassian Maria Spiridon contended that "the Master" simply lacked qualified commentators and that, when it came to writing, Țuțea "neither is nor wanted to be brilliant"[52] but rather aimed at using systematic language in a precise way. The most recent book on Țuțea's biography and writings was authored by Alexandru Popescu, who is steeped in devout Christianity and acknowledges that Țuțea's work is "in the tradition of the disciple who seeks to record the master's teachings and his life."[53] Popescu's book has merit in its details, but it is mostly a statement of faith as a sort of melancholy ode to a Christ-like "death-cell philosopher" whose "incantatory style resembling that of liturgical prayer" taught him, "often with

---

45 Gabriel Liiceanu, "Introducere," in *322 de Vorbe Memorabile*, 6.
46 Ibid., 7.
47 Ibid., 8–9.
48 Zigu Ornea, "Nevroza Țuțea" [The Țuțea Neurosis], *România Liberă*, 3 (1993).
49 Tudor B. Munteanu, "Foreword," in Petre Țuțea, *Mircea Eliade* (Cluj-Napoca: Eikon, 2013), 7.
50 Munteanu, "Foreword," 11.
51 Ibid.
52 Spiridon, *Petre Țuțea: Între Filosofie și Teologie*, 13.
53 Popescu, *Petre Țuțea: Between Sacrifice and Suicide*, 3.

prophetic solemnity," that the most important choice in life is "between spiritual self-sacrifice and moral suicide."[54]

Beyond extreme expressions of admiration, many of Țuțea's critics, even those who virtually dismiss his scholarly work, agree that Țuțea's oral legacy is a worthwhile guide to the formative power of independent thinking in the face of oppression. Liiceanu praises Țuțea's style for its trenchant and radical formulations which give the impression that "Țuțea independently rediscovers the few eternal truths of the world."[55] As Liiceanu points out, Țuțea was uniquely accessible as he "poured" into others and left behind "crystalline, polished by passion, suffering and intelligence, a few hundred 'memorable words'."[56] Neither critics nor hagiographers dwell very long on the essence of Țuțea's "crystalline" oral wisdom.

I argue that the outcome of the polarized characterizations of Țuțea as a Christic figure or a "folkloric" Socrates leads to a superficial treatment of some of his central messages, which renders Țuțea an ambivalent guide to independent political thinking in general, and to democratic politics in particular. It is Țuțea's political rather than what Țuțea calls his "teologal" thinking that is of interest here, not only because it is more clearly formulated, but also because it was the source of his broad popularity, and it offers a window into the kind of political ideas that found an eager audience in post-communist politics. Țuțea's political "system of thinking" has a better anchor in his oral legacy than in his theological work.[57] His *Treatise*, which is an extensive and rather opaque analytical exercise into the value of divine revelation in philosophical and theological thought, offers little beyond that, while the oral record is thick with critique, commentary, and conclusions that combine Țuțea's view of faith, interpretation of historical trends, and political inclinations. I examine the most contentious parts of Țuțea's thinking below.

Faith and Nationalism

Țuțea's post-1989 commentary distils and justifies his past dedication to the right wing, mostly in his ultra-nationalism, elitism, and categorical Christian Orthodoxy. But his thinking diverges from the radical right in

---

54 Ibid., xi and 6.
55 Liiceanu, *322 de Vorbe Memorabile*, 11.
56 Ibid., 14.
57 Țuțea himself acknowledges that his many written pages are "neither anthological nor eloquent regarding the spiritual evolution of my personality," cited in Liiceanu, *322 de Vorbe Memorabile*, 7.

both glimmers of support for a more openly democratic politics (as opposed to his earlier insistence on a strong central government) and his surprising support for American-style market economics (with a significant caveat: as long as it is "adapted" to fit Romanian nationalism and religiosity). Putting together Țuțea's political profile is difficult, mostly because he made contradictory statements on the virtues of democracy, which he said lacks a hierarchy of values. Some contradictions can be partly explained away by his extemporaneous style, as Țuțea did come back on some of his statements and even apologized for others. Overall, however, he was remarkably consistent in his view of religion, minorities, and a type of Romanian exceptionalism that amounts to what I identify as Tutea's protochronism.

The foundation of Țuțea's thinking is Christian dogma, mysticism, and revelation as the only sources of human understanding. Mystery, Țuțea says, "is the only form capable of liberating us from the anxiety of our personal limitations ... this is why freedom can only be dogmatically understood, in accordance with Christian doctrine, which is the religion of freedom."[58] Țuțea argues that theology, which he calls the science of Truth, excludes typical questioning and any attempt at a system of thinking. Modernity, secularism, and science follow the original sin—the human hubris of reaching knowledge outside of God. The one Truth cannot be searched for but only received by the grace of God, and even theologians need revelation to gather Truth.[59] The notion of human will independent from God is a dangerous illusion because it leaves humanity vulnerable to a fruitless search for meaning. The modern obsession with psychology and Freudianism are examples of man's lost path. The notion of human-led progress in art and science is illusory, and it can only become useful if combined with the dogmatic aspiration for mystery and revelation. In this context, human activities should always be rooted in the "living" tradition of religion and the Church. Ritual is a gate to an awareness of human limitation and an openness to revealed Truth. Țuțea insists on the necessity of a religious path in European thinking and unapologetically attributes much of the European cultural and scientific advance to the presence of religion (and its epistemic effect, revelation). "If you take the Bible out of Europe," Țuțea comments, "then Shakespeare becomes a tragic trickster, and Europeans, even Nobel laureates, are happy they are not sleeping in trees!"[60]

---

58 Țuțea, *Între Dumnezeu și Neamul Meu*, 14.
59 Țuțea, *Omul*, vol. I, 10.
60 Țuțea, *Între Dumnezeu și Neamul Meu*, 62.

Țuțea subordinates the state to the Church, or in his words, he "supraordinates religious order" to the state.[61] The political vision of the nation-state begins with the Christian Church, the vehicle of both morality and knowledge. Church institutions are meant to guide both political and personal evolution and combine the knowledge revealed to individuals into a useful moral scheme that supports a unitary Christian state. In the context of religion as the only possible organized path to knowledge, the Church is the ultimate arbiter of the Bible; in other words, the Church decides which portions of the Bible are revealed (rather than just inspired) knowledge. Revealed knowledge is canon and must be followed, which is why the state must be subordinate to the Church. While Țuțea believes that both Christian Orthodoxy and Catholicism fulfill this function "through the church," he is highly critical of other religions, including Protestantism, for its lack of attention to Church structures as immanent mediators.[62] Public morality is necessary and can only be made possible through the absolute rootedness of Christian morality in the state.[63]

Țuțea's radical Christian thinking leads him to profound skepticism toward science. Science can never be revealed as truth because it does not deal with the essential nature of existence, but science *can* be divinely inspired. Newton was given divine favor to discover the law of gravity, Țuțea argues, which is evident from the fact that many before him had the same experience but failed to reach that same (inspired) conclusion.[64] Inspired science is useful to the state and people, but Țuțea vehemently contests the claim of self-reliant, rational discovery through science. On the same Christian ground, Țuțea denies evolutionary theory and, in one of his more trenchant attacks, mocks evolutionary paleontology and calls Ernst Haeckel (the famous German biologist who expanded and popularized Darwin's work in Germany) "dimwitted."[65]

His skepticism of science, and especially scientists, combined with his belief that all knowledge is revelation leads Țuțea to an unresolved ontological tension. First, Țuțea recognizes the equality of human beings in the eyes of God. "The idiot," Țuțea says, "is first cousin with the genius before God."[66] But he also mentions that other than that, there is no equivalence between genius and idiot. Elsewhere, one of the most notorious

---

61 Ibid., 65.
62 Ibid., 67. Țuțea equates Protestantism with Lutheranism and ignores all other Protestant denominations.
63 Ibid., 93.
64 Ibid., 280.
65 Ibid., 101 and 277.
66 Ibid., 46.

and recurrent of Țuțea's many affirmations claims that "an old village woman, with dirty feet, kneeling before Mary's icon in church when compared to an atheist who is a Nobel Prize laureate: the old woman is a human being, and the Nobel prize laureate is a weasel. She dies a human being, he a weasel."[67] And in yet another interview he insists that his model of quintessential humanity is not Plato, Kant, or Hegel but a poor priest in Baragan (a rural, agricultural area of Romania).[68]

Țuțea constantly vacillates between two meanings of equality that are never conclusively integrated: an equality before God and a God-given inequality between intellects. This ambivalent attitude is also reflected in his ambivalence toward his friend Cioran. While he respects Cioran's intellect and calls him "his great friend," he frequently decries Cioran's turn away from religion and "feels sorry" for his unfulfilled, tragic existence, urging him to go back to his Christian roots. Țuțea frequently says that when he talks to an atheist, it is as if he is "talking to a door."[69] The believer is alive, and the atheist's soul is dead. Cioran is for Țuțea the exemplar of philosophy without faith, which is another hallmark of modernity. Philosophy alone, Țuțea argues, "leads us to the graveyard"[70] through the desperation Cioran experienced.

While Țuțea's Christian thinking leads him to profess that anyone can be the subject of God's revelation, he also insists that humans are essentially unequal and should occupy unequal positions in society. His Christian equalitarianism pertains to either the afterlife or a generic sphere of humanity that has little or no impact on earthly affairs. For Țuțea, God himself institutes this natural inequality, and while we might all be equal in the eyes of God, he does not create us as equal or grant us equal life experiences.[71] In a passage dedicated to a discussion of what it means to be a genius, Țuțea asserts that there is a celestial hierarchy of human species, and the idiot's role, also divinely selected, is to allow us to discern the presence of genius.[72] His thinking here is clearly moved by his early commitment to right-wing elitism infused with dogmatic Christianity.

Ideologically, Țuțea remains indebted to his earlier critique of democracy and what he calls its leveling effect. Only accident can produce a "great man" in democracy, because "the masses are absolute; every dim-

---

67 Țuțea, *322 de Vorbe Memorabile*, 20.
68 Țuțea, *Între Dumnezeu si Neamul Meu*, 303.
69 Ibid., 280.
70 Ibid., 330.
71 Ibid., 52.
72 Ibid., 332.

wit taken by himself is a dimwit and that's it ... but all these dimwits together become a historical principle."[73] Democracy, especially what Țuțea calls "absolute democracy," is a "historical graveyard," and the cradle of democracy, Europe, "can export technological know-how, prostitutes, science—politically, however, zero."[74] While Țuțea grants democracy a degree of transparency and participation, he claims that it gives too much undue access to power and needs to be moderated by classical liberalism. Liberal economic policies have an un-leveling effect, and free enterprise fosters the rise of a leading elite. Țuțea connects the rise of the elite with American liberalism, which he admires for its prosperity. You can never live in an equalitarian society, Țuțea argues, as well as "in the country of American billionaires."[75] American liberalism, Țuțea continues, is perfectly compatible with Christianity. Norms regulate both the behavior of liberalism and that of Christianity, and as long as Christianity takes precedence, the inequality of economic liberalism can be sustained through Christian ethics. God loves us equally but endows us differently, and according to Țuțea, this natural, divine order is the meeting point of Christianity and economic liberalism. The entrepreneur can exemplify Christian work ethics. While this logic might sound familiar, Țuțea's belief that the state is subordinate to the Church challenges mainstream American liberal economics. Free economic activity arguably requires expansive freedom, including freedom of religious belief and laws that do not deliberately favor ethnic or national groups. Țuțea is never clear about how the system is supposed to function, aside from the assumption that the Church is a custodian of ethics more than a regulator of economic activity. At face value, his view looks like a Christianized Schumpeterian elite theory, but it is unclear how Christian economic liberalism might look in practice, especially in the presence of a rigid social hierarchy. Țuțea's vision combines divine order and an elitism resulting in and from classical liberal economics. Țuțea's stronger discussion of liberalism is, in essence, a discourse of elite creation, not prosperity. Elites have a job in the national state: the job of "sorting out" society. Revolution, Țuțea argues, is mistakenly understood as a movement of the masses, but the reality is that the masses have the same role water has in a pitcher: they follow the movement of the vessel and nothing more. Elites are the essential movers of political re-creation.

---

73 Ibid., 298.
74 Ibid., 296.
75 Ibid., 66 and 281.

Essentialism and Exclusion

Țuțea takes his notion of a leading elite far to the right and praises Napoleon for supporting the natural order and getting rid of "street scum."[76] The implications of Țuțea's religious, hierarchical, and elitist thinking are far-reaching for the political place of religious and ethnic minorities. Țuțea's most extreme assertions regard Jews and Judaism. In sweeping allegations that offer stereotypical and polemic views, he frequently references Jews as the historical initiators of Marxism and secular humanism.[77] This charge undermines his otherwise self-professed admiration for the Judaic biblical tradition in laying the foundations of Christianity although Judaism is seen as essentially "giving way" to Christianity, the superior version of faith. In several interviews he claims that he cannot be an anti-Semite because to be anti-Semitic is to be anti-Christian, given the role Judaism played in the rise of Christianity.[78] At the same time he differentiates historical and modern Jews and Judaism and goes as far as saying that anti-Semitism is not a "spontaneous reaction of Romanians, Germans, Poles, Hungarians, Americans but is provoked by Jews through excess."[79] He accuses modern Jewish political ideology of anti-nationalism and decries what he considers Jewish efforts to impugn the figureheads of Romanian culture.[80] Țuțea's opinion was notable because it resonated with much of the extremism of transitional politics[81]:

> (Jews) provoke anti-Semitism. In fact, in Stalin's philosophical dictionary it is mentioned that everything that happened in history is caused by the 'nature' of the Jewish people. If even Stalin says this, who if I'm not mistaken, was married to a Jewish woman ... You only need a couple more like Rosen,[82] and that's it, the Jews will have to go into hiding even if there are only five of them. Why isn't he (Rosen) minding his business!? ... It is evident that the World Jewish Council rides to break the backs of the democratic herds in the United States. The Jewish Council forbids Kurt Waldheim, the head of the Austrian state, to enter the U.S. An offense given to a head of state![83]

---

76 Ibid., 298.
77 Ibid., 39 and 287, where Țuțea claims that Jews controlled the instauration of Russian Bolshevism.
78 Țuțea, *322 de Vorbe Memorabile*, 20.
79 Țuțea, *Între Dumnezeu si Neamul Meu*, 92.
80 Ibid., 92.
81 Tismăneanu, *Fantasies of Salvation*.
82 Moses Rosen, Chief Rabbi of Romania, 1912–1994; led Romanian Jews during communism, while the Ceaușescu regime pursued a harsh policy against Jewish national feelings. The controversy surrounding Rosen stemmed from the criticism that he did whatever it took to protect Romanian Jews, including collaboration with the Ceaușescu regime. After '89 he was an active political figure and continued to advocate emigration to Israel arguing that Romania was dominated by anti-Semitism and xenophobia.
83 Țuțea, *Între Dumnezeu si Neamul Meu*, 92.

Țuțea claims that Rabbi Moses Rosen is outright lying when he argues that there is anti-Semitism in Romania (and ignores extensive evidence showing otherwise).[84] The idea of a global Jewish conspiracy pervades his remarks, and Țuțea asserts that Jewish influence cultivated the rise of political extremes (both the left, because of their support, and the right, as a reaction to their "nature").[85] In contrast, Țuțea argues, this kind of extremism is no longer possible in Europe today because Christianity is dominating European politics. Țuțea relegates Jewish politics to a supra-national, global masonic order which is antireligious "and therefore anti-natural."[86]

In numerous contexts, Țuțea mentions that certain individuals are Jewish, usually to negatively depict them as agents of forces that eroded a historical effort at Romanian nationalism.[87] The idea of a global Jewish conspiracy coupled with the notion that crypto-Zionism destabilized Romanian nationalism gained overt public traction after 1989 when the "disease of communism" on the authentic Romanian body was cataloged as a foreign imposition. Communism is described as an un-Romanian (thus anti-natural) export brought in by the Russians (and their Jewish accomplices) grafted onto and polluting the Romanian nation. The role played by the Jews is mythologized in a rhetoric of renewed nationalism led by the resurgent right-wing political parties in post-communist Romania. Rehabilitating Romanian identity thus involves denying any local character of the communist order and finding those responsible for supporting it from the inside. This leads to a fifth-column rationalization of a non-Romanian group that buttressed Russian communism in the country; consequently Jews, Hungarians, and other national minorities become the target of suspicion.

Despite these straightforward assertions, more than one of Țuțea's commentators declares that Țuțea was not an anti-Semite but a nationalist.[88] In the introduction to *Petre Țuțea: Reflecții Religioase asupra Cunoașterii* (*Petre Țuțea: Religious Reflections about Knowledge*), Aurel Ion

---

84   Ibid., 292.
85   Ibid., 289; see also 351.
86   Ibid., 299.
87   The contexts are too numerous to mention, but he generally interprets Jewish presence as a negative historical influence, calling it in an interview the "Jewish dirt," 347. In one interview he mentions his discussion with a (supposedly) Jewish interrogator, saying that he responded to him by talking of Romanian nationalism, 114.
88   This is hardly an exculpatory argument, and Jews are the most prominent even though not the only target of Țuțea's nationalism. He extends the logic of exclusion to the Roma population, which he addresses with the (widely used) pejorative "țigani" (Gypsies), 28. He also considers the necessity for strong policies to "institute order" within the ranks of the Hungarian ethnics, 298.

Brumaru claims that "on the Jewish subject," in his most "animated moments, because he was prone to hasty outbursts," Țuțea went for a politics of assimilation in the tradition of Romanian inter-war politics (and earlier).[89] Țuțea's nationalism, Brumaru claims, was not chauvinism, but merely an expression of his belief that his "profession" was that of being Romanian. Brumaru also notes that Țuțea had attended the funeral of one of his friends, Oscar Lemnaru, a decision that was "paradoxical, because he was a Jew."[90] Other commentators either bracket the "Jewish issue" altogether or offer marginal and oblique insights. Liiceanu, who has no qualms about expressing a trenchantly harsh opinion about Țuțea's treatise, is otherwise reluctant to characterize Țuțea's opinions with more than a blanket assertion that they "sometimes remain downright contestable."[91] For Liiceanu, Țuțea's love of country suggests that "nationalism, as part and parcel of the natural economics of human society, can be practiced *courteously*,"[92] a curious depiction of a man who once noted that he was proud that "he did not go to prison for a Black tribe."[93]

Beyond the homogenous ethno-national outlook in which those who are Romanian "are born Romanian," Țuțea's nationalism is deeply imbued with faith. Around 1937, Țuțea is asked by Nae Ionescu what it means to be a true Romanian. He answers that the traits of a true Romanian are: 1. to be Christian; 2. to be willing to sacrifice one's life for Romania without any regrets; 3. to not cheat anyone; 4. to not defile any virgin, so as not to offend the majesty of Mary Mother of God; 5. to recognize one's limits and respect what others can do and one cannot.[94] Țuțea's nationalism remains virtually unchanged throughout the years. In his post-1989 interviews he reveals the same view of Romanianism as Christian, self-sacrificing, and masculine.[95] The outline reads more like a list of biblical commandments than a citizenship profile. The self-abnegation and

---

89   Aurel Ion Brumaru, "Introduction," in *Petre Țuțea: Religious Reflections about Knowledge*, 9.
90   Ibid., 8.
91   Liiceanu, "Introduction," 14.
92   Ibid., 12, emphasis added.
93   Țuțea states: "Everything I've lived through in prison…would have not known consolation if I hadn't lived with the certainty that I was honored to suffer for a great people. This is what saved me from madness. That is, I did not go to prison to represent a Black tribe, but a great people, heavy with history, and with a shining future," *Între Dumnezeu si Neamul Meu*, 341.
94   Cited in *Omul: Tratat de Antropologie Creștină*, vol I, 5.
95   The masculinity of Țuțea's nationalism is evident not only in his portrayal of a patriarchal religion as the center of the state but also in his vision of ethical and ideological teachings as the province of young men engaged in an emulation of the classical Athenian model, which he frequently referenced. Women are very rarely

moral norms that make up the core of Țuțea's Romanianness are united by their Christian core. Consequently, the profile of the quintessential Romanian is reflected in a patriarchal, theocratic political view, which squarely places the Church and church leadership (and therefore men) before the state. In a discussion about Romanian art, Țuțea characterizes the true Romanian artist as "first and foremost Christian"[96] and one who "situates the church before the state"[97] in order to project "true" value through his or her work.

Țuțea's nationalism is rooted in a protochronic myth of Romanian exceptionalism. "As a principle," Țuțea says, "I am convinced of the invincibility of the Romanian people."[98] History is proof of Romanian national endurance despite seemingly insurmountable odds. About the Romanian language, Țuțea bizarrely claims that it is a "universal, generally valid instrument" of expression that can encompass all world culture.[99] Language and the intellectual genius of the Romanian people can allow the Romanian spirit to "synchronize" itself with all human creations that can be brought to "Wallachian land."[100]

His pride in Romanian nationalism is expressed in his interviews in contexts that articulated the belief that his suffering was worthwhile because it served the Romanian nation. In a death-bed interview, Țuțea is asked about the necessity to reveal the horrible deeds that happened in the Romanian gulag. He responds that the truth should never be known "for the pride of the Romanian people" to be preserved. In a declaration reminiscent of the self-sacrificial element of Iron Guard ideology, he concludes: "Even now if you take me out and shove me to the wall for the

---

referenced in Țuțea's dialogues, and most times as ancillary characters in historical mishaps (*Între Dumnezeu și Neamul Meu*, 303, 313, 321, 344, 347, 362, 365). When he is directly asked about his view on women, his opinion is deeply conservative and in tune with Romanian social ideology both pre- and post-1989: "What man does not like women? Women must be loved for their charm, and because they make human beings," *322 Memorable Words*, 51. Elsewhere, Țuțea praises virtues like chivalry and heroism, further underscoring the masculinity of his nationalism, *Proiectul de Tratat: Eros*, 44–45.

96   Țuțea, *Între Dumnezeu și Neamul Meu*, 92; the same nationalist strand against the anti-nationalist Jewish presence is described in an account of his visit to a communist anti-religion Museum, where a woman (supposedly Jewish) asked him to sign the visitor's book, and he refused, citing his deep Christian beliefs.
97   Ibid., 93.
98   Ibid., 282. The argument about the superiority of the Romanian language is recurrent, and sometimes it is made "at the expense" of other languages; see 312 for a comparison with Russian. Also Țuțea, *Proiectul de Tratat: Eros*, 43–44.
99   Țuțea, *Între Dumnezeu și Neamul Meu*, 84.
100 Ibid., 281.

Romanian people I will shout 'Excelsior!'"[101] The Messianism of Țuțea's nationalism is evident in both the sacrificial element and his rhetoric about Romanians as chosen people. The idea of a privileged fate is grafted onto the discourse of a "Greater Romania" that must be reconstituted by "recapturing" the lands that Romania historically lost.[102] The idea of the rebirth of a historical Romania, popular with the communist government, mirrored the later populist trope that elicited the creation of a "Greater Romania" party, which enjoyed substantial political support and gained Parliamentary representation after 1989.

Implications

Marta Petreu remarked that the 1927 generation was intellectually split into three strands: far-right Legion members and sympathizers, far-left communists, and an apolitical and culturally-oriented group. "The most interesting thing about the 1927 generation," Petreu argued, was that many of its members vacillated between the two political extremes, or even successively committed themselves to both" without ever opting for democracy.[103] Such was the case of Țuțea, who moved from a "fanatical supporter of communism" to a far-right Legionnaire in 1933 and preserved his rightist, anti-democratic beliefs throughout communism. After 1989, Țuțea asserted that "I haven't changed at all" and extolled the virtues of "demophilia." "I am not a democrat," Țuțea claimed, "I am a demophile."[104] A term borrowed from Nichifor Crainic, a theorist of the so-called ethnocratic state, demophilia is love of one own's people, distinguished from democracy as a political system and accommodating nationalist and elitist sentiment.[105]

---

101 Memorialul Durerii (The Memorial of Pain), Episode 11. In another account of his Aiud imprisonment, Țuțea is reported to have said "Even if we die here, in chains and striped clothes, we are not the ones honoring the Romanian people, it is the Romanian People who honor us by allowing us to die for it," cited by Munteanu, *Între Dumnezeu și Neamul Meu*, 394.
102 Țuțea, *Între Dumnezeu și Neamul Meu*, 359–361 and 365.
103 Petreu, 216.
104 Țuțea, *Între Dumnezeu și Neamul Meu*, 293.
105 For a discussion of the history of elitism in Romania, see Sorin Adam Matei, *Boierii Minții: intelectualii români între grupurile de prestigiu si piața liberă a ideilor* (The Boyars of the Mind: Romanian intellectuals between prestige groups and the free market of ideas) (Bucharest: Compania, 2007); and Lucian Boia, *Capcanele Istoriei, Elita Intelectuală Românească Între 1930 și 1950* [The Romanian Intellectual Elite Between 1930 and 1950] (Bucharest: Humanitas, 2011).

Țuțea's elitism plucks a particular string in Romanian culture. Sorin Adam Matei and Mona Momescu argue that Romanian culture is particularly indebted to a mythology of intellectual elitism and abstruse access to knowledge, which they call "paramodernity."[106] Paramodernity is dominated by a public "fascinated with an intellectual model which, although it addresses modern subjects, is essentially traditional, prophetic, even sometimes outright feudal."[107] In Romania, paramodernity is anchored in the inter-war cultural model that obliterated the separation between the spiritual and the political, and self-exploration and political knowledge and inserted "myth into politics and connected it with a utopia of inner knowing"[108] thereby stifling the main ingredient of democratic debate: an open encounter of ideas and options. Ideas are not debated but posited. "It is not surprising," Matei and Momescu argue, "to refuse conflict and debate when you believe that the circumstances of your existence, like the place and religion you were born into, the language you speak, the intellectual models you grew up with as an adolescent or student, the personal taste transmitted by mentors or parents are the same thing as the immutable essence of the world."[109] Țuțea was particularly fit to rise as a public figure in this context: his essentialism appeared both accessible and learned from both the perspective of the martyr and that of torch bearer for a redeemed national image. Țuțea represented the self-sacrifice that rescued a purported national essence from the failed experience of communism. His ideological affinity for social and political hierarchy and dedication to a sacralized model of the nation were straightforwardly grafted onto the post-1989 impulse to convert the image of a Romania victimized by historical forces while also identifying those culpable for veering away from the "natural" road of national development. In the name of national preservation, Țuțea reified the strong leadership of the European right as a better alternative to communism, calling Hitler a "safety valve for order" against the rise of German communism. This attitude propped the widely-

---

106 Sorin Adam Matei and Mona Momescu, eds., *Idolii Forului: de ce o clasă de mijloc a spiritului e de preferat "elitei" intelectualilor publici* [Idols of the Forum: why a middle class of the sprit is preferable to the public intellectual "elite"] (Indianapolis: Ideagora, 2010). Also Roth, "Ethno-Nationalism: The Romanian Version," 17.
107 Sorin Adam Matei, "Idols of the Forum for a Middle Class of the Spirit," in Matei and Momescu, 34.
108 Stelu Șerban, "Politics Against Utopia. Intellectuals and Power in the History of Romanian Modernization," in Matei and Momescu, eds., *Idolii Forului*, 128.
109 Matei and Momescu, *Idolii Forului*, 34.

shared anti-Semitic sentiment that is well-documented in Romania, before, during and after communism.[110]

The post-revolutionary search for national values in Romania was framed around the double intent of "rescuing" tropes suppressed by Ceaușescu's dictatorship and strengthening the myth of national distinctiveness and authenticity. The result of this hermeneutic negotiation had a reactionary flavor that buttressed a protochronistic continuity that can be traced through both interwar and communist years. "For many nationalists," Totok and Macovei argue, "after 1990, Țuțea became a living example of the interbellum intellectual, stubborn and recalcitrant, who opposed Stalinist oppression without ever giving up his beliefs, which he imparted to others."[111] The "long durée" link represented by Țuțea speaks to some of the core antidemocratic inclinations that dominated 1989 politics. While eulogizing Romanianness, Țuțea relegated democracy to the "graveyard of history" because it could not possibly "guarantee the existence or sovereignty of the Romanian people."[112] Certainly, Țuțea's views do not exhaust the political options present in Romanian post-communist civil-society, but their popularity reflects a strong nationalistic strand in Romanian politics, colored by anti-Semitism and religiosity. Țuțea revived and distilled these inclinations "re-actualizing, decades later, the historical sensibility of the nationalist Right in the 1930s," articulated in the foundational mythologies combining leadership, Christian identity and the poetic voice of Romanian spirituality through their respective icons—Corneliu Zela Codreanu (The Captain), Stephen the Great (the great Voivode) and Mihai Eminescu (the national Poet).[113] Țuțea, "the most annotated man in Romania," framed a Romanian fantasy of salvation closely aligned with critics of democracy and a turn to the right. The man who suffered in communist prisons for over a decade survived to tell a tale of virile political resurgence through Orthodox faith in the service of ethno-nationalism. Petreu calls Țuțea's attitudes to democracy especially "surprising," yet the context of his views is firmly and consistently anti-democratic and illiberal. Like in Romania, the assumption that those who

---

110 Tismăneanu, *Fantasies of Salvation*; and Michael Shafir, *Între Negare și Trivializare prin Comparație. Negarea Holocaustului in Țările Postcomuniste din Europa Central și de Est* [Between Denial and Comparative Trivialization: Holocaust Denial in Central and East European Countries] (Iași: Polirom, 2002).
111 William Totok and Irina Macovei, *Intre Mit și Bagatelizare* [Between Myth and Bagatelle] (Iași: Polirom, 2016).
112 Țuțea, *Între Dumnezeu și Neamul Meu*, 289.
113 Boia, *History and Myth*, 214.

opposed communism would pave the way to liberal democracy was belied by the rise of figures like Victor Orban (a former dissident) in Hungary, Milos Zerman in the Czech Republic, or Jaroslav Kaczynski in Poland. The anti-democratic politics of the right persist, grafted onto the echoes of old but familiar ideological strands and extending the shelf-life of deeply entrenched illiberal and antidemocratic politics that have become all but normalized in current European politics.

What Is too Long and When Is too Late for Transitional Justice? Observations from the Case of Romania

Cynthia M. Horne

Abstract: *Nearly 30 years after the end of Nicolae Ceaușescu's regime, what is too long and when is too late to use public disclosures about secret police complicity in the past to influence the composition of public office holders in the present? This article examines Romania's public disclosure measures from 2010 to the present, drawing on the reports of the secret police file repository agency—the C.N.S.A.S.—in order to better understand the temporal parameters surrounding their continued use. First, the article shows that despite contentions that there are no more spies left to unmask, Romania's vetting process continues to disclose the collaborator backgrounds of current political candidates, at both the national and local levels, and individuals being considered for appointments in high-ranking political and social institutions. Second, contrary to expectations that citizens might be too fatigued with the public disclosure process to consider them politically salient, citizen engagement with their personal files remains robust. Together, these findings suggest that preconceived temporal parameters for this type of transitional justice measure might have underestimated the duration of its utility and political relevance.*

Temporal assumptions regarding the timing and duration of certain transitional justice measures affect how academics and policy-makers think about their purpose, utility and impact. This is particularly true with respect to personnel reforms designed to catalyze bureaucratic turnover in the wake of a regime transition. In the case of post-communist transitions, personnel reform measures, like lustration and public disclosures, have relied on the contents of the communist-era secret police files to inform current employment screening processes.[1] Embed-

---

Research for this article was generously supported by the Division of Social Sciences within the Research Institute of the University of Bucharest, where the author was a visiting professor in residence during the summer of 2018. I would like to especially thank Marian Zulean for his support of this project and assistance during my residency at ICUB.

ded in debates surrounding the conditions under which the past can and should inform future employment are two temporal assumptions.[2] First, the timing of the onset of these measures is often linked to policy efficacy, with late measures generally perceived as less efficacious, possibly even counter-productive, but certainly suboptimal compared to measures enacted early in the transition.[3] Second, these types of personnel reforms are considered more important during transitions but less necessary or appropriate after democracy has been consolidated.[4] However, what do we really know about the relationship between the timing and duration of personnel reform measures and efficacy? Little scholarship has actually questioned our *a priori* temporal assumptions or problematized how the timing and duration of transitional justice might condition outcomes.[5] Addressing these lacunae in the literature, this article focuses on temporal parameters surrounding one type of transitional justice—public disclosures—in the context of Romania's post-communist transition.

---

1 Lavinia Stan, ed., *Transitional Justice in Eastern Europe and the Former Soviet Union: Reckoning with the Communist Past* (New York: Routledge, 2009).
2 Lustration as a transitional justice process has provoked fierce debates surrounding its legality, appropriateness, and implementation. See Stan, ed., *Transitional Justice in Eastern Europe and the Former Soviet Union*; Roman David, "Transitional injustice? Criteria for conformity of lustration to the right to political expression," *Europe-Asia Studies* 56, no. 6 (2004): 789–912; and Cynthia M. Horne, "International Legal Rulings on Lustration Policies in Central and Eastern Europe: Rule of Law in Historical Context," *Law & Social Inquiry* 34, no. 3 (2009): 713–44.
3 Pablo de Greiff and Alexander Mayer-Rieckh, eds., *Justice as Prevention: Vetting Public Employees in Transitional Societies* (New York: Social Science Research Council, 2007); Sang Wook and Daniel Han, "Transitional Justice: When Justice Strikes back—Case Studies of Delayed Justice in Argentina and South Korea," *Houston Journal of International Law*, 30 (2007–8): 653–700; *Rule of Law Tools for Post-Conflict States. Vetting: An Operational Framework* (New York: Office of the United Nations High Commissioner on Human Rights, 2006), HR/PUB/06/5.
4 Council of Europe, *Measures to Dismantle the Heritage of Former Communist Totalitarian Systems.* Resolution 1096 and Doc. 7568, 3 June (Strasbourg, France: Parliamentary Assembly, 1996); and European Court of Human Rights, *Case of Sidabras and Dziautas v. Lithuania*, Final 55480/00 and 59330/00, 27 July 2004 (Strasbourg: Council of Europe, 2004).
5 Exceptions include Thomas Obel Hansen, "The Time and Space of Transitional Justice," in *Research Handbook of Transitional Justice,* eds. Cheryl Lawther, Luke Moffett, and Dov Jacobs (Cheltenham, UK: Edward Elgar, 2017), 34–51; Cynthia M. Horne, "Late Lustration Programs in Romania and Poland: Supporting or Undermining Democratic Transitions?" *Democratization*, 16, no. 2 (2009): 344–76; and Cynthia M. Horne, "The Timing of Transitional Justice Measures," in *Post-Communist Transitional Justice: Lessons from 25 Years of Experience*, eds. Lavinia Stan and Nadya Nedelsky (New York: Cambridge University Press, 2015), 123–47.

Public disclosure measures are related to broader post-communist lustration programs. Lustration measures are legally prescribed transitional justice methods in which the communist-era secret police files are used to review the backgrounds of both public and semi-public officials and political candidates for evidence of membership in or collaboration with the communist security services and/or high-ranking communist party positions. In Central and Eastern Europe, consequences for such collaboration vary but have included public disclosures and/or removal from positions of power under the new regime.[6] The Czech Republic's use of compulsory employment dismissal as part of its lustration law is often juxtaposed against Poland's less punitive, more truth-telling approach or Hungary's very limited and short lustration program, in order to illustrate a range of lustration programs in practice.[7] In the absence of formal lustration laws, countries like Romania, Bulgaria and Slovakia have turned to public disclosure processes, functioning as a type of informal lustration, replicating some of the procedures and goals of regional post-communist measures.[8]

Public disclosures draw on the contents of the secret police files, reviewing the background of public office holders and candidates, appointed civil positions, and individuals in positions of public importance for evidence of collaboration with the communist security services. However, there are no formal, direct employment consequences, like many lustration measures. Instead the threat of public disclosure is intended to catalyze bureaucratic and employment change. Individuals might self-select out of public office or candidacy to prevent the shame of being disclosed, political parties could opt not to put candidates forward with collaborator backgrounds, voters could choose not to vote into office known secret police operatives, and employers could fail to hire or appoint individuals with said backgrounds. The similarity between public disclosures and regional lustration laws led to the process being dubbed a type of "silent lustration" by the Bulgarian secret police

---

6   Stan, ed., *Transitional Justice in Eastern Europe and the Former Soviet Union*.
7   Roman David, *Lustration and Transitional Justice: Personnel Systems in the Czech Republic, Hungary, and Poland* (Philadelphia: University of Pennsylvania Press, 2011).
8   Dragoş Petrescu, "Opening of the Securitate Files in Post-1989 Romania: Legal and Institutional Aspects," paper presented at the Association for Slavic, East European & Eurasian Studies annual conference, Boston, 7 December 2018; and Cynthia M. Horne, "'Silent Lustration': Public Disclosures as Informal Lustration Mechanisms in Bulgaria and Romania," *Problems of Post-Communism*, 62, May (2015): 131–44.

file repository agency (the Dossier Commission).⁹ As such, public disclosures can be defined as a variant of lustration with similar goals, drawing on similar information sources but with different constitutional mandates and legal constraints.

The public disclosure programs in Romania, Bulgaria, and Slovakia share some common elements. All three countries had heavily politicized lustration processes, repeatedly proposing and vetoing the passage of formal laws or thwarting their implementation. All three countries delimited or ruled against formal lustration: Romania's Constitutional Court struck down the lustration laws in 2008 and blocked lustration provisions; Bulgaria amended its constitution to officially ban lustration; and Slovakia allowed its lustration law inherited from Czechoslovakia to expire without implementation in 1996.¹⁰ Despite the rejection of lustration, the three countries eventually passed and implemented public disclosure procedures, which in many ways mimicked the lustration programs of their neighbors. All three countries were relatively late to engage in authentic public disclosures, with the processes starting in earnest around 2006–8.¹¹ As such all three are examples of delayed transitional justice. Finally, public disclosure processes have been primarily implemented by the secret police file repository agencies in each country, all of which are members of the European Network of Official Authorities in Charge of the Secret Police Files.¹² As such there is a shared sense of mission, a sharing of information about how to organ-

---

9   Horne, "Silent Lustration."
10   See the website of the Bulgarian Dossier Commission for legal limitations on lustration, available at: http://www.comdos.bg/, accessed on 2 February 2019; *Law for Access and Disclosure of the Documents and* Announcing *Affiliations of Bulgarian Citizens to the State Security and the Intelligence Services of the Bulgarian National Army*, December 2006, available at: http://lex.bg/bg/laws/ldoc/213 5540283, accessed on 2 February 2019; Constitutional Court Decision 820/2010 "On the objection of unconstitutionality of provisions of the lustration law to limit temporary access to certain positions and titles for people who were part of the structures of power and the repressive apparatus of the communist regime from March 6, 1945 to December 22, 1989," *Monitorul Oficial* 420, 23 June 2010; and R. Leśkiewicz and P. Žáček, eds., *Handbook of the European Network of Official Authorities in Charge of the Secret Police Files* (Prague: Institute for the Study of Totalitarian Regimes and Institute of National Remembrance, 2013).
11   Cynthia M. Horne, *Building Trust and Democracy: Transitional Justice in Post-Communist Countries* (New York: Oxford University Press, 2017).
12   Poland, Hungary, the Czech Republic, Romania, Bulgaria, Germany, and Slovakia were founding members. See European Network of Official Authorities in Charge of the Secret Police Files, *A Reader on Their Legal Foundations, Structures and Activities* (Berlin: Die Bundesbeauftragte für die Unterlagen des Staatssicherheitsdienstes der ehemaligen Deutschen Demokratischen Republik, 2009).

ize and preserve the files, and even a shared sense of accountability across the member organizations.[13]

While public disclosure measures have been shown to support aspects of trust-building and democratization in the post-communist region, albeit with weaker effects than more compulsory and punitive lustration measures, what remains unclear is whether there are temporal parameters delimiting a time period for their appropriate use.[14] Public disclosures are politically complicated, institutionally expensive, morally contested, and entail quasi-punitive employment consequences for those found 'guilty' of secret police collaboration. Since they are costly, their duration bears empirical consideration. Moreover, one of their primary goals is to promote trust—in vetted public institutions, political office holders, and government.[15] If the measures are no longer relevant or perceived as legitimate, they will fail to positively affect perceptions of the state. What is too long and when is too late to use the secret police files for current employment vetting considerations?

To address these temporal conditions, this article engages a series of sub-questions drawing on Romania's use of its secret police files from 2010 to the present. First, demographically speaking, are there any public office holders or political candidates left to publicly disclose nearly thirty years since the fall of the communist regime? The old guard may have aged out of political consideration, already been unmasked, or self-selected out of political consideration, rendering an employment vetting process based on information in the secret police files from 30 to 50+ years ago somewhat anachronistic and possibly obsolete. Second, for truth-telling measures to be effective they must be valued by citizens. Are citizens still interested in access to the secret police files, both their own and those of political candidates? After several decades, citizen fatigue with the duration of measures might have rendered them less politically salient and less useful in building public trust. In short, focus-

---

13 The Czech Institute for the Study of Totalitarian Regimes was reprimanded in 2014 and threatened with suspension over allegations that it did not properly vet members of its own file repository agency. Jan Richter, "Agency Administering Secret Police Files Threatens to Quit International Network," *Radio Praha*, 23 January 2014, available at: https://www.radio.cz/en/section/curraffrs/agency-administering-secret-police-files-threatens-to-quit-international-network, accessed 2 February 2019.
14 Horne, Building Trust and Democracy; and Lavinia Stan, *Transitional Justice in Post-Communist Romania: The Politics of Memory* (New York: Cambridge University Press, 2013).
15 *Rule of Law Tools*; de Greiff and Mayer-Reickh, *Justice as Prevention*; Horne, *Building Trust and Democracy*; and David, *Lustration and Transitional Justice*.

ing on the use of public disclosure measures in Romania permits a fine-grained analysis of the temporal conditions associated with this regional transitional justice method, with possible policy implications for other post-communist countries still using public disclosures (Bulgaria) or countries using late lustration measures (Ukraine and Poland).

To preview the main findings, Romania's vetting process continues to disclose the collaborator backgrounds of current political candidates, individuals being considered for current appointments in political and social institutions, and others holding high-ranking public positions. While there is evidence of a declining number of former collaborators and operatives vying for public positions, Romania has not reached the predicted demographic cliff. The old guard has not quite aged out or been shamed out of public positions of trust, suggesting continued policy relevance to public disclosures. Additionally, citizen interest in the secret police files remains strong with respect to both personal files and the files of political candidates. Predicted citizen fatigue has not rendered file access and file disclosure obsolete just yet. These findings suggest that preconceived temporal expiration dates for this transitional justice method might have underestimated its utility and public relevance. However, the number of former collaborators and operatives publicly disclosed is declining, suggesting that the cost/benefit calculation associated with public disclosures might be shifting. While the article highlights Romania's experience, it potentially informs our understanding of temporal parameters surrounding personnel reform programs as transitional justice measures more broadly.

Thinking Theoretically about Timing

The perception of the time sensitivity of personnel reform measures, particularly lustration, appeared in scholarship at the beginning of post-communist transitions before there was even significant implementation.[16] The Council of Europe issued guidelines in 1996 recommending no more than a decade for lustration, despite the limited implementation at that time and the fact that many countries had not started their personnel reform measures yet (Czechoslovakia was the first country to

---

16 Samuel Huntington, *The Third Wave Democratization in the Late Twentieth Century* (Norman: University of Oklahoma Press, 1991); John Moran, "The Communist Torturers of Eastern Europe: Prosecute and Punish or Forgive and Forget," *Communist and Post-Communist Studies* 27, no. 1 (1994): 95–109.

pass laws in 1991).[17] The rationale for why early reforms were better than later measures was strengthened when lustration became politicized in the mid-1990s in several countries, including Hungary and Romania, giving rise to concerns about possible extralegal manipulation of these measures.[18] As such, the two-pronged assumptions that early measures were the most efficacious and that there was a built-in expiration date for the measures developed before we had even amassed empirical evidence about the impact of these transitional justice methods.

There are several reasons why lustration and public disclosures might be particularly time-sensitive transitional justice methods. First, personnel reform seeks to change the composition of personnel in positions of power to support the regime transition. This is less useful if there are significant delays enacting the reforms, and some might argue that they are not useful late into a transition because corrupt or compromised personnel have been allowed to remain in positions of power. Delayed measures are therefore viewed as less efficacious than reforms enacted in the wake of a regime change.[19]

Second, the aftermath of a transition is often described as a period of "extraordinary politics."[20] Normal politics and rules might be suspended in order to push through reforms necessary to support a democratic transition. The European Court of Human Rights (ECtHR) has expressed this understanding of lustration laws, highlighting that the measures might be legally inappropriate once democracy is consolidated.[21] According to this line of reasoning, as more time passes from the initial transition, such measures become less legally appropriate. In addition, over time citizens are expected to be more interested in forward- rather than backward-looking justice measures.[22] Citizens could become fatigued with policies that focus on the past rather than policies

---

17 Council of Europe, *Measures to Dismantle the Heritage of Former Communist Totalitarian Systems.*
18 Csilla Kiss, "The Misuses of Manipulation: The Failure of Transitional Justice in Post-Communist Hungary," *Europe-Asia Studies,* 58, no. 6 (2006), 925–40 and Stan, *Transitional Justice in Post-Communist Romania.*
19 Claus Offe, *Varieties of Transition: The East European and East Germany Experience* (Cambridge: Cambridge University Press, 1996).
20 Leszek Balcerowcz, *Socialism, Capitalism, Transformation* (Budapest: Central European University Press, 1995).
21 European Court of Human Rights, *Case of Bobek v. Poland,* § 62. 68761/01, 17 July 2007 (Strasbourg: Council of Europe, 2007); European Court of Human Rights, *Case of Matyjek v. Poland,* § 69. 38184/03. 24 April 2007 (Strasbourg: Council of Europe, 2007).
22 Jon Elster, *Closing the Books: Transitional Justice in Historical Perspective* (New York: Cambridge University Press, 2004).

correcting political, social, or economic problems in the present. Citizen fatigue, as measured by loss of citizen engagement with the process, could signal that the measures are considered less salient, or worse, no longer legitimate areas on which to focus scarce state resources.[23] Therefore, earlier measures rather than later or longer measures are seen as ways to avoid a loss of citizen engagement.

Third, there is a concern that personnel reforms could be instrumentalized by political parties. Lustration and public disclosures reveal the collaborator backgrounds of candidates for public office and individuals in positions of political power, making them potentially ripe for instrumental use by political parties against rivals. The manipulation of post-communist transitional justice in Hungary, Romania, and Poland illustrates the politicization of lustration.[24] Concerns that later and longer measures would be more prone to politicization contribute to our temporal assumptions that earlier measures are most appropriate.

Fourth, there are self-selection mechanisms which might reduce the benefits of public disclosures compared to the political and economic costs. Demographically speaking, the pool of former secret police agents and collaborators will eventually age out of politics. Top bureaucrats, apparatchiki, and secret police officers would likely have been middle-aged at the height of their communist careers and peak influence, placing them in their 70s and 80s now. Perhaps the natural aging process has rendered public disclosures increasingly obsolete? A related argument is that over time individuals recognize that their backgrounds will be revealed through vetting, so individuals might self-select out of positions to avoid public disclosure. Alternately, political parties might avoid putting forward known collaborators as candidates to avoid negative press, or institutions might decide against appointing former collaborators to avoid tainting their image. These self-selection mechanisms might point to an appropriate end date to measures.

There are also expectations about the appropriate duration of lustration and public disclosures. The very term 'transitional justice' implies that the measures are used during the transition period after a

---

23   There is evidence of this predicted citizen fatigue in the Former Soviet Union. Cynthia M. Horne and Lavinia Stan, eds., *Transitional Justice and the Former Soviet Union: Reviewing the Past, Looking toward the Future* (New York: Cambridge University Press, 2018).

24   Kiss, "The Misuses of Manipulation"; Stan, *Transitional Justice in Post-Communist Romania*; and Aleks Szczerbiak, "Explaining Late Lustration Programs: Lessons from the Polish Case," in *Post-Communist Transitional Justice: Lessons from 25 Years of Experience*, eds. Lavinia Stan and Nadya Nedelsky (New York: Cambridge University Press, 2015).

regime change.[25] The Council of Europe suggested a ten-year period for the use of lustration in post-communist countries, arguing that more than a decade was too long to continue such 'transitional' justice.[26] While the ECtHR did not give a specific number of years, it similarly argued that once democracy was consolidated, such measures would become less legally appropriate.[27] An assumption that a decade was an appropriate duration for measures has remained a benchmark for evaluating personnel reforms although subsequent ECtHR rulings and the European Commission for Democracy through Law (the Venice Commission) have issued broader interpretations of the duration of the measures in practice.[28] For example, in 2017 the ECtHR sided with Bulgaria in a case raised by a citizen negatively affected by public disclosure, ruling that the on-going public disclosures were legal and appropriate even in 2017.[29] The Venice Commission has taken a more temporally lenient view toward Ukraine's 2014 lustration laws as well.

If we are to apply some of these temporal considerations to Romania, we might question if there remains utility to its public disclosure program, namely, is there anyone left to publicly disclose? Second, do these measures resonate with citizens? Are citizens engaged with the process, or has it become politically irrelevant to them? Romania is an interesting case to explore with regard to temporal conditions of transitional justice because by regional post-communist standards it has had a very late, long, and informal approach. Before examining the empirical evidence related to Romania's current public disclosures, I first provide some background information on the agency charged with administering Romania's secret police files—the National Council for the Study of the Securitate Archives.

---

25 Ruti Teitel, *Transitional Justice* (New York: Oxford University Press, 2000).
26 Council of Europe, "Guidelines to ensure that lustration laws and similar administrative measures comply with the requirements of a state based on the rule of law," in *Measures to Dismantle the Heritage*, §g.
27 European Court of Human Rights, *Case of Matyvek v. Poland*. 38184/03, 24 April 2007 (Strasbourg, France: Council of Europe, 2007).
28 European Commission for Democracy through Law (Venice Commission), *Final Opinion on the Law on* Government *Cleansing (Lustration Law) of Ukraine*, Opinion 788/2014, CDL-AD (2015)012, Venice, 19 June 2015.
29 European Court of Human Rights, *Anchev v. Bulgaria*, Applications 38334/08 and 68242/16, ECHR 011 (2017), 11 January 2018.

C.N.S.A.S.'s Structure and Function

The National Council for the Study of the Securitate Archives (Consiliul Național pentru Studierea Arhivelor Securității, C.N.S.A.S.) manages the archives of the former communist secret police, the Securitate. Drawing on information in the files, its determinations of collaboration and complicity are the basis for Romania's current public disclosure program.[30] This section overviews the changes to the legal mandate and scope of activities of the C.N.S.A.S. over time in order to contextualize its current activities.[31]

The C.N.S.A.S. was created in 1999 and charged with managing file access, screening political candidates and office holders for evidence of collaboration with the Securitate, and publicly disclosing this information although it did not have the authority to remove individuals from employment.[32] These functions were similar in design to other already established lustration agencies, like the Institute of National Remembrance in Poland and the Historical Archive in Hungary.[33] Despite the legal mandate, the C.N.S.A.S.'s ability to execute its functions was limited from its inception; it lacked funding, a building in which to work, broad political support, and direct access to the secret police files.[34] Despite its structural hobbling, the C.N.S.A.S. reviewed some cases and issued rulings, but the judgments often appeared politically biased.[35] This is partially a function of the method of appointing members to the decision-making C.N.S.A.S. Collegium. The Collegium members are politically appointed, proportional to the parties in power, with the intention that

---

30 For a description of its charter, see C.N.S.A.S., Official website, available at: http://www.cnsas.ro/, accessed on 4 February 2019.
31 For details about the domestic political environment that has shaped the evolution of the C.N.S.A.S., see Dragoș Petrescu, "Dilemmas of Transitional Justice in Post-1989 Romania," in *Lustration and Consolidation of Democracy and the Rule of Law in Central and Eastern Europe*, eds. Vladimira Dvořáková and Anđelko Milardović (Zagreb: Political Science Research Center, 2007), 127–52 and Lavinia Stan, "Reckoning with the Communist Past in Romania: A Scorecard," *Europe-Asia Studies*, 65, no. 1 (2013): 127–46.
32 Law 187/1999 on Access to the Personal File and Disclosure of Securitate as Political Police, 9 December 1999, available at: http://lege5.ro/Gratuit/gmzdqnzthe/law-nr-187-1999-on-the-access-to-the-personal-file-and-the-disclosure-of-the-securitate-as-a-political-police, accessed on 25 January 2014.
33 Leśkiewicz and Žáček, eds., *Handbook of the European Network*.
34 Stan, *Transitional Justice in Post-Communist Romania*, 92.
35 Lavinia Stan, "Moral Cleansing Romanian Style," *Problems of Post Communism* 49, no. 4 (2002): 52–62.

the C.N.S.A.S. represents a range of political views.³⁶ However, since collaboration rulings are decided by majority vote, the decisions advanced can and did reflect Romanian politics, thereby undermining perceptions that the C.N.S.A.S. was making authentic and politically autonomous rulings.³⁷ In short, although the C.N.S.A.S. was structured like other file agencies in the European Network and nominally processed files, its limited number of decisions and politicized rulings undermined its credibility.

A confluence of domestic and international factors shifted the political landscape and support for the C.N.S.A.S. in 2006.³⁸ First, the National Liberal Party, as part of the ruling Justice and Truth Alliance, pushed the passage of a more expansive lustration law to support greater accountability for the past.³⁹ Second, the Tismăneanu Commission researched and presented a report documenting and condemning the abuses committed against the Romanian people by the communist regime.⁴⁰ Third, President Traian Băsescu endorsed the report and condemned aspects of the communist dictatorship, thereby creating a domestic political environment favorable toward more accountability. President Băsescu also had 60,000 files transferred to the C.N.S.A.S. in 2005/2006, thereby finally providing the C.N.S.A.S. with the information they needed to screen political candidates and office holders.⁴¹ Fourth, these domestic changes coincided with Romania's accession to the European Union, with some suggesting the timing of the measures showed

---

36   A Collegium of eleven individuals, nine nominated by political parties proportionate to their representation in the Senate, one appointed by the President, and one by the Prime Minister, has authority over the personnel employed at the C.N.S.A.S.
37   Comments by Dragoș Petrescu, Panel Discussion "Remembering Past Atrocities," Society for Romanian Studies international conference, Bucharest, Romania, 27 June 2018.
38   Horne reviews the domestic politics surrounding these changes in "Informal Lustration."
39   For election information, see European Election Database, Norsk Senter for Forskningsdata, available at: http://www.nsd.uib.no/european_election_databas e/country/romania/introduction.html, accessed 4 February 2019.
40   There are disagreements in Romanian society regarding aspects of the report. Cosmina Tănăsoiu, "The Tismăneanu Report: Romania Revisits Its Past," *Problems of Post-Communism* 54, no. 4 (2007):60–9.
41   Leśkiewicz and Žáček, eds., *Handbook of the European Network of Official Authorities*, 226.

they were designed to secure EU membership by demonstrating Romania's commitment to transparency and accountability.[42]

The 2008 legislative elections shifted domestic politics once again, bringing into power the Social Democratic Party (with known ties to the former Romanian Communist Party and the Securitate) and the Democratic Liberal Party, both of which were less favorable to transitional justice. In this politically charged environment, the Constitutional Court struck down elements of the lustration law in 2008 and stripped the C.N.S.A.S. of its legal mandate for lustration.[43] The decision, which contracted the Court's previous rulings on the legality of lustration, was seen as a politically motivated attempt to quash disclosures that could negatively impact the grand coalition in power, or even unseat Court members with collaborator pasts.[44] The C.N.S.A.S. was not dissolved but instead given a new, diminished mandate to reflect the Court decisions. The C.N.S.A.S. continued to verify the background of individuals and publicly disclose the information, but the Bucharest Court of Appeals was the legal authority making finalized, irrevocable collaboration decisions.[45]

Since 2009 the C.N.S.A.S. has operated under this new mandate, managing the secret police files, reviewing tens of thousands of files, and issuing thousands of affirmative verdicts for further consideration by the Bucharest Court of Appeals.[46] Its four main functions are: 1) "to ensure the free access of individuals to their personal files"; 2) to facilitate the "vetting of individuals seeking public office"; 3) "to expose publicly the former agents and informal collaborators of the Securitate in accordance with rule of law principles"; and 4) "to develop research and education activities ... about the repressive actions of the Securitate."[47] The protocols governing the file review and public disclosures provide

---

42 Florin Abraham, "Three Decades of Transitional Justice in post-communist Europe," paper presented at the Society for Romanian Studies international conference, Bucharest, Romania, 27 June 2018.
43 Constitutional Court Decision 51 of 31 January 2008 declaring Law 187/1999 unconstitutional, in Leśkiewicz and Žáček, *Handbook of the European Network of Official Authorities*, 226; and Constitutional Court Decision 820/2010.
44 Bogdan Iancu, "Post-Accession Constitutionalism with a Human Face: Judicial Reform and Lustration in Romania," *European Constitutional Law Review*, 6, no. 1 (2010):28–58 and Stan, *Transitional Justice in Post-Communist Romania*, 96.
45 Leśkiewicz and Žáček, *Handbook of the European Network of Official Authorities*, 220–30.
46 See the CNSAS website for annual reports detailing the files reviewed and decisions rendered. Available at: http://www.cnsas.ro/, accessed on 4 February 2019.
47 Consiliul Național Pentru Studierea Arhivelor Securității, *2017 Raport de activitate privind anul* (Bucharest: C.N.S.A.S., 2017), 127, available at: http://www.cnsas.ro/rapoarte.html, accessed on 27 August 2018.

for four stages: 1) the C.N.S.A.S. completes a preliminary investigation and finds evidence of collaboration; 2) a final determination is completed and approved by the C.N.S.A.S. Collegium[48]; 3) the Collegium decides which of the final determinations are forwarded to the Bucharest Court of Appeals for review and due process procedures, including granting the accused the right to a hearing and appeal; 4) only after the full legal process is completed can a positive determination of official and irrevocable regime collaboration be rendered by the Bucharest Court of Appeals and subsequently published in the *Official Gazette*.[49] The next section turns to an empirical examination of the stages of the file review process, testing whether the vetting mandate has become anachronistic several decades after the transition.

Public Disclosures: Has Time Run out?

The C.N.S.A.S. reportedly verified files on 5,731 operatives and issued 3,729 public disclosures of regime complicity during 2008–2014. As of 27 February 2018, there were 3,505 security officers and non-commissioned officers and 508 Securitate employees publicly disclosed on the C.N.S.A.S. website.[50] These substantial figures illustrate the part the C.N.S.A.S. has played in Romania's accountability efforts. Is there anyone left to publicly disclose?

Data on both preliminary and final C.N.S.A.S. determinations, as well as irrevocable judgments of collaboration conferred by the Bucharest Court of Appeals, provide information on the number of individuals for whom evidence of collaboration/complicity has been found and for whom final determinations of collaboration have been published. The focus is on data over the past decade as this captures the temporal element of the research question: is there anyone left to publicly disclose?

---

48 The Collegium is the top consultative group within C.N.S.A.S., comprised of the President, the Vice-President, the Secretary, and members of the different investigative units. See organizational chart, available at: http://www.cnsas.ro/documente/2012.03.01%20-%20Organigrama%20CNSAS.pdf, accessed on 30 May 2018.

49 These procedures, including the appeals process, are detailed on the C.N.S.A.S. main webpage, available at: http://www.CNSAS.ro/index.html, accessed on 30 May 2018. The Bucharest Court of Appeals is in charge of overseeing the due process safeguards of individuals and their right to appeal.

50 C.N.S.A.S., "Fosta Securitate: Cadre și Colaboratori," no date, available at: http://www.cnsas.ro/fosta_securitate.html, accessed on 5 February 2019.

Figure 1: Cases of collaboration/complicity initiated for investigation and preliminary findings

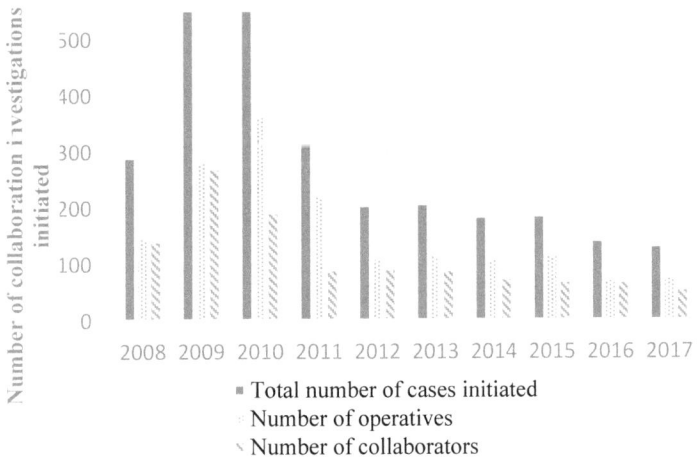

■ Total number of cases initiated
Number of operatives
Number of collaborators

Source: Author compiled from C.N.S.A.S. Annual Activitiy Reports, 2008–2017, http://www.C.N.S.A.S..ro/

Figure 1 presents the number of preliminary collaboration determinations over 2008–2017, with the total number of cases broken down by the number of operatives and collaborators disclosed. Years 2009 and 2010 saw the highest number of cases initiated, reflecting both the increase in the number of files transmitted to the C.N.S.A.S. after the 2006 institutional restructuring and improvements in managing and deciphering information in the files.[51] As predicted, there is a steady decline in the number of cases, suggesting there are fewer individuals left to publicly disclose. The number of cases has declined over time, but 2017 still yielded more than 100 public officials with preliminary determinations of collaboration. To merit such a determination there must be evidence in the files, the file must include a signature of the operative/agent demonstrating involvement, and the nature of the collaboration must violate the human rights of the victim.

---

51 Consiliul Național pentru Studierea Arhivelor Securității, *2016 Raport de activitate privind anul* (Bucharest: C.N.S.A.S., 2016), available at: http://www.cnsas.ro/rapoarte.html, accessed on 27 August 2018.

Following preliminary collaboration determinations, the C.N.S.A.S. Collegium evaluates the available information and issues a final determination, which can then be forwarded to the Bucharest Court of Appeals for judicial review. Figure 2 presents a breakdown of these final determinations by year.[52] The number of operatives and collaborators officially confirmed in the past four years of data remains significant. The total number of individuals in 2014 (343) was the highest of the recent four years, with declining numbers over time.[53] The ratio of informants and collaborators found in the files remained consistent over time as well. Do these figures suggest that demographically speaking previous collaborators and operatives have aged out of positions of power or public trust, or that individuals are self-selecting out of public office? While there is clear evidence of a decline in total numbers, nearly thirty years after the end of communism there remains a robust number of individuals to vet for future positions of power.

Figure 2: Cases of collaboration/complicity: final determinations by C.N.S.A.S.

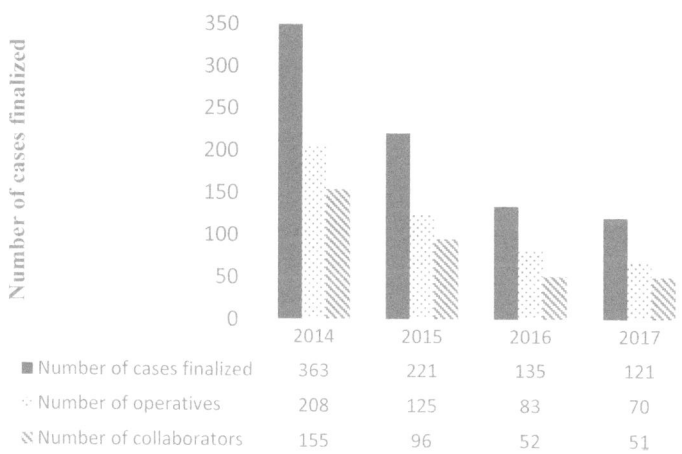

	2014	2015	2016	2017
Number of cases finalized	363	221	135	121
Number of operatives	208	125	83	70
Number of collaborators	155	96	52	51

Source: Author compiled from C.N.S.A.S. Annual Activity Reports, 2014-2017, www.C.N.S.A.S..ro

---

52 The total number of political police collaborators and informants was higher in the finalized figures than in the preliminary determinations because some years involve addressing or finalizing investigations started in previous years. For additional information, see C.N.S.A.S., *2017 Raport de activitate privind anul*.
53 Consiliul Național Pentru Studierea Arhivelor Securității, *2014 Raport de activitate privind anul* (Bucharest: C.N.S.A.S., 2014), available at: http://www.cnsas.ro/rapoarte.html, accessed on 27 August 2018.

Once the C.N.S.A.S. Collegium has issued a final determination, it can forward the case to the Bucharest Court of Appeals for review, potential appeal, and final judgment. During 2008–2014, the C.N.S.A.S. advanced 1,406 cases to the Bucharest Court of Appeals, and the Court issued 1,366 final irrevocable judgments by 2016.[54] The identities of another 220 former security officers were slated for publication in the *Official Gazette* in 2017.[55] The C.N.S.A.S. has gradually adopted a strategy of only advancing cases for which there is broad internal consensus regarding the quality of evidence of material collaboration, resulting in higher rates of success obtaining final affirmative Court judgments.[56] Some 90 percent of forwarded cases resulted in judicial determinations of collaboration, with a success rate of 98 percent in recent years.[57] The comportment both within the C.N.S.A.S. and between the C.N.S.A.S. and the Bucharest Court of Appeals regarding assessments of collaboration has contributed to perceptions of the legitimacy of decisions.

Figure 3 presents the number of definitive and irrevocable court determinations during 2009–2015. The number of Court finalized cases peaked in 2011 and 2012 with 214 and 205 determinations, respectively, halving in 2013, with a total of 124 individuals, and nearly halving again in 2014, with 74 total cases. The 2015 numbers were only nine cases. This suggests a winnowing of cases over time, confirming the anticipated temporal drop off in the number of individuals to be publicly disclosed.

Figure 3 also speaks to another critique of lustration in general and late lustration and public disclosures in particular, namely that the process largely misses the most egregious cases because the files of important agents and collaborators were destroyed both prior to and in the chaotic aftermath of the transition. The remaining files are only on less materially important collaborators and informants, rendering the process somewhat inert. Figure 3 shows that these court-finalized determinations were publicly disclosed by both Securitate operatives and collaborators involved in current political life. The number of operatives receiving finalized court decisions consistently exceeded the number of cases against collaborators each year, further suggesting that the vetting net was capturing individuals who were important to the Securitate.[58]

---

54 C.N.S.A.S., 2016 *Raport de activitate privind anul*.
55 Ibid. Decisions are published in the *Official Gazette*. Budget limitations were cited in the activity report as a constraint on the timely publication of decisions.
56 Personal communication with Florin Abraham, former C.N.S.A.S. Collegium member, Bucharest, Romania, 2 July 2018.
57 C.N.S.A.S., 2017 *Raport de activitate privind anul*.
58 The total distribution of operatives and collaborators disclosed by the C.N.S.A.S. is available under "Fosta Securitate: Cadre și Colaboratori," showing many more collaborators than operatives.

Figure 3: Definitive and Irrevocable Decisions: Court Finalized

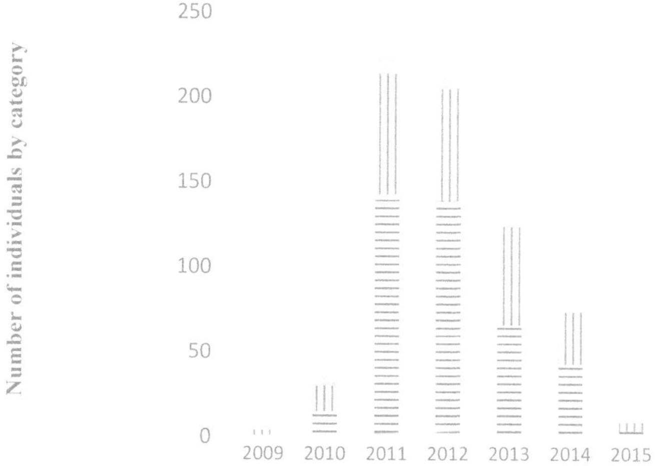

	2009	2010	2011	2012	2013	2014	2015
Reject CNSAS decisions	0	6	9	6	0	0	0
Definitive and Irrevocable Decisions: Collaborators	3	15	71	66	58	31	5
Definitive and Irrevocable Decisions: Operatives	1	15	143	139	66	43	4

Reject CNSAS decisions

Definitive and Irrevocable Decisions: Collaborators

Source: Author compiled from C.N.S.A.S. Annual Activity Reports, 2009-2015, www.C.N.S.A.S..ro

Moreover, all determinations require definitive proof that an individual's actions violated the human rights of a victim, therefore, almost by definition, anyone who is irrevocably found to be an operative or collaborator is guilty of human rights violations. The files are incomplete and certainly there are people who have escaped investigation, but all of the publicly disclosed individuals (both operatives and collaborators) perpetrated material offenses against others under communism, and were investigated because they were candidates for or in positions of current public trust. These findings refute the contention that the quality of informants/collaborators/operatives is so low as to dilute the benefits of the process.

In sum, this section reviewed three stages of the public disclosure process, including preliminary determinations, final determinations, and the irrevocable finalized judgements. In terms of temporal conditions, there has been declining utility to this process evident in the finalized court judgments, but the twenty-five-year mark was still yielding significant numbers of affirmative collaboration determinations. In short, there are former collaborators and operatives who are politically active, proving that demographically speaking the process has not quite reached its temporal cliff, although there is evidence that it is approaching. The next section turns to the vetting of public office holders and candidates in 2016 and 2017 and focuses more narrowly on the most temporally proximate period for collaboration evaluations.

Recent Elections and Appointments of Public Officials

Vetting New Candidates for Elected Positions

One of the primary responsibilities of the C.N.S.A.S. is to verify the background of political candidates for national and local elections. Part of the rationale for vetting candidates is to publicly disclose information prior to elections, such that voters can then make informed election choices. This review of political candidates results in thousands of C.N.S.A.S. verifications during election cycles. In 2006 and 2007 the C.N.S.A.S. performed 4,697 and 17,734 checks, respectively.[59] In the 2016 election year, it received information on 24,112 electoral candidates to review: 18,600 for local elections and 5,532 for parliamentary elections. The 2017 election year included the verification of 23,125 candidates: 16,278 individuals in local elections and 5,693 in national elections. These numbers illustrate the sheer number of candidates to screen, at both significant time and financial cost. This begs the question: are there any former operatives or collaborators left to catch in the electoral vetting net so many years after the regime change? Are these positions of high political importance meriting a continuation of the program?

In the 2016 election cycle, the C.N.S.A.S. identified and published the names of six candidates previously verified as collaborators, and

---

59 Consiliul Național pentru Studierea Arhivelor Securității, *2006 Raport de activitate privind anul* (Bucharest: C.N.S.A.S., 2006), available at: http://www.cnsas.ro/rapoarte.html, accessed on 27 August 2018; C.N.S.A.S., *2007 Raport de* activitate *privind anul*; C.N.S.A.S., *2008 Raport de activitate privind anul* (Bucharest: C.N.S.A.S., 2008), available at: http://www.cnsas.ro/rapoarte.html, accessed on 27 August 2018.

identified secret police file information on 6,525 other candidates, resulting in the further investigation of 158 individuals who showed evidence of material collaboration with the Securitate.[60] In the 2017 electoral candidate list, there was no information in the files on 13,621 people, removing them from further investigation. Another 3,974 clean certificates were issued, suggesting a lack of evidence of individual collaboration. After file review, 134 candidates merited additional investigation, including 77 former cadres and 57 Securitate employees. In the end, files on fifteen candidates were transferred to the Court for further review and potential action, with thirty-six candidates in local elections already having been found guilty of collaboration. Additionally, in 2015–2017 the C.N.S.A.S. documented 131 candidates lying on their verification certificates, thereby serving a significant oversight function for the process of vetting political candidates as well.[61]

Table 1 presents 2013–2017 data on collaborator/operative determinations for candidates for public office and elected officials at the national and local levels. The columns separate three categories: 1) candidates for elected office; 2) individuals in elected positions of power at the national level, generally confined to the Senate and the Chamber of Deputies; and 3) individuals in local or regional elected positions, including council members and mayors.[62]

---

60 C.N.S.A.S., *2016 Raport de activitate privind anul*.
61 C.N.S.A.S., *2017 Raport de activitate privind anul*.
62 Some years present initial and others present final C.N.S.A.S. determinations, due to data availability. There is no double counting across the categories.

Table 1: Individuals vetted for office, positions, or certifications with positive collaborator/operative determinations by C.N.S.A.S.

Year[1]	Candidates for elected office	National elected positions[2]	Local/regional elected positions
2017 final determination	1 operative 2 collaborators (1 Chamber of Deputies candidate; 2 local positions)	1 collaborator (Cabinet Chief, Chamber of Deputies)	2 operatives 29 collaborators
2016 final determination	0 operatives 3 collaborators (1 Chamber of Deputies candidate; 2 local positions)	0 operatives 0 collaborators	0 operatives 15 collaborators
2015 final determination	1 operative 9 collaborators (including 4 Senate candidates, 3 Chamber of Deputies candidates (1 also a European Parliament candidate))	0 operatives 0 collaborators	2 operatives 28 collaborators
2014 initial[3]	0 operatives 4 collaborators (3 candidates for Senate, 1 Chamber of Deputies candidate)	0 operatives 0 collaborators	0 operatives 29 collaborators
2013 initial[3]	1 operative (Chamber of Deputies candidate) 8 collaborators (includes 3 Chamber of Deputies candidates; 1 for Senate; and various local elections candidates including Mayor of Bucharest)	0 operatives[4] 0 collaborators	1 operative 29 collaborators

[1] Recently C.N.S.A.S. released the names and positions for their initial and final determinations. Due to overlap in reporting, I only count the final reports by year.
[2] One operative appeared in the 2017 finalized list at a high-ranking government position—Secretary of State, Ministry of Defense. This is not a directly elected position registered in the national level of elected positions, but it refers to a high-ranking position being occupied by a former operative.
[3] The position breakdown was not published with the 2014 or 2013 annual reports for the final determinations—only the initial determination. Therefore, the initial determinations are reported here.
[4] There were no directly elected former operatives, the Chief of Services of the Chamber of Deputies and a Supreme Court judge were disclosed as former *Securitate* operatives. These appointed positions are examples of persons in current positions of power with known operative backgrounds.
Data compiled by author from the C.N.S.A.S. annual activity reports, various years.

The first column, which presents figures on disclosures for candidates in national and local elections, includes a mixture of operatives and collaborators publicly disclosed in each year, with the majority of disclosures being related to collaborators. The positions are politically important, including candidates for the Chamber of Deputies, the Senate, and the European Parliament. The second and third columns speak to whether the pre-screening and public disclosure of candidates might affect who is ultimately elected to office. There is a stark difference between column one (candidates) and column two (elected national positions). In only one of the five years (2017) is there a case of a nationally elected individual with a known collaborator background. To rephrase, there are collaborators/operatives who put themselves forward for elected positions (column one), showing that this group has not aged out or self-selected out of consideration for public office. But there are almost no former collaborators/operatives (column two) who are actually elected at the national level, suggesting that this information might affect citizen voting. At the local level the numbers tell a slightly different story. There are significantly more individuals with collaborator backgrounds at the local level (column three) than at the national level (column two), although the number of operatives in locally elected positions remains low and the number of collaborators relatively constant.

What do these findings suggest? One must be cautious attributing too much of a causal impact on public disclosures as a means of keeping former collaborators from public office, as there are clearly collaborators and operatives vying for elected office (column one) and in elected positions of power at the local level (column three). Table 1 also includes information on political appointees with known collaboration/operative backgrounds: in 2017 the Cabinet Chief in the Chamber of Deputies was revealed to have a collaborator background, and in 2013 the previous operative status of both the Chief of Services of the Chamber of Deputies and a Judge in the Supreme Court was disclosed. These are politically important and influential positions of power, and the fact that they are occupied by tainted individuals suggests that the mere revelation of previous regime complicity does not necessarily force their removal. Nonetheless, the very limited number of individuals in elected positions of power at the national level compared to candidates for positions suggests that public disclosures affect, but do not determine, the composition of current public office holders. Taken together these findings illustrate the continued utility of public disclosures as a form of forward-looking transitional justice.

Table 2: Screening of Appointed Positions: Affirmative Cases 2015–2017

Public Office Holders	Civil Society Positions
Magistrates, Members of Judiciary	Director, Public Heath (regional level)
Secretary State in the Ministry of Defense	Decan, Orthodox Theological Faculty
Military Prosecutor's Office	President, Free Trade Union of Educators
	Chief Director, Regional Public Finance (various regions)
Minister of Transport	National Agency Land Improvement
Local Council Members (regional, various)	Museum Director (regional level)
Ambassadors	Head of Journal (weekly)
	Radio Journalism
	Founding Member, National Association of Detectives
	Pastor, His Assembly of God (stationed in USA)
	Director, Center for Financial Training—Millennium
	Union, Member of Committee of Drivers
	President, Association of Property Owners (regional)
	President, Association of Former Political Prisoners of Romania (regional offices)
	VP, Authority of Fiscal Surveillance (regional)

Data compiled by author from the C.N.S.A.S. annual activity reports, various years.

Appointed Positions: Office Holders and Civil Society Positions

Public disclosures are not confined to elected public officials; the C.N.S.A.S. is legally required to vet individuals holding certain appointed positions in public and semi-public institutions and associations.[63] Over time personnel in these institutions have been screened, therefore the focus is on new personnel. However, vetting does apply to all persons from this legally prescribed list of positions and institutions. This is consistent with the post-communist lustration of an array of positions in universities, schools, churches, unions, banks, and other broadly defined organizations and institutions of public trust.[64]

---

63 Personal interview with Adrian Cioflâncă, C.N.S.A.S. Collegium member, Bucharest, 17 October 2012; Personal communication with Florin Abraham, 2 July 2018. The C.N.S.A.S. website lists agencies subject to vetting and documents requests by employers. See the three foundational laws for details on the scope of vetting.

64 Stan, *Transitional Justice in Eastern Europe and the Former Soviet Union*; David, *Lustration and Transitional Justice*.

Table 2 presents an array of recent (2015–2017) affirmative collaboration determinations of individuals in appointed positions at the national and local levels. Positions within the judiciary, such as magistrates, members of national and local courts and prosecutors, individuals with oversight over finances, including regional public finance positions and financial organizations, and directors in public health institutions have been verified as former collaborators or operatives. Within academia, professors, rectors, and presidents have been disclosed. Print journalists as well as radio broadcast positions have also appeared in the list of recently disclosed positions. Union leaders, museum directors, land management officials, and even pastors are also screened and revealed as collaborators. Table 2 is confined to disclosures between 2015 and 2017, suggesting that demographically speaking we have not yet seen an aging out of former collaborators and operatives in broadly understood positions of public trust.

This article engages the temporal question, is there anyone left to publicly disclose? The 2015–2017 determinations illustrate positive collaboration findings across political candidates, elected officials, and appointed positions. There remain individuals at all ranks of government and authority to screen, and the process affects the selection of final elected officials at the national level. However, at some point there will be fewer and fewer individuals to disclose. This naturally prompts questions about the benefits of engaging in such reviews given the operational costs associated with vetting thousands of political candidates and appointees as compared to the returns to society. There are hints in the data that the process is reaching the end of its temporal parameters.

Gauging Citizen Fatigue

Post-communist public disclosures not only reveal the background of high-ranking political figures but include more personal revelations about the complicity of friends, colleagues, and loved-ones. These personal revelations are emotional, politically sensitive, and potentially socially divisive.[65] Have Romanian citizens grown tired of the secret police files and the years of public disclosures? As time passes, one might assume a natural waning of interest in file access and public disclosures as revelations become less socially shocking and politically

---

65 Cynthia M. Horne, "Lustration, Transitional Justice, and Social Trust in Post-Communist Countries. Repairing and Wresting the Ties that Bind?," *Europe-Asia Studies*, 66, no. 2 (2014): 225–54.

salient. What do the trends show regarding citizen interest in the secret police files?

Figure 4 compares two measures of citizen engagement with the files: the number of viewing sessions at the C.N.S.A.S. reading room and the number of people who first exercised the right to review their own file in a given year. Both measures reflect individual engagement with personal files (their own files or files of relatives for which they have access). These numbers do not include individuals who would like to review the files of public officials, nor do they include researchers with a scholarly interest in the files. There are space limitations in the viewing rooms, restricting the number of individuals who can be accommodated, and therefore the numbers do not reflect the total demand.[66] As such, they are proxies for citizen interest in the files on a personal level.

Figure 4:   **Citizen Direct Engagement with Files**

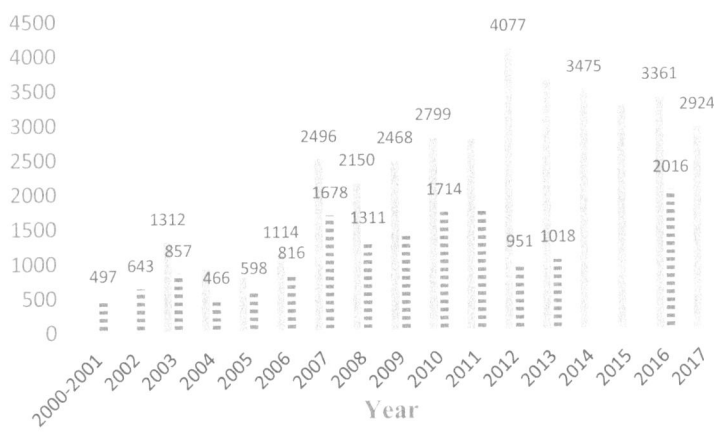

Number of viewing sessions (visitors to reading room--access own files)

— Number of new people to first exericse right access their own files

Source: Author compiled from C.N.S.A.S. Annual Activity Reports, 2002-2017, www.C.N.S.A.S..ro

---

66 Data was not available in the annual reports on the number of people who were turned away due to space limitations. Since 2014, on-line visitors and on-line data access have reduced the need for in-personal physical review of some files, thereby taking up some of the excess demand. On-line file access is another proxy for citizen interest.

Figure 4 shows that the number of file viewing sessions remained quite high in 2017. While the number of viewing sessions peaked in 2012 at 4,077, the 2017 figure still puts the number of viewing sessions at nearly 3,000, which remains very high in comparison to other periods. The number of individuals who first exercised the right to access their own file in a given year was higher in 2016 than in any of the previous years. Data suggests that citizen interest in the files remains strong and appears to be higher than it was when files first became available in the early 2000s. In short, the data do not show citizen fatigue with the files.

Figure 5:   Copies Provided of Pages in the Secret Police Files

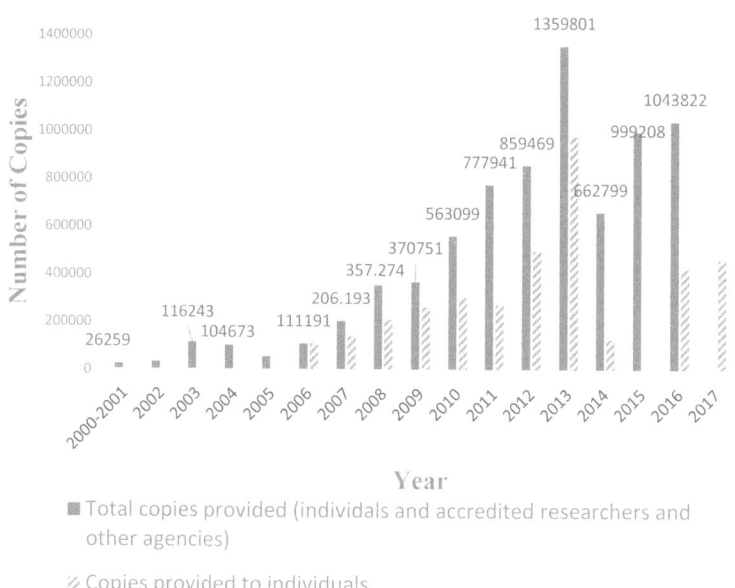

Source: Author compiled from C.N.S.A.S. Annual Activity Reports, 2002-2017, www.C.N.S.A.S..ro

Figure 5 also speaks to the level of interest in the files. It shows both the number of copies the C.N.S.A.S. provided to individuals related to their personal files and the total number of copies provided to both individuals and researchers in a given year. One should interpret absolute numbers with caution, due to the C.N.S.A.S.'s resource and capacity limitations to meet all file requests.[67] However, Figure 5 shows that the total number of copies provided to individuals and researchers increased for more than a decade, topping off at 1.3 million copies in 2013. Fewer copies were requested after 2013, perhaps due to the fact that individuals had more expansive on-line access and therefore did not need to rely solely on printed copies any longer. Even given the post-2013 expanded web access, in 2016 and 2017 nearly a half a million copies were provided to individuals reviewing their files each year, suggesting that both citizen and scholarly interest in the files remain robust.

There has also been an expansion in on-line file access and web views. In 2013 the number of recorded on-line visitors was 37,844, increasing to 80,522 in 2015, and 71,880 in 2016. The number of on-line visitors declined in 2017 to 56,896 but it was accompanied by a significant increase in web hits for the C.N.S.A.S. to more than 300,000. As such, there appears to be continued engagement with the files by citizens and researchers both in person and on-line. The number of first-time users is unexpectedly robust and individuals remain engaged with personal files.

Individuals may also submit requests for information about the identity of informants or agents found in their personal files. If information exists (as many files were destroyed), the C.N.S.A.S. formally notifies petitioners in writing about the identity of said informers or collaborators.[68] Figure 6 presents figures on this proxy measure of citizen engagement with the files, documenting the number of informers disclosed per year directly to individual petitioners. Note that this is not the total number of inquiries received by the C.N.S.A.S. but only the fraction of total inquiries for which there was information to report. As Figure 6 shows, the number of such disclosures has continued to increase with time, reflecting both the institutional capacity of the C.N.S.A.S. to process more files and sustained citizen interest in the files.

---

67 Consiliul Național Pentru Studierea Arhivelor Securității, *2015 Raport de activitate privind anul* (Bucharest: C.N.S.A.S, 2015), available at: http://www.cnsas.ro/rapoarte.html, accessed on 27 August 2018; and C.N.S.A.S., *2017 Raport de activitate privind anul*.
68 The C.N.S.A.S. repeatedly emphasizes that notifications to individuals about regime complicity in their files is not equivalent to a formal collaborator designation because it has not completed all legal steps and due process components. C.N.S.A.S., *2016 Raport de activitate privind anul*.

Figure 6: Individuals whose past regime involvement officially disclosed to petitioners

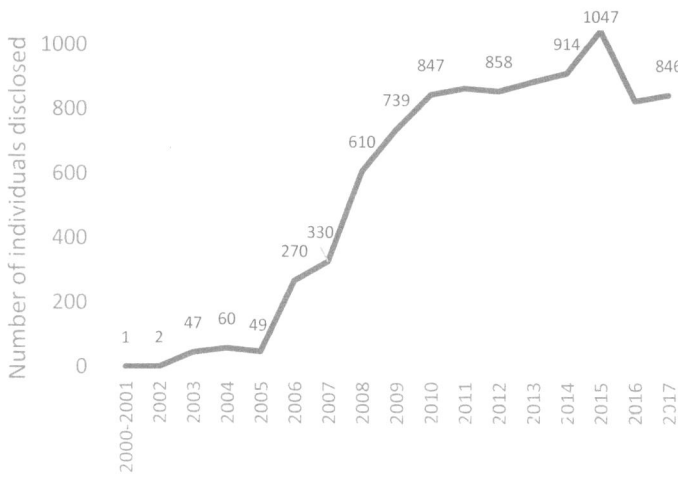

Source: Author compiled from C.N.S.A.S. Annual Activity Reports, 2002-2017, www.C.N.S.A.S..ro

The number of such affirmative disclosures peaked in 2015, a time quite late in Romania's transition. While the number of disclosures decreased in 2016 and 2017, both years remain very high and consistent with the number of operatives disclosed in 2010–2017. In sum, nearly thirty years into the transition, the three different proxy measures of citizen engagement with the files illustrate continued high levels of citizen interest.

Conclusion

What is too long and when is too late for public disclosures as transitional justice measures? This article empirically explored some of the assumptions regarding the late transition use of public disclosure measures as personnel reforms. In particular, it examined the contention that public disclosures are not useful or even appropriate so long after a regime change because there is no one left to publicly disclose, at least no one of real importance. Related to this, predicted citizen fatigue with the process after so many years of on-going revelations might undermine its potential political saliency. The evidence presented here does not support the contention that public disclosures have a built-in expiration date as personnel reforms. To the contrary, the findings suggest a need to think more flexibly about our temporal assumptions with respect to this transitional justice method.

First, the C.N.S.A.S. vetting process has continued to publicly disclose candidates running for public office, including individuals vying for seats in the Senate and the Chamber of Deputies, electoral candidates for mayoral positions, and appointed positions in the judiciary and law enforcement. While the number of public disclosures has declined over time, hinting at the declining utility of this process in the future, they have not reached such a low threshold as to appear trivial as of 2018. Second, public disclosures continue to reveal former collaborators and operatives in high-ranking positions of public and social trust across the financial services, union leadership, media and public broadcasting, and universities. These types of semi-public and social institutions are often described as critical foundations for a robust civil society. To the extent that public disclosures bring transparency, accountability, and potential personnel turnover to these institutions of social and political trust, there remain possible benefits for a relatively low trust society like Romania.[69] In short, former collaborators and operatives have not selected out or aged out of the political process in Romania just yet.

Third, while this article could not evaluate the impact of the threat of public disclosures on potential office holders, there was preliminary evidence that former collaborators put themselves forward as political *candidates* but few obtained *elected national* positions. Thus, the revelations resonate with political parties and voters and continue to be politically relevant indicators of integrity. Fourth, while there was preliminary evidence that Romania might be reaching its outer limits on the utility of public disclosures as seen in a marked decrease in the number of finalized, irrevocable court decisions (Figure 3), Romania has not reached this temporal limit just yet. Taken together the five proxy measures (Tables 1 and 2, Figures 1, 2, and 3) show a significant number of public disclosures of office holders and political candidates, illustrating that former collaborators and informants remain politically active decades after the transition. The fact that the revelations are of high-ranking elected positions and appointed positions in the government and public service today points to the current political salience of the measures, refuting contentions that only small fry are still being outed.

---

69 Horne, *Building Trust and Democracy* and Horne, "Lustration, Transitional Justice, and Social Trust."

Fifth, the paper looked for evidence of expected citizen fatigue with the secret police files, which might signal a loss of utility or political saliency to the public disclosure process. This article presented five separate measures of citizen engagement to triangulate these questions. All of the measures demonstrated continued high levels of citizen engagement with the files as of 2018. Citizen interest in their own files and in public disclosures remained on par with pubic interest measures from a decade prior, refuting a citizen fatigue hypothesis. To the extent that citizen interest speaks to the legitimacy of the process, we have evidence that the measures continue to resonate as forms of accountability.

It is not clear what continues to drive Romanians' personal engagement with the files, although a similar interest with the files is evident in other neighboring countries as well. For example, Bulgarians' engagement with their personal files remains high as of 2018. Moreover, a public opinion poll in 2017 showed that 61.4 percent of Bulgarians thought elected office holders and candidates should continue to be screened with the secret police files.[70] While this interest in the files might be partially explained by the incomplete nature of the transition in Bulgaria and Romania, the 2019 file revelations in Latvia of the contents of the 'Cheka bags' similarly point to the political salience of the use of the files as both personnel reform and accountability measures.[71] As such, why post-communist citizens remain personally and politically interested in the content of the files and for how long remain questions open for further scholarly inquiry.

What does the case of Romania tell us about the temporal parameters of these types of public disclosures and file access measures? First, the Council of Europe originally suggested a ten-year time period for lustration and the ECtHR echoed a need to end vetting once the transition was secured, but even thirty years is insufficient time for the former cadre to opt out of or age out of the political process. Lustration/public disclosures might need to take place over a much longer period than originally imagined. This suggests a need to rethink these durable *a priori* assumptions about the duration of personnel reform measures, since they were formed before we had such an empirically rich understanding about their use and limitations in practice.

---

70 National Center for the Study of Public Opinion, Social Barometer Bulgaria, *Public Opinion on the work of the Dossier Commission*, no date, available at: https://www.comdos.bg/Социологически_барометър, accessed on 9 February 2019.
71 Andrew Higgins, "4,141 Latvians were just outed as K.G.B. informants," *The New York Times*, 18 January 2019.

Second, incomplete files, destroyed files, and problems with file transfers all hampered Romania's public disclosure and file access measures early in the transition, a problem other post-communist countries had as well. Over time the C.N.S.A.S. improved its management of the files, and ability to extract information from partial files. Building on the knowledge from the other European Network file repository agencies, the C.N.S.A.S. developed file cross-checking techniques, which have permitted determinations that might have previously been impossible due to incomplete information. For example, in 2016 the C.N.S.A.S. extracted relevant information on 130 people without files by combing and cross-checking information from 93,565 related dossiers.[72] The C.N.S.A.S. has gotten better at managing information and rendering judgments, and citizen interest in the files has remained high, challenging assumptions that later measures are necessarily less politically salient or legitimate than earlier measures. This is a lesson that might be applied to other post-conflict or post-authoritarian justice programs, as many lack the capacity or resources to manage personnel reform information in the immediate transition period.

Third, the more temporally contentious components of the C.N.S.A.S.'s mandate involve forward-looking justice elements, namely how its revelations from the secret police files might shape future office holders and political candidates. The past affects perceptions of current integrity and capabilities for employment, potentially resulting in self-vetting, institutional removal, or public shaming to catalyze removal. Looking to the future, using information in the secret police files as a proxy for integrity will become anachronistic, even if the vetting or public disclosures do not. It bears consideration to ask *when* (not if) new integrity criteria are required, transforming this transitional justice method into a prospective form of employment vetting and merging the past with the future. Whether C.N.S.A.S. is equipped or appropriate to play such a prospective role is questionable given its firm placement as a repository of the past.

---

72 C.N.S.A.S., *2016 Raport de activitate privind anul*; and C.N.S.A.S., *2017 Raport de activitate privind anul*.

Searching for a Future: Mass Media and the Uncertain Construction of Democracy in Romania

Brindusa Armanca and Peter Gross

Abstract: *To date, Romania's democracy and the news media's professionalization have not met indigenous and foreign expectations, as both have failed to assume their social responsibility. The persistent crisis in ethics, enveloped in the illiberal culture and political culture, is victimizing democratization and the media's independence and professionalization and, thus, their ability to serve the still ongoing democratic transformation. This article chronicles the crisis, its causes and outcomes. Finally, it concludes that the country's emerging civil society, coupled with the small groups of independent, professionalizing media and journalists are the key to the country's liberal democratic future.*

Christophe Deloire, the head of Reporters Without Borders, considers Walter Lippmann's nearly century-old assessment that the "crisis of Western democracy is a crisis of journalism" to be a valid explanation for the critical point at which the world's democracies find themselves today.[1] Deloire's statement appears to address a liberal democracy that, with all of its permutations, embraces the common notions of free and fair elections, protection of human rights, and respect for the rule of law.[2] Yet, the nature of full democracies versus semi-democracies and hybrid ones is different and, therefore, the media systems and the journalism practices are expressions of those differences, as well as of the (general and professional) culture established in each nation.[3] Theoretically, media in liberal democracies are to be independent of all other societal institutions so that they can, and should be, objective and unbiased in their reporting

---

1   Christophe Deloire, "The Crisis of Western Democracy Is a Crisis of Journalism," in openDemocracy (25 January 2018), available at: https://www.opendemocracy.net/can-europe-make-it/christophe-deloire/crisis-of-western-democracy-is-crisis-of-journalism, accessed on 5 December 2018.
2   Arend Lijphart, *Patterns of Democracy: Government Forms and Performance in Thirty-Six Countries* (New Haven: Yale University Press, 2012); Larry Diamond and Leonardo Morlino, "The Quality of Democracy," in *In Search of Democracy*, ed. by Larry Diamond (London: Routledge, 2016), 32–45.
3   For example, Marieke de Mooij, *Human and Mediated Communication around the World* (New York: Springer, 2014).

of news and information.[4] The practices of the media and their journalism in the varied types of liberal democracies and semi-democracies do not always meet theoretical expectations, not only because of the nature of the democracies they reflect but also because of choices individual media outlets and journalists make.

While we agree that there is a significant interdependence between an independent, professional news media and liberal democracy, we posit that (1) the illiberal calamity faced by the budding democracies of Central and Eastern Europe and their news media is assignable to severe deficiencies in professional and general ethics and in the culture that cradles them, and (2) by itself the media are unable to sustain or affect major changes in the political system and its ethics.[5]

Using secondary sources, the analyses of the 28-year-old promotion of democracy and the evolution of news media in Romania, and particularly the developments in 2017–2018, offers corroboration of our hypothesis. We briefly examine the nature of Romanian democracy, its political system and culture, and then delve into the characteristics of the media system and the practices of journalism in that country. We explain how the relationship between the media and democracy functions in the midst of a still ongoing transformation, which continues to be affected by socio-political, economic and cultural crises. This allows us to clarify the role and influence of the media, and explain the interdependencies between culture, political culture and the evolution of the media. It permits us to shed light on the media system's initial tentative growth and then decline, as well as the serpentine and often unpredictable route that this transformation takes, reflecting both cultural conformity and the related ethical challenges of society.

The Democracy Project, the Political System, and Culture

The evolution of Romania's political system did not proceed along Western hopes or indigenous expectations. Democracy was at best a murky concept for Romanians given the absence of understanding, or a misunderstanding, of the accompanying liberal values and attitudes upon which

---

4   James Carey, "Mass Media and Democracy between the Modern and the Postmodern," *Journal of International Affairs*, 47 (Summer 1993): 1–21.
5   For example, Lanka Bustikova and Petra Guasti, "The Illiberal Turn or Swerve in Central Europe?," *Politics and Governance*, 5:4 (2017): 166–76. By ethics we mean the set of principled rules according to which individuals and groups are to behave, conduct public and private activities, and practice professional activities.

the system must be based to make it compatible with its Western counterparts. This should not be a surprise in a country that only experienced an incipient and short-lived democratic experiment in the 1920s.[6]

The architecture of the new democratic system was designed by former communist officials, handicapped by their un-democratic tendencies and mentalities and bolstered for nearly half a century by the quasi-criminal, unethical Marxist-Leninist state and government, and all their institutions. By the mid-1990s, these custodians of the democracy-building process morphed into, and were partnered with, newly minted business-media oligarchs massively ambitious for economic gain that they considered achievable only by pursuing direct or indirect control of the political system. Thus, the politician-businessmen and politician-media owners arose as dominant players, exploiting both the political and the media systems of their own making for their own purposes. To their dismay, by 2017 more aggressively and before that more cautiously, they were increasingly challenged by a growing and maturing civil society.[7]

Romania is a semi-presidential republic with a bi-cameral parliament. It has been alternately labeled "semi-democratic?" or "semi-consolidated," "partly free," "illiberal," or a "hybrid" democracy.[8] To bring a modicum of precision to characterizing the country's democracy, and thus the context of our examination of the news media, we define it as a competitive authoritarian system. Such a system is distinguished from the other hybrid types by its employment of democratic institutions to exercise political authority and is a "post-Cold War phenomenon," despite its existence during the interwar period in some of the region's countries, including Romania.[9] This political authority does not constitute full-blown authoritarianism but a milder, "diminished" kind[10] that "affects the behavior and expectations of political actors."[11]

---

6   Keith Hitchins, *A Concise History of Romania* (New York: Cambridge University Press, 2014).
7   Romania's elites and the system they have created have also been continually challenged—with little success—by the European Union whose ranks they joined in 2007. Romania's civil society began flexing its growing muscles by January 2017. See Peter Gross, "The New 'Normal:' Romania's New Political Crisis," *Social Europe* (10 January 2017), available at: https://www.socialeurope.eu/new-normal-romanias-latest-political-crisis-within-continuum-corruption, accessed on 5 December 2018.
8   Steven Levitsky and Lucan A. Way, *Competitive Authoritarianism: Hybrid Regimes after the Cold War* (New York: Cambridge University Press, 2010). Romania does not fit the hybrid types of constitutional oligarchies or exclusive republics, tutelary regimes, restricted or semi-competitive democracies.
9   Levitsky and Way, *Competitive Authoritarianism*, 15–7, and footnote 87.
10 Juan J. Linz, *Totalitarian and Authoritarian Regimes* (Boulder, Colo.: Lynne Rienner, 2000), 34.
11 Levitsky and Way, *Competitive Authoritarianism*, 16.

We posit that these effects are mutually shared by politicians, businessmen, media owners and leading journalistic figures; furthermore, that behaviors, expectations, and practices are derivatives of culture, i.e. values, beliefs, orientations, attitudes, and life's underlying assumption, shared also by the majority of members of a society. This culture is fashioned by the "vagaries of history that are passed on from generation to generation" and creates the environment for the type of democracy Romania has today.[12]

Romania's pre-communist period had its own ethical challenges affecting an uncertain, temporary experimental democracy in the 1920s, as already mentioned, partly because of the young state's struggles to define its national and cultural identity after gaining independence from the Ottoman Empire in 1877.[13] From that point on until the communists imprisoned the country in 1947, Romania's democratic experiment sputtered on without a significant record of amelioration in its culture, until its brief spasm of fascism that plunged it into the depth of immorality.[14] The communist regime that lasted until 1989 added to the cultural shortcomings of both leaders and ordinary citizens. It should be no surprise that after a mere 28 years of democratization, Romania remains one of the most corrupt countries in Europe.[15] Measured against the corruption in former communist countries (not including the Caucasus and Central Asian), Romania ranks in the upper half on Transparency International's Corruption Index.[16]

---

12   Lawrence E. Harrison, *The Central Liberal Truth. How Politics Can Change a Culture and Save It from Itself* (Oxford, England: Oxford University Press, 2016), 6.
13   Hitchins, *A Concise History of Romania*.
14   The specifics of Romanian culture have been noted by authors like Mircea Eliade, Constantin Noica, Ion Luca Caragiale, and Emil Cioran, among many others. See also Adrian Marino, *Politică și cultură: pentru o nouă cultură romănă* (Iasi: Polirom, 1996); Adrian Marino, *Revenirea în Europa* (Cluj-Napoca: Aius, 1996); Adrian Marino, *Pentru Europa: Integrarea României. Aspecte ideologice și culturale* (Iasi: Polirom, 1995); Lucian Boia, *De ce este Romănia altfel?* (Bucharest: Humanitas, 2012); and Lucian Boia, *Capcanele Istoriei. Elita intelectuală romăneanscă între 1930 si 1950* (Bucharest: Humanitas, 2011).
15   Michael Peel, "Romania Corruption Battle Exposes the Limits of EU's Influence," *The Financial Times* (22 February 2018), available at: https://www.ft.com/content/bc9c43dc-1703-11e8-9376-4a6390addb44, accessed on 26 February 2018; and Palko Karasz, "In Romania, Corruption's Tentacles Grip Daily Life," *New York Times* (8 February 2017), available at: https://www.nytimes.com/2017/02/09/world/europe/romania-corruption-coruptie-guvern-justitie.html, accessed on 3 August 2017.
16   Transparency International, "Corruption Index 2017," 2017, available at: https://tradingeconomics.com/country-list/corruption-index?continent=europe, accessed on 3 November 2018.

Found in every walk of life and at every strata of society, corruption is related in a significant measure to the absence of a sense of social responsibility, and exercised in a myriad of ways, including the reliance on *pile-cunoștințe-relații* in everyday life that is linked to the "typical Romanian characteristics" of "injecting the personal in values."[17] Parochial, authoritarian, and hierarchical inclinations remain core values, attitudes, behaviors and practices, particularly of the elites.[18] Whether this culture is or is not shared by other corrupt nations in Central and Eastern Europe is a matter of debate and left for other studies to determine.

An example of how these Romanian cultural values combine in public life and define the ways of the socio-economic and political elites is represented by the attempts of the ruling Social Democratic Party (PSD)—Alliance of Liberals and Democrats (ALDE) since taking power in January 2017 to change criminal laws for personal reasons, in addition to attacking the National Anti-Corruption Directorate (Directia Nationala Anticoruptie, DNA), partly by trying to dismiss its very effective head, Laura Codruta Kovesi, in order to render it harmless. Changes in the General Prosecutor's Office and threats made by politicians against Lucian Lazar, the prosecutor general, round out what many see as the PSD-ALDE coalition's only coherent, yet higly negative, "policies."[19] The primary goals of the political elites' consistently venomous attacks on all individuals, groups and institutions that oppose or criticize them is to diminish their independence. The few professional media and journalists that accurately cover the misdeeds of these elite members are their primary and permanent targets. Citizens have lost confidence in the state, in its institutions; in 2018, 79 percent distrusted parliament and 85 percent distrusted political parties.[20]

Throughout 2017 and up to the time of this writing, parliamentary activities were subordinated to the corrupt interests of senior political

---

17 Adrian Marino, *Al treilu discurs. Cultură, ideologie și politica in Romania. Adrian Marino în dialog cu Sorin Antohi* (Iasi: Polirom, 2001), 111. *Pile*—a file—is a metaphor for smoothing the way for yourself, relatives and friends; *cunostinte* are acquaintances and *relații* are connections.
18 Lucian Boia, *History and Myth in Romanian Consciousness* (Budapest: Central European University Press, 2001), 238.
19 The DNA's relative success brought about the ire of the ruling PSD-ALDE, in control of the government at the time of this writing. See Mihai Mares, "Bribery and Corruption 2019: Romania," Global Legal Insights, 2018, available at: https://www.globallegalinsights.com/practice-areas/bribery-and-corruption-laws-and-regulations/romania, accessed on 5 December 2018.
20 Ana Adi, "Protester Profiles," in *#REZIST. Romania's Anticorruption Protests: Causes, Development and Implications*, ed. By Ana Adi and D. G. Lilleker (Berlin: Bournemouth University and Quadriga University of Applied Sciences, 2017), 165.

leaders, some under investigation or indictment, and others already convicted felons, like the leader of the PSD and President of the Chamber of Deputies, Liviu Dragnea, and the Senate Speaker, Calin Popescu Tariceanu. Adding ethical breaches to their substantial illegalities, they abused their powers to set up special committees tasked with amending the penal code to enable their exoneration and the full enjoyment of the privileges and fortunes they nefariouslly accumulated.[21]

The PSD-ALDE government resuscitated a type of "neo-bolshevism" exemplified by contempt for state institutions and the law; by authoritarian reactions to any forms of criticism of the notion that the party is always right; and by their obsession with "permanent revolution" and manipulative efforts to confuse citizens and incriminate the "class enemy."[22] Dragnea, who as a convicted felon cannot become prime minister and therefore manipulates the government in not too subtle ways, is the target of particularly negative judgements. As Andrei Cornea emphatically insists, Dragnea

> longs to lead the whole country, like Ceausescu, forever and forever. He would like to have no Constitution to respect, not to care for justice, human rights, or international engagements, if it is not convenient to him. He does not want to have any more troubles with [challenges to] corruption and with the enrichment of the party's nomenclature. Perhaps he dreams of ... putting a muzzle on the hostile press.[23]

The politicization of governmental and state institutions and of all points of influence over society intensified after 2000 by which time the political class had secured its power by employing the laws and the privileges it acquired since 1990, extending its influence throughout the country. Nepotism and political clientelism eliminated competence and expertise as standards for employment and advancement. As the Romanian Institute for Evaluation and Strategy's (IRES) poll shows, 70 percent of those interviewed say success has little do do with merit, and promotions are perceived as a consequence of luck or relationships that lack integrity, e.g. corruption and clientelism.[24]

---

21 "Parlament/Comisia specială pe legile justiției a aprobat modificările la Codul de procedură civilă," Agerpres (19 May 2018), available at: https://www.agerpres.ro/politica/2018/05/23/parlament-comisia-speciala-pe-legile-justitiei-a-aprobat-modificarile-la-codul-de-procedura-civila--114472, accessed on 15 November 2018.
22 Andrei Cornea, "Neobolșevism pe picioare de lut," Revista 22 (13 February 2018), available at: https://revista22.ro/70269481/neobolsevism-pe-picioare-de-lut.html, accessed on 14 February 2018.
23 Ibid.
24 Ibid, 167.

The ramifications for liberalization or the enlightenment of a culture and political culture that cumulatively embrace the most negative of characteristics from the pre-communist and communist periods, and add new versions in the contemporary environment, are best summarized as follows:

> The moral and ethical impoverishment wrought by the tolerance of corruption in a nation can run its length and breath. People become inured to transgressions as seemingly insignificant as cheating on an exam …, using family connections to circumvent the normal hiring process, buying one's way out of a speeding ticket. The next thing you know the betrayal of the public trust and theft of society's resources can leave the nation quite literally, bankrupt. [25]

In fact, Romania declined from its 6.64 score in 2016 to 6.44 in 2017 in the Democracy Index, the lowest score since indexing began in 2006. As such, the country is ranked among "flawed" democracies. [26] The decline reflects the ruling coalition's continuing machinations "to weaken the independence and effectiveness of the judiciary and to block the efforts of some bodies to tackle corruption," the report said. Other assessments also place Romania among the "semi-consolidated" democracies.[27] The elites are not the only authors of this denouement. A study of perceptions of integrity in Romania suggests a societal atmosphere that tolerates corruption and dishonesty, seeing them as organic to everyday life, and to which ordinary citizens contribute. For example, 86.9 percent of a survey's respondents believe that an "honest person is a loser"; 84.19 percent believe that one "cannot be impartial today"; 90.69 percent admit to making "small [ethical] compromises"; 87.05 percent "admire the winners in all circumstances"; and 82.07 percent believe that "rules are for stupid people."[28]

The cultural legacies of the communist regime are difficult to eradicate and are exemplified in the behaviors of the majority of Romanians, including chronic opportunism, which delayed the genesis of an active,

---

25 James A. Mitchell, "Corruption, the Electoral Process, and the Politics of Transition in Romania," *Romanian Journal of Society and Politics* (16 December 2010), available at: http://rjsp.eu/corruption-electoral-process-politics-transition-romania.html, accessed on 3 November 2011.
26 The Economist Intelligence Unit, *Democracy Index 2017: Free Speech Under Attack*, 2018, available at: www.eiu.com/democracy2017, accessed on 4 March 2018.
27 Freedom House, *Nations in Transit 2017*, 2017, available at: https://freedomhouse.org/report/nations-transit/nations-transit-2017, accessed on 31 January 2018.
28 *Study on the Culture of Honesty & Integrity in Romania, 2010–2014*, available at: https://d25d2506sfb94s.cloudfront.net/cumulus_uploads/docment/rkjk42ib1o/YG-Archive-Eurotrack-May-results-290513-honesty.pdf, accessed on 5 December 2018.

democracy-oriented citizenry. However, by 2016–2017, Romania, "always surprising" as the slogan of a tourist campaign extols the country, has finally found its voice against the current offensively illiberal, antidemocratic government. Civil society, spearheaded by the growing middle class, launched continuous street demonstrations beginning in January 2017 against an abusive Emergency Ordinance, attempts to undo the anti-corruption battle, and other specific and general proposals, policies and behaviors of the PSD-ALDE government and parliament. The #Rezist movement is the expression of the dissatisfaction with the corrupt and incompetent political classes and the campaign to remove any and all liberal democratic values from public life.[29]

The individuals who nurture this kind of civic consciousness are described by the Germany-based researcher Ana Adi as "Romanian in spirit, heritage or nationality, generally tech-savvy, with a global focus and understanding, with a checkered record of civic engagement but so enraged and disappointed by the current state of affairs in Romanian politics that they are determined to get involved and do more."[30] Active today in defending European justice and values, the resistance movement has been met with an unprecedented strategy of deceit and manipulation by a ruling political class whose ability to influence and divide society is highly honed. As in other countries in Central and Eastern Europe, imaginary enemies have been invented to distract and deflect attention from the political elites' misbehaviors, supposed authors of anti-Romanianism like the "parallel state," the ubiquitous mischief-maker George Soros, "binom," foreign embassies, or multinationals.[31] The parliament and government-driven anti-rezistance? campaign have strong media allies who are funded with public money—a process that is wholly opaque—and by powerful businessmen. As a generalization, Romania's media are both witting and unintentional products of and contributors to the extant culture, political culture, and partner to the political class's ambitions.

---

29 The resistance's profile appears in an IRES survey. Young people and adults below 50 years of age, with average (30%) and high (40%) education levels, urban dwellers, working mainly in the private sector (76%), or students (11%). See Vasile Dancu, "Protestez, deci exist," *Sinteza Magazine*, 38 (March–April 2017), 11–18, available at: http://revistasinteza.ro/protestez-deci-exist/, accessed on 5 December 2018.
30 Adi,"Protester Profiles."
31 "Binom" (in Romanian), taken from algebra (the sum of two terms), is the nickname to the DNA/Kovesi team by its political enemies.

The Media and Their Post-1989 Era

The system

When the communist regime ended in December 1989, Romania's media system underwent an almost instant transformation. Print media were quickly taken over by individuals and groups, and new newspapers appeared; radio followed suit; and state television became, unofficially, a public service outlet. Journalism was practiced by some old and mostly new, self-appointed journalists; neither group knew how to do journalism akin to how it was done in the West.[32]

A handful of the leaders of the communist newspapers that quickly re-branded themselves after 1989 used the opportunity offered by "privatization" to take over the left-over media infrastructure of the Romanian Communist Party, and profited the most from the change in political systems. The take-over affected headquarters, printing houses, paper stocks, and so on. As the 1990s progressed, they sold shares in their new media business, joining the club of those whom transition enriched beyond their wildest dreams. Among them were leaders of the Communist Party daily, *Scânteia/The Spark* (today called *Adevărul/Truth*), and at the local level, *Drapelul Roșu/Red Flag* (now *Renașterea bănățeană/Banat Renaissance*) in Timișoara.

This almost instantly established commercial press functioned side by side with a plethora of party newspapers that appeared in the first four months of 1990, this time representing an aray of political parties, and lasting only till the middle of the decade. Quite aside from the short-lived party press, political control over the media quickly manifested itself in 1990 when media owners began collaborating with political parties and politicians. Then politicians themselves entered the media business, acquiring national and local/regional media companies. A hyper kind of political parallelism firmly established itself and continues to this day, with the notable exceptions of a handful of Internet-based and traditional media outlets and individual journalists.[33] It [This political parallelism?] was finally diluted by the economic troubles the country and the media expe-

---

32 Peter Gross, *Mass Media in Revolution and National Development: The Romanian Laboratory* (Ames, IA: Iowa State University Press, 1996).
33 Ioana Coman and Peter Gross, "Uncommonly Common or Truly Exceptional? An Alternative to the Political System-Based Explanation of the Romanian Mass Media," *International Journal of Press/Politics*, 17:4 (October 2012): 457–79.

rienced starting in 2008–2009, which caused both the number of newspapers and their readership to decline.[34] The bulk of the press's political, entertainment, and sensationalist content became quasi-non-political, even more sensationalist and entertainment-oriented as economic opportunism grew among the journalists and editors who were not among the approximately 7,000 editorial workers who lost their jobs.

The establishment of the DNA in 1992 and the first broadcast law, followed by its new iteration in 1994, brought the first commercial television stations in 1993 (Canal 31, and Mediapro, which became ProTV) and 1994 (Tele7abc). In 1992, state television officially became a public service institution. Co-optated by the ruling parties in successive governments is a firmament of its character, the state television remains a controversial disseminator of news and information given its dependence on the government.[35]

The number of licenses registered with the National Audiovisual Council shows that in 2017 there were over 450 active television licenses and over 600 radio licenses.[36] In 2017, television claimed over 65 percent of the 400 million Euro market; the rest was divided among radio, online, the Out of Home Advertising, and the declining number of print media.[37] Given this imbalance, it is no wonder that some media outlets have already closed. Those that continue to operate despite the insufficiency of income confirm that many TV channels are not self-financing, but are funded by other businesses for purposes other than pure news and information, including the preponderant political one. In 2016–2017, the majority of news media ran deficits; the highest newspaper circulation was 33,000 copies per day in a nation of 18 million citizens. Five television news channels competed "for slightly over 500,000 viewers, a small advertising market. The share of online advertising is also insignificant, too."[38]

---

34 "BRAT: Tirajele ziarelor continua să scada; Doar trei publicatii au avut cresteri in T3 din 2014," *Wall Street (Romania)* (3 December 2014), available at: https://www.wall-street.ro/articol/Marketing-PR/188270/top-ziare-vanzarile-si-tirajele-au-scazut-cu-o-treime-fata-de-2008-inainte-de-criza.html, accessed on 3 April 2018.
35 Peter Gross, *Intoarcere în laboratorul românesc. Mass media* (Bucharest: Nemira, 2015).
36 Consiliul Național al Audiovizualului, *Situația numărului de licențe TV_SITE*, no date, available at: http://www.cna.ro/IMG/pdf/Situatia_numarului_de_licente_TV_SITE-3.pdf, accessed on 1 March 2018.
37 Media Fact Book 2017, available at: http://www.mediafactbook.ro/, accessed on 4 March 2018.
38 Freedom House, Nations in Transit 2017.

The media and journalists' culture

Whereas the press became less political by 2000—although its agenda was shaped by political controlers, via editors-in-chief, editorial directors or the press' leading opinion-makers—local and national broadcasting remained decidedly politicized. A 2014 study by ActiveWatch maps the geography of the ethical disaster in local broadcasting, where the content is "imposed by the owner, dictated by politicians, paid from public money and by blackmail ... and [where] the journalists' independence is out of the question."[39]

Towing the political line is advantageous for editors-in-chief, editorial directors and the star opinion-makers who are paid far above the average salaries. For example, the image makers of Antena 3 who shill for owner Dan Voiculescu's political and business interests and orchestrate mediated hostilities against his oponents earn monthly salaries between 10,000 and 30,000 Euros at a time when other reporters' average wages do not exceed 1500 Euros. International reports have highlighted the "excessive politicization" of the media and its instrumentalization, achieved through "corrupt financing mechanisms, editorial policies subordinated to the owner's interests and the [Romanian] intelligence agency's infiltration of staff—such was the impact of media transformation on political propaganda tools."[40]

Romania's media began their post-communist journey with heart, hope, determination and a lack of experience in practicing the kind of professional journalism meant to serve democracy. The slow and uncertain process of "professionalisation" has not yet restrained the media from militating on behalf of political interests, persuading via opinion-based journalism, and being generally counterproductive to encouraging and informing civil society and upholding liberal democratic values.

The similar but not identical socio-professional routes taken by Central and Eastern European media show that the idealized, overstated role of journalists during and immediately after the 1989 revolutions, annointed as "saviors," has diminished their opportunity to play central roles as informers of public opinion. The shock of finding that these sav-

---

39   Liana Ganea, ed., *Harta politică a televiziunilor locale*, ActiveWatch (January 2014), 13, available at: http://activewatch.ro/Assets/Upload/files/Harta%20Politica%20a%20Televiziunilor%20Locale%20-%20ActiveWatch%20Ian%202014.pdf, accessed on 5 December 2018.

40   Reporters Without Borders, *World Press Freedom Index*, 2017, available at: https://rsf.org/en/ranking, accessed on 5 December 2018. Romania is ranked 46th among the 180 countries assessed.

ior-journalists were ordinary people, worse yet, unprofessional, dismissive of common standards and rules, and co-opted by the political elites or willingly complicit with them, marginalized journalists. This has been observed by scholars who studied the media in the region—Mihai Coman, Colin Sparks, Marian Petcu, Walery Pisarek, Karol Jakubowicz, Manuela Preoteasa, Dusan Reljic, Slavko Splichal, Peter Bajomi-Lazar, and others—who noted the journalists' loss of credibility. They saw the pendulum swing from the idea of the inviolability of freedom of expression and the independence of journalists to the condition of quasi-slavery on the plantation of media moguls; from the acknowledgement of the need for skills to be learned in an academic setting to the reality of "workplace qualification" as judged by media owners; and finally, from the initial enthusiasm to the reality of economic and professional crisis.

Mihai Coman accurately describes the hard lessons learned by journalists whose "status depends on two capricious entities: the public and the owner."[41] In the midst of the economic crisis of 2008–2009?—when publications, radio and television stations began disappearing, when unemployment in the ranks of journalists grew vertiginously and when vassalage often became compulsory to keep one's job—the media found out that it has nothing on which to depend: no effective legal protection and professional unions, no professional unity, and having to live with accusations that they practice manipulation, sensationalism, and deception thanks to their collusion with the powers-that-be. The profession "lost control" by not having authority over its resources: the financial wherewithal is under the control of owners who play the money game in ... political and dubious business, and the journalist's autonomy is narrowly decided by owners.[42]

The portrait of the opportunistic journalist is thus shaped by the vision of him/her being frightened by the lack of professionalism, a mercenary figure ready to figuratively liquidate anyone for money, social position, visibility. The lack of consolidated professional principles, the individualism towards which he pushed the paradigm shift of the profession through digitization and the intervention of new technologies—this sentence is incomplete.

Television still dominates news consumption

Approximately 85 percent of Romanians get their information from television. In 2017, 49 percent of Romanians spent two to three hours per day watching television and one in five watched four to six hours during the

---

41 Mihai Coman, *Mass-media în România post-comunistă* (Iasi: Polirom, 2003), 151.
42 Ibid, 159.

week, exceeding the average daily global television consumption of about three hours.[43]

The manipulative news policies of television channels, reflecting the political polarization of society to which they contribute and which they aggravate, have created the phenomenon of captive audiences. They are dependent on these news channels and unable to look critically at what is being offered them.[44] The political aims of television are camouflaged with the manipulative notion that the news and information offered to the audiences is in the "public interest." It includes fake news such as President Iohannis sells children; European Parlament member and former prosecutor, Monica Macovei, is a traitor to her the country and its enemy; the DNA serves foreign interests; or former Prime Minister Dacian Cioloș, a Dragnea oponent, is the illegitimate son of George Soros. Fake news extended to the suggestion that the protests in the winter of 2017 were sponsored by Soros (and as a result, adults received 100 Lei, children 50 Lei, dogs 30 Lei). The response embraced a satirical strategy that temporarily dominated the public sphere, suprising Dragnea and his supporters, subverting their narrative, and "undermining governmental conventions": "Dragnea's statement that American billionaire George Soros was funding the protests, including dogs [that were at the protests], was met with dry replies ... Placards showing giraffes or cats asking for payment, the picture of a dog displaying the following message: Soros, where is my money?"[45]

Antena 3 and RTV, and periodically also B1 TV and TVR, conduct anti-anti-corruption and anti-DNA campaigns. As already noted, the so-called public television, politicized since 1990, is detached from the public mission for which it was established. TVR's politically beholden administrators and managers drove the institution into bankrupcy by 2016, where it has lingered for the past ten years, having amassed a deficit of 150 million euros.[46] In 2017, the PSD-ALDE parliamentary majority de-

---

43 *Indexul consumului de televiziune în România 2017*—we need full details for this. Mercury Research for Astra România based on a representative national sample of 402 people over the age of 18 who are television service users; the margin of error was + 5%.
44 The phenomenon of TV addiction is quite new in the agenda of media researchers. S. Sussman and M. Moran, "Hidden Addiction: Television," *Journal of Behavioral Addictions*, 2:3 (September 2013): 125–32.
45 Brindusa Armanca, "Humor as a Form of Symbolic Communication during the February 2017 Protests in Romania," in *#Rezist. Romania's 2017 Anticorruption Protests. Causes, Development and Implications*, 105.
46 Claudia Pirvoiu and Costin Ionescu, "Soarta TVR a fost decisă: Insolvența. Procedura ar putea fi demarată în maxim o lună," HotNews.ro, March 3, 2016, available at: https://economie.hotnews.ro/stiri-media_publicitate-20840883-soarta-tvr-fo

cided to change the funding model of the public television (TVR), jettisoning the radio-TV tax and financing TVR with public funds, definitively tying public media to the political powers.

Corruption

The anti-corruption strategy assumed by Romania at the time of joining the European Union in 2007 had consequences that were difficult to predict. Most of the major media "moguls" ended up under investigation in the last few years, were found guilty of various illegalities and condemned to prison terms, making Romania an exception in this regard in the European Union. Such convictions also illustrate the moral and financial vulnerability of the Romanian media. As early as 2006, journalist Dan Tapalagă concluded that media owners, who become oligarchic and corrupt over the years, represent the very dishonesty that defines the media, and are the "faces of the same system."[47] These authorities in political and financial manipulations focused their efforts on and journalists in television stations, specifically *Realitatea, Intact*, and *MediaPro*. These stations indefatigably involve themselves in corruption, exemplified by

> politics, ex-Securitate [people], tax havens, business, all ingeniously braided [together]. All three have to defend vast territories of illegitimate interests and a skewed past. How will they do it? In crucial moments and on essential themes: [relying on] elections, justice, reforms. Subtly controlling the topics of public discourse, fine tuning, [controlling its] tone and hue.[48]

Foreign investors like Bodo Hombach, the president of the *Westdeutsche Allgemeine Zeitung*, noted that both in Romania and in other Central and Eastern European countries the oligarchs are "buying their newspapers and magazines more and more, not so much to make money, but in order to get political influence."[49] By 2009, the insecurity of the media industry grew, and the media companies of the moguls appeared to begin teetering on the edge of disaster. Several publications and televisions stations like *Adevărul, Evenimentul zilei, România liberă*, and Realitatea TV are owned by bankrupt companies. The fact that they still publish and broadcast calls

st-decisa-insolventa-procedura-putea-demarata-maxim-luna-surse.htm, accessed on Dec. 6, 2018.
47 Dan Tapalaga, "Starea vremii în presă," *HotNews.ro*, 31 May 2006, available at: https://www.hotnews.ro/stiri-arhiva-1176453-starea-vremii-presa-dan-tapalaga.htm, accessed on 4 March 2018.
48 Ibid.
49 Stetka, Vaclav Stetka, "From multinationals to business tycoons: Media ownership and journalistic autonomy in Central and Eastern Europe," *International Journal of Press/Politics*, 2012, 17(4), 433–456.

into question their sources of financing, and the guarantees of freedom of the press.

A sampling of media enterprises and owners who have been investigated, indicted or already convicted of illegalities include the following. The Intact Media Group (which includes Antena 1, Antena 3, Happy TV, Radio Zu, *National Journal*, Romantic Radio, *Gazeta Sporturilor*, gsp.ro) is owned by Dan Voiculescu and his family. Voiculescu is a former member of the Securitate, a former leader of the Conservative Party, ex-Senator, convicted in 2014 to a ten-year prison term for corruption, and released on parole in 2017. His daughter Camelia Voiculescu was sentenced in 2016 to a two-year prison term for blackmail.[50] Realitatea Media (which includes Realitatea TV, *Cațavencu*, and *Cotidianul*) is owned by Sorin Ovidiu Vântu, a former Securitate "snitch" with considerable influence in politics. In 2015, Vântu was convicted for corruption to six years and four months in prison. His estimated fortune reached 50–60 million Euro in 201? (according to Forbes Top 500) and 100–150 million Euro in 2012–2013 (according to Capital Top 300). The new owners of Realitatea Media are Cosmin Gușa, former PSD politician; Maricel Păcurariu, convicted in 2014 to a four-year prison term and released on parole in 2017; and Elan Schwatzenberg, prosecuted for fraud but escaped to Israel before his trial. Romania TV is owned by Sebastian Ghiță, a former PSD legislator suspected of links to the secret services, and a beneficiary of public money. He was prosecuted in 2016, but escaped to Belgrade, Serbia, where he was imprisoned for money laundering, bribery and facilitating access to secret information. Adevărul Holding (*Adevărul*, *Click*, *Dilema*) is owned by Dinu Patriciu, a founder of the Liberal Party and former legislator who also owns the large oil business, Rompetrol. He was convicted of fraud in 2012 and sentenced to a two-year and six months prison term. He died in 2014. The new owner of Adevărul Holding, Cristian Burci, who also owns Prima TV and Kiss FM, is related to the secret services, and a sponsor of politicians. He was prosecuted for corruption in 2016; the case is still in the courts. The *România liberă* newspaper, owned by Dan Adamescu, together with Medien Holding, ASTRA insurance, several shopping centers, and other businesses. Adamescu was convicted of fraud in 2016 and sentenced to a four-year and four-month prison term. He died in 2017. The newspaper was inherited by his son, Alexander, himself prosecuted for fraud and detained in London in March 2018, where he still awaits extradition to Romania to stand trial. The MEDIA Pro (including PRO TV, Acasa

---

50   The Securitate was Romania's version of the Soviet KGB.

TV, Pro Cinema, MTV Ro, Media Pro, Pro FM, Info Pro, and Mediafax) is owned by Adrian Sârbu, a former CEO and owner of the American media company CME, who has high political contacts. He was indicted for fraud in 2015 and his trial is ongoing. The tabloid TV channel OTV is owned by Dan Diaconescu, founder of the People's Party, which was represented in parliament until it merged into the National Union for the Progress of Romania in 2015, the year its founder began serving a five year and six month prison term for blackmail.[51] Diaconescu was convicted of blackmail in 2015, sentenced to a five-year and six-month prison term, and released on parole in 2017. Other media owners indicted for various offenses include Dan Andronic (*Evenimentul zilei*), Radu Mazăre and Sorin Strutinsky (Neptun TV and *Ziua de Constanța*), Sorin Roșca Stănescu (*Ziua*), Radu Budeanu (*Cancan*), Cristian Sima (*Hotnews*), as well as Mihai Ghezea and Florin Paraschivescu (*Atac de Buzău*).

The Voiculescu case illustrates the owners' control over editorial policy. Voiculescu converted his Intact Media, whose Antena 3 serves as the tip of his political lance and slingshot, into a weapon against state institutions, particularly the judiciary and the DNA. Specifically, Antena 3 carries out journalistic campaigns against the judges who condemned Voiculescu, his daughter and son-in-law; the former head of the DNA, Kovesi, and the prosecutors who investigated and indicted them; the journalists who report on their case; all of his enemies and political and market competitors. It broadcasts fake debates to stimulate public interest in a particular issue. IntactMedia uses deceptive methods to enhance its professional prestige and credibility by purchasing American awards, or claiming prestigious affiliations that remain unconfirmed (from APTR awards to affiliation with CNN International).[52]

International reports do not mince words in diagnosing the problem faced by Romanian media and their journalists: they are "instruments of political goals." This assessment leads to the overall perception that journalists do not work for a particular media outlet but for its owner and, therefore, their work has deleterious professional consequences: "journalistic professional standards are often disregarded and journalists, editors, and media managers, in fear of losing their jobs, practice a high level of self-censorship."[53]

---

51 He was released from prison in November 2017.
52 I.B., "Reporter Virtual: Cum se cumpăra premiile cu care se laudă Antena 3. Mic ghid pentru doritori," *HotNews.ro* (10 February 2014), available at: https://economie.hotnews.ro/stiri-media_publicitate-16584981-antena-1-antena-3-10-nominalizari-pentru-premiera-observator.htm, accessed on 4 April 2018.
53 Freedom House, *Nations in Transit 2017*.

Romanian media's democratic, financial, and professional shortcomings are not unique in the region.[54] Studies confirm the precarious relationships between owners and journalists throughout Central and Eastern Europe since 1989, none better expressed by the European Commission's 2014 Final Report on Media and Democracy in Central and Eastern Europe.[55] The Report points to insufficient transparency regarding media ownership and the deficiencies in the journalists' training and funding, leading to their being "divided and disoriented." The report concludes that this diminishes the media's abilities to act as "independent and unbiased" purveyors of news and information, concurrently recognizing that they are not simply "innocent victims of political and economic manipulation," but "often have sided with their business or political patrons, indulging in propaganda, misinformation, or even smear campaigns."[56]

Regulation and ethics

Romanian journalists prefer self-regulation. From a professional perspective, this has been a failure, but they vigorously reject political attempts to draft press laws since December 1989, after the communist Press Law 3/1974 was quickly abolished. Had they succeded in parliament, such proposals would have established legal constraints on them. The following examples illustrate their authoritarian nature and the illiberal mentalities of their authors.

The 1992 Draft Law on the Press, authored by Senators Vasile Mois (of the anti-Semitic Greater Romania Party, PRM) and Ion Plătică (representing the PDS) included three articles: "Newspapers and periodicals are obliged to send one copy [of each edition] before dissemination to the County Prefecture and to the County Police Inspectorate in whose territorial jurisdiction they are headquartered and publish" (Article 45); "The participation of journalists in shoutouts or seditious songs uttered in public places or meetings shall be punished by imprisonment from 6 months

---

54 Péter Bajomi-Lázár, *Media in Third-Wave Democracies. Southern and Central/Eastern Europe in Comparative Perspective* (Budapest: L'Harmattan, 2017); and Peter Gross, "Media, Journalism, and the Third Wave of Democratization in Former Communist Countries," *Central and Southeast European Politics Since 1989*, ed. by Sabrina P. Ramet and Christine M. Hassenstab (New York, NY: Cambridge University Press, 2019), 2nd edition.
55 Jan Zielonka, *Final Report Summary—MDCEE (Media and Democracy in Central and Eastern Europe: Qualities of Democracy, Qualities of Media)*, 9 March 2016, available at: https://cordis.europa.eu/result/rcn/180378_en.html, accessed on 5 February 2014.
56 Ibid.

to 3 years or a fine from 500 000 to 2 000 000 Lei" (Article 74); and "An offense brought to the President of Romania ... shall be punished by imprisonment from 6 months to 3 years or a fine from 500,000 to 2,000,000 Lei" (Article 75).[57]

The 1998 Draft Law on the Exercise of the Profession of Journalist, initiated by deputy Petre Țurlea (of the National Salvation Front and then the chauvinistic Romanian National Unity Party, PUNR) and the Union of Professional Journalists in Romania (Uniunea Ziariștilor Profesioniști, UZP), gave the UZP a monopoly to legitimate journalists and the right to exclude them from the profession.[58] The 2008 Draft Law on Positive News, proposed by Senator Ioan Ghișhe (of the National Liberal Party) and Gheorghe Funar (PRM), established a socio-political standard for the media's gatekeeping: "The news programs of television and radio stations must contain an equal measure of positive and negative news" (Article 28).[59] In 2010, a group of Liberal Democratic Party legislators headed by Silviu Prigoană, introduced a bill according to which publications were to be licensed by the National Broadcasting Council. Publications could thus be banned, although Article 30 of the Constitution stipulates that "No publication can be suppressed."[60] Also in 2010, the Draft Law of the Journalist, authored by Senator Ioan Ghișhe (National Liberal Party), read that "A press offense means a civil offense commited by inserting information, reflections or comments in the mass media, about facts that have no implications for society and have caused material or moral damage to a person"; "'Offense' means any fact (illicit) and harmful to the person, accomplished by action or omission committed with the intention of harming another person. A quasi-offense is also an illicit and harmful fact, but committed without intentions to harm." (Article 68). The same article says:

> Journalists may be disciplined, in relation to the seriousness of the facts, by a reprimand, warning, fined [at the level of] two to ten times average salaries, prohibited from exercising their profession for one month to one year [or] excluded from the profession. The act of publishing material that is likely to prejudice a legitimate right

---

57 Brîndușa Armanca, "Etica mass-media și dilemele autoreglementării. Studiu comparativ de aplicare a normelor deontologice în presa din România și Germania," *SAECULUM*, serie nouă, Anul XV(XVII), Nr.2 (42)/2016, 273–284.
58 Ibid.
59 Alina Mungiu-Pippidi and Cristian Ghinea, "Struggling with Media Capture: Romania." Evangelia Psychogiopoulou, ed., *Understanding Media Policies: A European Perspective, 2012, 172;* Rupert Wolfe Murray, "In Romania, Even Good News Can Be Bad, Radio Free Europe/Radio Liberty, July 15, 2008, available at: https://www.rferl.org/a/Romanian_Good_News_Can_Be_Bad/1183803.html, accessed on 9 November 2018.
60 Armanca, "Etica mass-media și dilemele ...," 2016.

of a person shall be sanctioned by a fine of 6 to 12 times an average salary, and the act of a representative of a public authority who provides erroneous data to journalists shall be sanctioned by a fine of 6 to 12 average salaries per economy.[61]

The 2015–2016 Draft Defamation Law, titled "Legislative Proposal on Promoting Human Dignity and Tolerance Towards Group Differences" by Dragnea, specified that social defamation was a contravention sanctioned with fines between 60,000 and 100,000 Lei.[62] In 2017, changes to Law 41/1994 on the Organization and Functioning of the Romanian Radio (SRR) and the Romanian Television (SRTV) legalized the politicization of the public media by allowing members of political parties to become members of the Board of Directors.[63] That same year, the online publication PressOne acquired a document showing that a consultation in the PSD-ALDE government aimed at repealing Law 544/2001 on Free Access to Information of Public Interest, which allows any petitioner to request data and information from a state institution about spending of public money, contracts, organizational charts, auctions, and reports.[64]

The attempts of the political elites to legislate the work of the media suggest they reject the professional functioning of the media system, or their ignorance of the need for it to do so. The same can be said of the elites' conviction they should control the "Fourth Estate." Their ill-advised, illiberal attitudes and actions also affect the roughly ten existing codes of ethics, which remain no more than aspirational ideas set in writting.

The ethics committees of TVR and SRR are exceptions, sometimes used to intimidate journalists who are too vocal on some subjects.[65] In 2009, the Media Organizations Convention, which brought together 42 media organizations from across the country, published the Uniform Code

---

61 Ibid.
62 The law would punish any negative references to a group, including political parties. For example, journalists could not characterize the PSD, the PNL, or any other political party in negative terms. Because they are defined as "social groups."
63 Cătălina Mănoiu, "CCR: Membrii consiliilor de administrație al TVR și SRR pot fi înscriși în partide politice," Mediafax, 12 July 2017, available at: https://www.mediafax.ro/politic/ccr-membrii-consiliilor-de-administratie-ale-tvr-si-srr-pot-fi-ins crisi-in-partide-politice-16584158?fbclid=IwAR1mI9had9yy9nRaT0E1UMXLTq2 Pq2aOp01ZStVVHriswxYR9ZROgZf6JkM, accessed on 13 September 2018.
64 "Guvernul vrea să schimbe legea accesului la informații publice UPDATE: Ce spune ministrul Consultării Publice," Ziare.com, June 9, 2017, available at: http://www.ziare.com/politica/guvernul-sorin-grindeanu/guvernul-vrea-sa-puna-bete-in-ro ate-presei-se-pregateste-o-modificare-a-legii-accesului-la-informatii-publice-146 8929, accessed on 12 December 2018.
65 Public media entitites are legally required to have Ethics Committees. When management controls the committee through obedient journalists, they can put pressure on journalists.

of Conduct subsequently negotiated with the Romanian Press Owners' Club. In the absence of Ethics Councils (Consilii de Onoare) to make effective judgments on ethical violations, the code remains a mere theoretical reference and didactic material for journalism classes. The elusive idea of journalistic ethics, and even more so of their application, seriously damages the credibility of the news media system, which is not trusted to serve the public interest.

Society's loss of interest in the rigors of data and fact-based truth—hastened by the invasion of the digital world—is a form of "Truth Decay" that exibits four trends shared by Romania with the rest of the world: (1) increasing disagreement about facts and analytical interpretations of facts and data; (2) a blurring of the line between opinion and fact; (3) the relative growing volume and influence of opinion and personal experience over facts; as well as (4) declining trust in formerly respected sources of factual information."[66]

The division, polarization, and radicalization of the media

Instrumentalization, clientelism and politicization of and in the media have deeply divided the media system, partly because the latter embraces the former two in various ways or not at all. For instance, instrumentalization and clientelism exist without politicization, serving an array of masters who employ media for non-political ends. Thus, Romania has media (1) that are subservient to the political-economic interests of the owners/politicians and abide by few, if any, professional standards and ethics, (2) the few who aim at serving a variedly defined notion of social responsibility and attempt to retain a professional, ethical editorial policy, and (3) those who have neither professional and ethical standards nor political obligations to their owners and simply aim at making money. The tabloid press, whose online presence has grown, exemplifies the latter group; it relies on *clicks* and *likes* for its goal of making money.

The financing of each of the three media groups has a different source. The politicized/political press may be supported as any other commercial venture and/or be subsidized by politicians or political parties and/or by other commercial ventures owned by politicians. The essential point is that the financing of these outlets is quasi- or wholly non-transparent. The (somewhat) independent press relies on the vicissitudes of the market. The purely money-oriented press depends on the audience.

---

66 Jennifer Kavanagh and Michael D. Rich, *Truth Decay: An Exploration of the Diminishing Role of Facts and Analysis in American Public Life* (Santa Monica, CA: Rand Corporation, 2018), x-xi.

From a news and information perspective, too, these are major divisions. The politicized press and broadcasting are focused on propagandizing, manipulating and distracting audiences, and the discrediting of the (somewhat) independent press. This (somewhat) independent press is mostly focused on news and information in an environment created by sources, unresponsive state and government institutions, as well as economic pressures that restrict its purpose. The money-oriented media concentrate on sensationalism and entertainment.

The divisions in the media system are spurred on by the proliferation of fake news—for political, sensationalist, and entertainment purposes—and by campaigns to denigrate independent journalists who are ridiculed as "ethicists," "Sorosists" and "journalists with epaulettes," and allusion to some working for the security services. Add to that the language that is being used in these campaigns, the aggressive, injurious style with which they are prosecuted, and the illiberal attitudes that it exemplifies. All these turn the media, particularly the television, into a media cesspool.

In 2014, in a rare show of solidarity, more than 600 journalists signed a proclamation protesting the deterioration of good journalistic practices, and expressing their deep revulsion with

> The violations of the Code of Ethics, the insult, libel, lie, manipulation and, in general, contempt for ethical norms have become a common practice. The serious damage to dignity and public image, the overthrow of professional reputations in the case of important personalities in cultural life, including journalists, have exceeded all limits. Injuries, ... denigrations, intrusions into private life, the violence of language [used], the trivial and the premeditated falsification of truth are unspeakable practices. We believe that they diminish the entire [professional] guild and must cease. We reject the induced confusion that everything is reduced to different political positions and that all journalists are equally guilty of degrading the professional morale and the public space. [67]

The protest summarizes Romanian media and journalists' essential problems and what divides them into two camps, that is, the ethical and moral shortcomings and not the ideological or even political differences.

The Shock of New Technologies

Adding to the challenges the Romanian media face in contributing to the progress of society are the very changes brought about by the dramatic rise of digital technologies to the media system and to journalism. Digital technologies created an enormously expanded communication capability,

---

67 "Protest al jurnalistilor împotriva practicilor degradante din presă," *Revista 22* (20 January 2014), available at: https://www.revista22.ro/protest-al-jurnali350tilor-mpotriva-practicilor-degradante-din-presa-36864.html, accessed on 4 March 2017.

lessening the influence of the press, despite their concurrent increase in platforms for the traditional media. Independent and quasi-independent digital outlets that compete and provide counterpoints to their traditional cousins are the main beneficiaries.[68] Non-partisan journalists wishing to distance themselves from the majority of the less-than-independent traditional media outlets set up blogs, online publications and independent journalism projects that have significantly added to civil society's more professional information and news. Among these are Republica (https://republica/ro), Vice (vice.ro), and the Rise Project (riseproject.ro). Importantly, digital technologies provided a modality for bringing together local joint journalism projects intent on eliminating clientelism, instrumentalization and parallelism, like PressHub (presshub.ro) and the Clean Voices project (https://www.civicmedia.ro/voci-curate-i/).

These new journalistic outlets and possibilities are reconfiguring not only the way people are informed, but how they inform themselves. They continue to give birth to fresh news and information dependencies, as well as social loyalties. They are also contributing to audience fragmentation, challenging the ability of digital media to stimulate social solidarity and cultural dialogue. Adding to this doubt is "the volatility of networked digital media environments" that testifies to "the limits of social media for public debate."[69]

Roughly 88 percent of Romanians go online to receive news and information—this includes the 65 percent who access digital media.[70] The expansion of broadband Internet and a rapid growth in social networking users—9,600,000 Facebook users in January 2017, with a 15.66 percent increase from the previous year, most of them under 55 years of age—left businesses unprepared to operate in and use the new digital world.[71] For example, their purchase of online advertising is slow, which from an economic perspective also damages media development and in some cases

---

68   Nick Couldry, Clemencia Rodriguez, Göran Bolin, Julie Cohen, Gerard Goggin, Marwan Kraidy, Koichi Iwabuchi, Kwang-Suk Lee, Jack Qiu, Ingrid Volkmer, Herman Wasserman, Yuezhi Zhao, Olessia Koltsova, Inaya Rakhmani, Omar Rincón, Claudia Magallanes-Blanco and Pradip Thomas, "Chapter 13: Media and Communications," in *Rethinking Society for the 21st Century* (in press), available at: https://www.ipsp.org/download/chapter-13, accessed on 3 March 2018.
69   Ibid, 51.
70   Raluca Radu, "Romania," *Reuters Institute Digital Report 2017*, 88 (2017), available at: http://www.digitalnewsreport.org/survey/2017/romania-2017/, accessed on 25 January 2018.
71   "9,6 milioane de conturi de utilizator de Facebook in Romania," Facebrands.ro (10 January 2017), available at: http://www.facebrands.ro/blog/2017/01/9-6-milioane-conturi-utilizator-facebook-romania/, accessed on 4 March 2018.

even causes bankrupcies.[72] Younger Romanians are better educated in the use of the Internet and other digital media when compared to the older generations; the better educated are apt to have greater digital skills, as do people in urban environments when compared to those in rural setting.[73]

The shrinking of the print media that began in 2009 has caused a decline in advertising revenue. Of "every 100 euros" in advertising revenues collected? in 2008, "only 15 euros" remained available to newspapers by 2013; this included the revenues they earned from their online advertising.[74] The increase in online advertising revenue—18 percent in 2017, from 366 million Euros in 2016 to 403 million Euros in 2017—is insufficient to support the numerous publications and websites. Web-based journalism does not earn money for Romania's newspapers, instead the major news clearing and host platforms are the profitmakers: Google earned US$109.6 billion worldwide in 2017 and Facebook US$40,653 million.[75] The traditional media's "privilege" exists to a different extent [meaning it is drastically reduced?] today, compared to the period when the traditional press was supreme, because the Digital Era involves new forms of communication, but also new obstacles (data protection, suveillance, etc.).[76]

---

72 *Jurnalul național* (Intact Publishing) is bankrupt, *Realitatea Media* is insolvent, and the biggest television stations have large debts. In 2014–2015, Adevarul Holding, *Evenimentul zilei* and *Capital* became insolvent. See Alina Mungiu-Pippidi, "Libertatea presei, această fraudă națională (II)," *Romania Libera* (11 September 2014), available at: http://romanialibera.ro/opinii/comentarii/libertatea-presei-—aceasta-frauda-nationala--ii--349450?c=q2561, accessed on 4 March 2018.
73 "9,6 milioane de conturi."
74 Cătălin Tolontan, "Ideea care durează de 90 de ani," Tolo.ro (8 January 2014), available at: www.tolo.ro/2014/01/08/Ideea-care-dureaza-de-90-de-ani/, accessed on 25 March 2018.
75 "Google's Revenue Worldwide from 2002 to 2017 (in billion U.S. dollars)." Statista.com (2018). Available at: https://www.statista.com/statistics/266206/googles-annual-global-revenue/, and "Facebook's Annual Revenue and Net Income from 2007 to 2017 (in million U.S. dollars)," Statista.com (2018), available at: https://www.statista.com/statistics/277229/facebooks-annual-revenue-and-net-income/, accessed on 25 March 2018,
76 "Media privilege" is understood to mean all provisions that guaranteed by special information rights, the ability to fulfill their opinion-shaping function, legal protections for media freedoms against state interference and against individuals who may want to suppress reporting by refering to general provisions of civil or criminal law, without any consideration of the media's freedom to communicate.

Conclusion—The future ... if there is one?

To date, the country's democracy and news media's professionalization have not met indigenous and foreign expectations, as both have failed to assume their social responsibility. The persistent crisis in ethics, enveloped in the illiberal culture and political culture, is victimizing democratization and the media's independence and journalistic professionalization.

There are two Romanias today. The Romania of the democratic civil society, which militates for transparency in government and state institutions that run democratically on behalf of voters, and yearns for an enlightened political leadership capable of establishing transparency and accountability in government. This Romania has a few media outlets and journalists who assume the responsibilities of their profession, respect and abide by its ethics, and strive to inform their audiences. The other Romania has a corrupt political elite governing on its own behalf, clouding the state they control, without being responsible to citizens. The media and journalists cater to this elite are not allowed and are unwilling to abide by professional standards and ethics. Instead, they serve as propagandists and political instruments to beffudle, mis-inform, and dis-inform audiences and thus oppose civil society and democratization.

The media's failure to make game-changing contributions to democratization is not surprising. They are expressions of the political-economic systems that, in turn, are the children of the culture and political culture whose transformation is infinitely slower than the transition from one political system to another. This is a truism demonstrated across Central and Eastern Europe. Romania's emerging civil society, coupled with the small groups of independent, professionalizing media and journalists are the key to the country's liberal democratic future.

Ionuț Butoi, Mircea Vulcănescu. O microistorie a interbelicului românesc. București: EIKON, 2015. 375 pp.

Review by Emanuel Copilaș, West University of Timișoara, Romania

Ionuț Butoi's book brings to the forefront analytical methods rarely used in contemporary Romanian historiography. His micro-historical approach judiciously places within the national and international contexts different tendencies, personalities and social categories from the interwar period. It also offers new and rich perspectives on an era that Romanian historiography has often treated either in a unilateral, reductionist fashion or aprioristically considered as an almost natural creation of the ideological tendencies of the time.[1] Indeed, much of what has been written about this period fails to give sufficient weight to the crucial connections between the ideas and social groups of the 1920s and 1930s. Butoi's work shows that these connections were more diverse and dynamic than previously portrayed.

Accordingly, the author reassesses the socio-economic and political environment of the interwar period through the perspectives afforded by Mircea Vulcănescu's (1904–1952) life and work. A sociologist and economist with an abiding interest in the rural world, Vulcănescu was affiliated with the Bucharest Sociological School led by Dimitrie Gusti (1880–1955). Butoi's analysis of Vulcănescu's personal, intellectual and political trajectory seeks to reconstruct the interwar social milieu "from the inside", namely both in the manner in which "historical realities were perceived and signified by the actors themselves" and in "their structural, contextual dimensions" (p. 304). The analysis is organized into three main chapters titled "Incursions into the History and Problematic of the Young Interwar Generation", "The Interwar Romanian Village: A Terra Incognita", and "A Different Mircea Vulcănescu". Thus, Vulcănescu emerges from Butoi's narrative as an iconoclastic figure, one who was actively engaged in trying to provide a viable institutional alternative to the chauvinistic, authoritarian right-wing currents increasingly manifest in academia and other institutions.

As a scholar, Vulcănescu produced consistent analyses of the ways in which Romanian villages were organized and functioned, often related

---

1 Examples include Ioan Scurtu and Gheorghe Buzatu, *Istoria Românilor în secolul XX* (Editura Paideia, București, 1999); Dan Dungaciu, *Elita interbelică. Sociologia românească în context european* (Editura Mica Valahie, București, 2003).

to the analyses of the Marxist sociologist Henri Stahl, despite the fact that the two authors did not share the same ideological principles. Influenced by Nae Ionescu, of whom he was nevertheless critical, and by the reinvigorated and actualized Orthodoxism 'the Professor' elaborated, which he adopted without its anti-Semitism, Vulcănescu vehemently critiqued both the Romanian state's modernizing perspective towards peasants, which saw them as a cheap, competitive source of crops for the international market, and the romantic rural imagery prevalent amongst the traditionalist Right. Consequently, Butoi's emphasis on Vulcănescu' sociological work and political activities as opposed to the hitherto dominant historiographical focus on his role as a philosopher of culture yields several important insights about the era under examination.[2] It is in this context that the well-known dispute between 'autochtonists' and 'westernizers' gains new meanings.

Vulcănescu carefully deconstructed the cold portrayal of peasants as aspiring small entrepreneurs. For example, to the official puzzlement regarding the low productivity of some agricultural fields which benefited from state sponsored modern technologies, Vulcănescu answered by denying the existence of work for profit in the capitalist sense within the rural world: peasants produced for subsistence, not for commerce. Their productivity was part of a symbolic horizon which, although unintelligible from the outside, possessed a very well-articulated social logic of its own. Therefore, after receiving new agricultural equipment, the peasants preferred to reduce their working time in order to obtain the same production, sometimes even less, using the surplus of time obtained for other different lucrative purposes (pp. 168–181, 205–206). Hence, just as Vulcănescu did in his own time, Butoi justifiably dismisses simple explanations that attribute interwar Romania's underdevelopment to the structural dependency towards Western capitalism, taking into account important internal factors that propelled this ultimately unavoidable dependency.

On the other hand, Butoi convincingly argues that the modern Romanian state was to a significant extent a creation of the great Western powers designed as part of a geopolitical belt against Tsarist expansionism, and for half a century against Bolshevik expansionism (p. 32). Autochtonist nationalism, directly contributing to the legitimation and the consolidation of the new state, was significantly induced from outside, due to the geopolitical reason mentioned above. This is precisely why the

---

[2] For example, see Marin Diaconu, *Mircea Vulcănescu. Profil spiritual* (Editura Eminescu, București, 2001).

book would have benefited from a short overview of the cultural factors like German romanticism, for example, which constituted in the second half of the 19th century the main instrument of Romania's modernizing elites in the process of creation of a primordialist national mythology, in its turn well-suited to the institutional objective of state consolidation. The right-wing ideological core that influenced many student movements did not appear out of nowhere, as an expression of the deep irrationality somehow inexplicably characterizing the interwar period; it had deep and complex roots.

Indeed, Butoi's effort to analyze the autochthonous, nationalist and fascist dimensions of interwar youth radicalization by going beyond shallow "culturalist" explanations is one of the most important contributions of the book. The author shows how the economic crisis of the 1930s institutionally impacted the Romanian state, forcing it to drastically reduce the number of positions from the administrative and educational sectors. It thereby condemned many university graduates to unemployment, their numbers rising massively after the First World War due to economic reasons (the allotment of peasants through land reform, which generated a certain increase of the number of students from rural areas, although not a significant one when compared to the whole student population), and political reasons (the introduction of universal suffrage in 1918, even if only for men). Consequently, the universities were forced to accept a growing number of young people, attracted to this environment by aspirations for social mobility despite the huge tuition fees and ungenerous financial aid provided by the state (pp. 61, 63).

Ethnic Romanian students gradually began to develop resentments towards Jewish students, whose families had been integrated in the urban environment for many generations and who did not have to endure the same hardships. In these conditions, as the state proved itself increasingly helpless and uninspired, the dynamic potential of students was gradually channeled towards Orthodoxism and nationalist political movements led by university professors such as A. C. Cuza and, later on, Nae Ionescu. Here it is important to note that Vulcănescu himself was part of a Christian student association. But ASCR (The Association of Christian Romanian Students) had an entirely different trajectory than that of the radical right student movement. In fact, ASCR was the first student organization that collaborated with Dimitrie Gusti in establishing the University Office (Oficiul Universitar). This was a center dedicated to helping students with housing, medical care, legal assistance etc. That being said, the greatest beneficiary of student discontent was the Legionary Movement, which had well-defined and functional organizational structures. The Legion's call to glorify deeds, not words, appeared to offer the moral, social and ideological guidance which established institutions could no longer offer, promising also a new world, which would continue the mystical and spiritual past of the fatherland.

All in all, Butoi's book represents a well-researched, nuanced and innovative contribution to the historiography of Romania's interwar period. The book debunks many preconceptions about this epoch as the golden age of incipient democracy, brutally annihilated by the advent of the communist regime. On the contrary, the interwar and the communist period are more united by their political authoritarianism and censorship rather than divided by their different ideological principles.

Henry P. Rammelt. Activistes protestataires en Hongrie et en Roumanie. Paris: L'Harmattan, 2018. 210 pp.

Review by Dana S. Trif, Babeș-Bolyai University, Cluj-Napoca, Romania

Henry Rammelt's book, *Activistes protestataires en Hongrie et en Roumanie* ('Protest Activists in Hungary and Romania') is a comprehensive study of the waves of protests in Hungary and Romania between 2008 and 2015. The book is a welcome attempt at closing a large research gap in the academic literature. Scientific studies have so far largely ignored the unusual revival at the beginning of the 21st century of mass protests in these two Eastern European countries, which often rank low in terms of civic engagement. Their 'transition' from authoritarianism to democracy has of late also appeared to reverse its course.

The period itself warrants a more focused type of scientific inquiry: from smaller scale anti-NATO demonstrations in Romania in 2008, to mass protests against migration and corruption, Romanian and Hungarian citizens seemed to defy scientific expectations of civic apathy. Or did they? The author sets to answer this question by exploring the sociopolitical factors behind largely self-organized and borderline legal protests.

Rammelt's theoretical framework, grounded in the social movement's literature, relies on approaches and concepts such as cultural and political opportunity structures, resource mobilization, framework, as well as structural, relational, and cognitive social capital analyses. His comparative study benefits from a multi-method research design, which successfully combines survey data, from sources such as the World Value Survey, with qualitative data collection and analysis methods. Semi-structured interviews with protest activists help recreate the local, political and cultural opportunity structures as perceived by these participants. They also assist with mapping the movements' internal organization, ability to mobilize resources, digital expertise and growing social and online networks.

The Romanian case study covers three landmark events: the 2008 anti-NATO demonstrations, the 2011/2012 anti-austerity protests, and the 2013 'Romanian Fall'. The latter was generated by a mix of environmental and anti-corruption concerns that ultimately blocked the privatization of the Roșia Montană silver mine. Hungarian protests are historically divided according to two cut-off points: the scandal involving the Socialist Prime Minister of Hungary, Ferenc Gyurcsany, in September

2006, which triggered countrywide protests against the alleged corruption of the 'old' political elites; and, in 2010, the elections won by Viktor Orban's Fidesz party, generally considered to be a negative turning point for Hungarian democracy.

In Hungary, pre-2010 activism led to the rise of the right-wing Jobbik ('Movement for a better Hungary'), but also of the left-leaning LMP ('Politics can be different'), a party rooted in the local environmental movement. After 2010, the country witnessed a series of thematic protests and issue-driven social movements: the demonstrations against the controversial 2013 Constitutional changes introduced by Viktor Orban's government; the Milla movement and Facebook page (2010/2014), a unique case of early social media activism; and the short-lived 'anti-internet tax' movement (2014/2015) generated by a bill that was ultimately never adopted.

Rammelt presents the findings of his comparative case study in a comprehensive and easily readable way. For anyone interested in the history and politics of this region, or in the medium and long-term effects of a 'transition' to democracy, Rammelt's book is a must read. The birth (Romania) or re-birth (Hungary) of civic engagement in two former Communist dictatorships is a lesson in the *how*s and *why*s such a phenomenon can happen.

Romania's case is relatively straightforward. The first generation of protest activists found their calling during the 2008 anti-NATO demonstrations. Through a process of internal and external learning, the initial small group of dedicated young activists grew ever bigger. They would eventually put their mobilization abilities to use during the 2013 Roșia Montană protests, when Romania witnessed its first big wave of mass demonstrations after 1989. The activists used social platforms such as Facebook to grow their networks, build a strong collective identity and reach out to previously inactive citizens.

Hungary's history of protests is a bit more complicated, and also longer. According to Rammelt, the old and young generation of activists are mixed together, often displaying strong ideological preferences. Although the digital technologies used to mobilize large number of sympathizers are similar (and comparable to the Romanian cases), the events of 2006 and 2010 ultimately triggered divisions between right and left-wing activists. This fractured ideological landscape and the strong attachment of various activists' groups to a particular ideology has hampered the movements' internal coherence and ultimate success.

The signs of a newly emerging 'culture of protest' is, however, what brings both groups together. This is perhaps one of the study's most interesting findings. While Romanians did indeed build on previous achievements and successfully created strong social and online networks (mostly free of any particular ideology, but very resourceful in their mobilizing ability), 'protest as a way of life' is something characteristic to Romanian and Hungarian activists alike. One of the strongest points of Henry Rammelt's book is that it successfully draws the picture of this 'thick' protest culture. Differentiating itself through social media savviness and ability to draw large numbers of sympathizers into fully-fledged participants, this new way of protesting flourishes despite the governments' perceived democratic backsliding.

Even if the author does not explicitly say it, the younger generation of protesters in these former Communist countries challenge the pessimism of studies bemoaning the reversibility of 'transitions' to democracy. Whether these youngsters will ultimately be successful politically remains an open question. The cases of LMP and Jobbik can be used to argue that new social movements and a revived sense of civic engagement may or may not strengthen democracy. Undoubtedly, however, Henry Rammelt's book offers the reader solid evidence and a good historical overview of the former's (re)emergence in Hungary and Romania. The scientific rigor applied in this research lends even more credibility to his findings, and offers food for thought to anyone interested in the democratization processes of Eastern Europe, as well as in democratization processes in general.

EAST EUROPEAN STUDIES: JOURNALS AND BOOK SERIES

Soviet and Post-Soviet Politics and Society

Editor: Andreas Umland

Founded in 2004 and refereed since 2007, SPPS makes available, to the academic community and general public, affordable English-, German- and Russian-language scholarly studies of various empirical aspects of the recent history and current affairs of the former Soviet bloc from the late Tsarist period to today. It publishes approximately 15–20 volumes per year, and focuses on issues in transitions to and from democracy such as economic crisis, identity formation, civil society development, and constitutional reform in CEE and the NIS. SPPS also aims to highlight so far understudied themes in East European studies such as right-wing radicalism, religious life, higher education, or human rights protection.

Journal of Soviet and Post-Soviet Politics and Society

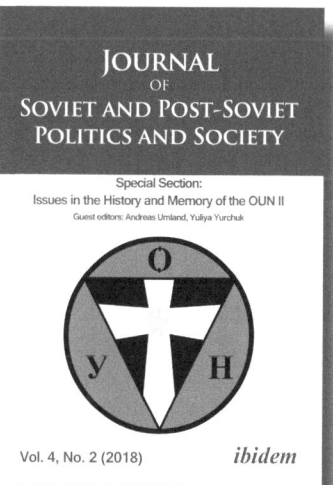

Editors: Andreas Umland, Julie Fedor, Andrey Makarychev, George Soroka, Tomasz Stępniewski

The Journal of Soviet and Post-Soviet Politics and Society is a new bi-annual journal that was launched in April 2015 as a companion journal to the Soviet and Post-Soviet Politics and Society book series (founded 2004 and edited by Andreas Umland, Dr. phil., PhD). Like the book series, the journal will provide an interdisciplinary forum for new original research on the Soviet and post-Soviet world. The journal aims to become known for publishing creative, intelligent, and lively writing tackling and illuminating significant issues and capable of engaging wider educated audiences beyond the academy.

CHANGING EUROPE

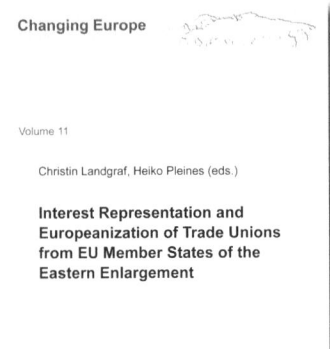

Editors: Dr. Sabine Fischer, Prof. Dr. Heiko Pleines, Prof. Dr. Hans-Henning Schröder

The book series Changing Europe contains edited volumes dealing with current political, economic and social affairs in Eastern Europe and the enlarged EU. The core of the series is formed by contributions to the Changing Europe Summer Schools, which are being organised by the Research Centre for East European Studies at the University of Bremen.

FORUM FÜR OSTEUROPÄISCHE IDEEN- UND ZEITGESCHICHTE

Editors: Leonid Luks, Gunter Dehnert, Nikolaus Lobkowicz, Alexei Rybakow, Andreas Umland

FORUM features interdisciplinary discussions by political scientists—literary, legal, and economic scholars—and philosophers on the history of ideas, and it reviews books on Central and Eastern European history. Through the translation and publication of documents and contributions from Russian, Polish, and Czech researchers, the journal offers Western readers critical insight into scientific discourses across Eastern Europe.

ibidem Press | Leuschnerstr. 40 | 30457 Hannover | Germany
Phone: +49 (0) 511 2 62 22 00 | Fax: +49 (0) 511 2 62 22 00 | sales@ibidem.eu

LITERATURE AND CULTURE IN CENTRAL AND EASTERN EUROPE

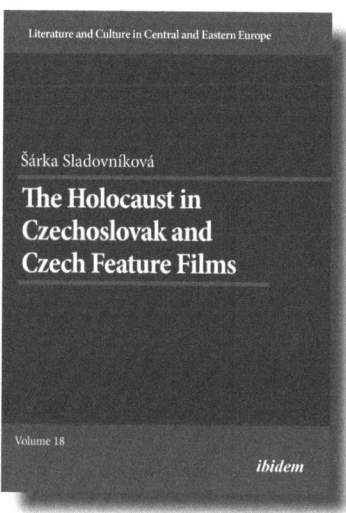

Editor: Prof. Dr. Reinhard Ibler

This series was founded to give a platform for the contemporary research into Literature and Culture of Middle and Eastern Europe. The profile of the series is geographical rather than philological, thriving on a variety of content and methods. Central subjects include the literary and cultural processing of the Holocaust, a focus born out of the successful Gießen project on comparative research of this important and productive issue, using Polish, Czech, Slovakian, and German material. Further, defining subjects are the discourse on modernity and avant-garde, questions of genre typology and history, as well as interdisciplinary aspects of aesthetics and literary and cultural theory, as far as it is grounded in Middle and Eastern European intellectual tradition.

IN STATU NASCENDI

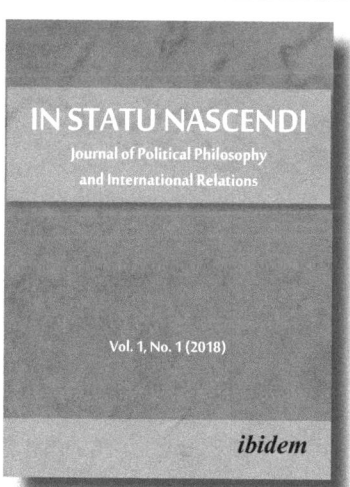

Editor: Piotr Pietrzak

In Statu Nascendi is a new peer-reviewed journal aspiring to provide a world-class scholarly platform, which encompasses original academic research dedicated to the circle of Political Philosophy, Cultural Studies, Theory of International Relations, Foreign Policy, and the political Decision-making process. The journal investigates specific issues through a socio-cultural, philosophical, and anthropological approach to raise a new type of civic awareness about the complexity of contemporary crisis, instabilities, and warfare situations, where the "stage-of-becoming" plays a vital role.

ibidem.eu